P9-CQG-206

DISCARD

BLOOMINGTON PUBLIC LIBRARY

205 E. OLIVE STREET

POST OFFICE BOX 3308

BLOOMINGTON, ILLINOIS 61701

JAN 03

AMAZON SWEET SEA

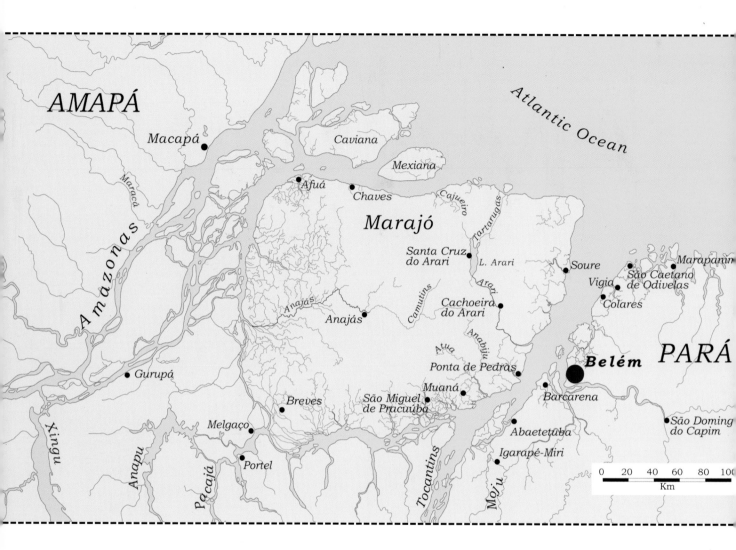

AMAPÁ

Macapá

Caviana

Mexiana

Atlantic Ocean

Amazonas

Maracá

Afuá

Chaves

Cajueiro

Marajó

Tartarugas

Santa Cruz
do Arari

L. Arari

Soure

Marapanim

São Caetano
de Odivelas

Vigia

Arari

Colares

Camutins

Anajás

Anajás

Cachoeira
do Arari

Anabiju

Afua

Belém

PARÁ

Gurupá

Ponta de Pedras

Barcarena

Muaná

Breves

São Miguel
de Pracuúba

Xingu

Melgaço

Abaetetuba

São Domingo
do Capim

Anapu

Portel

Igarapé-Miri

Pacajá

Tocantins

Moju

0   20   40   60   80 100

Km

BY NIGEL J. H. SMITH

AMAZON
Sweet Sea

LAND, LIFE, AND WATER

AT THE RIVER'S MOUTH

BLOOMINGTON, ILLINOIS
PUBLIC LIBRARY

UNIVERSITY OF TEXAS PRESS, AUSTIN

304.2
Sm 1

Publication of this book was aided by generous
subsidies from M. K. Hage and Roger Fullington.

Copyright © 2002 by the University of Texas Press
All rights reserved
Printed in China
First edition, 2002

Requests for permission to reproduce material from
this work should be sent to Permissions, University of
Texas Press, P.O. Box 7819, Austin, TX 78713-7819.

∞ The paper used in this book meets the minimum
requirements of ANSI/NISO z39.48-1992 (R1997)
(Permanence of Paper).

Library of Congress Cataloging-in-Publication Data

Smith, Nigel J. H., 1949–
Amazon sweet sea : land, life, and water at the river's
mouth / by Nigel J. H. Smith.
p.   cm.
Includes bibliographical references (p.   ).
ISBN 0-292-77770-1 (hardcover : alk. paper)
1. Human ecology—Amazon River Valley   2. Rain
forest ecology—Amazon River Valley.
3. Environmental degradation—Amazon River Valley.
4. Environmental policy—Amazon River Valley.
5. Landscape changes—Amazon River Valley.
6. International economic relations—Amazon River
Valley.   7. Amazon River Valley—Environmental
conditions.   8. Amazon River Valley—
Economic conditions.   I. Title.
GF532.A4 S65 2002
304.2'09811—dc21
2001008473

To the memory of
Antônio Vizeu da Costa Lima
(1925–1993)
Geographer and tireless promoter
of education in the Amazon

Contents

Preface

When the first Europeans sailed near the mouth of the Amazon, they marveled at the colossal size of the river that seemed to push back the salty waters of the Atlantic and at the rich store of natural resources waiting to be exploited. In 1499, still far out to sea off the mouth of the Amazon, a Spanish explorer had a crew member dip a bucket into the ocean and found the water drinkable. Vicente Yáñez Pinzón, awestruck at so much freshwater with land nowhere in sight, described those parts as a *mar dulce* (sweet sea). Another early explorer near the mouth of the Amazon, Pedro Álvars Cabral—the "discoverer" of Brazil—also did not tarry long but remarked that the forests in the estuary were so thick they could supply virtually unlimited timber to the navies of Iberia.

The image of the Amazon's mouth as a vast natural warehouse of biological treasures persists today. This book explores how the use of these natural resources has altered in the light of technological change, rapid urban growth, and accelerated market integration. Often such developments are identified as major threats to the environment, but in the case of the Amazon estuary they have diversified agriculture and helped to save floodplain forests from wanton destruction. People have transformed "natural" forests into cultural forests by rearranging the biological furniture. Over generations, locals have deflected the normal fallow cycle in slash-and-burn farming and created agroforests rich in economic species. By so doing, they have retained a biologically diverse landscape that benefits not only wildlife but also their own livelihoods.

In spite of the relatively good news with respect to human-induced landscape changes in the estuary—in stark contrast to many other parts of the Amazon basin—several trends recently have emerged that do not augur well for the resiliency of the land and its people. Historically, cattle production in the Amazon estuary has been confined to seasonally flooded savannas, especially on Marajó. But pockets of pasture have started to appear in areas hitherto dominated by forests. Should this trend accelerate, the productivity of fisheries could be threatened because many species of fish important in commerce and subsistence need floodplain forest to feed and breed. Forests also provide locals with important supplements to their subsistence and income, including game. Another trend that could undercut the productivity of extractive activities is the removal of mangroves in some areas to make way for urban development. Mangroves in the estuary are critical habitat for crabs, the basis of an important commercial activity.

These trends are analyzed from a historical and natural history perspective. One of the principal objectives of this book is to underscore the importance of the estuary's diverse habitats for local folk and, through trade, for urban dwellers as well. Yet many of the plant and animal resources tapped locally do not enter markets and are thus undervalued. Policy makers may thus be tempted to promote development schemes that do not take into account the value of biodiversity to locals. A major aim of this book is to highlight some of the little-known plants and animals that not only enrich the lives of people today but also could become the next generation's crop plants and livestock—if they survive.

Another theme threading through the chapters dealing with how people use and sometimes abuse the natural resources in the Amazon estuary is the changing perceptions of nature over time and what this means for how people relate to the environment. In spite of rampant globalization, many ideas about respect for wild plants and animals still surface in tales recounted by hunters and fishers. Often folk beliefs are dismissed as mere superstition, but they influence the way people hunt and fish and are a means of transmitting a conservation message to future generations.

Scientific names are relegated to appendixes to render the text more readable to nonspecialists. The scientific names provided in the appendixes are best bets only, because many groups of plants and animals in the Amazon are in need of taxonomic revision. Literature is not cited in the text so as to improve its flow; published material consulted for this project is listed under "Further Reading."

Unless otherwise stated, all photographs are my own. I have found that the camera serves as a medium for breaking the ice as I take pictures of people and ask about what they are doing. Far from being an intrusion in their lives, most rural people with whom I interact find my photographic interest in their livelihoods equally intriguing. On returning from the field and scrutinizing the slides, I am often delighted to find details about plants and animals, or the size and shape of objects manufactured from local plants, that I had missed in my notes. In my thirty years of fieldwork in the Amazon, I can remember only two or three instances when people did not want to be photographed, and of course I respected their wishes. On return visits, I always make a point of bringing families samples of my photographs, which usually generate a great deal of excitement and laughter, including remarks about how large so and so's nose appears and denials that they really look like that.

I have undertaken fieldwork in the Amazon estuary intermittently since 1970. In the dry season of 1970, I spent several days on Fazenda Livramento, Marajó Island, during a field excursion organized by Hilgard O'Reilly Sternberg, now professor emeritus, Department of Geography, University of California, Berkeley. I also visited Macapá and its vicinity while on this field trip. Between 1970 and 2001 I made numerous short trips to town and country in the Amazon estuary. Most of the observations for this book, however, were made during a more concentrated period of fieldwork between 1994 and 2001. Although all the visits were brief, lasting between a few days and three weeks, I experienced the Amazon estuary during all seasons and in years of exceptionally heavy rains (1999) as well as in years that were relatively dry (1997).

Numerous organizations and individuals provided logistical support or were otherwise helpful in planning my trips, helping me to identify plants and animals from photographs, and exchanging ideas. I am especially grateful to the following individuals for their assistance and insights: Milton Abreu Filho, secretary of culture, Vigia Municipal government; Dita Acatauassú, Fazenda Tapera, Marajó; Samuel Almeida, Museu Goeldi, Belém; Scott Anderson, Museu Goeldi, Belém; Ronaldo Baena, EMBRAPA, Belém; Lindalva Barbosa, seamstress and homemaker, Portel; Pedro Barbosa, sawmill owner, Portel; Washington "Jorge" Rodrigues Barbosa, town councilor, Portel; Tuffi Barra, vice-mayor, Afuá, Marajó; Eduardo Paulo Furtado de Barros, entrepreneur, Afuá, Marajó; Michael Binford, University of Florida, Gainesville; Demetro Ferreira Cardoso, Fazenda Vitória near Melgaço; Antonio "Toni" de Carvalho Brabo, Muaná, Marajó; Miguel Santana de Castro, mayor, Afuá, Marajó; David Cleary, the Nature Conservancy, Brasília; Charles Clement, INPA, Manaus; Narrinah Coelho, town councilor, Afuá, Marajó; Jef Le Cornec, Pousada Ekinox, Macapá; Zenaldo Coutinho, federal deputy from Pará, Brasília; Juarez Damasceno, ABED sawmill, Portel; Antonio Cardoso Denorio, Portel; Mauri Deschamps, Agropecuária Ilha de Nazaré, Antônio Lemos, Pará; Jean Dubois, REBRAF, Rio de Janeiro; Italo Falesi, EMATER, Belém; Louis Forline, Museu Goeldi, Belém; Walbert Gabriel, secretary for agriculture, Abaetetuba municipal government; Giovanni Gallo, Cachoeira do Arari, Marajó); Carlos Gondim, FCAP, Belém; Michael Goulding, Amazon Conservation Association, Gainesville, Florida; Vera Guapindaia, Museu Goeldi, Belém; Luis Umberto Freitas Guimarães, entrepreneur, São Miguel de Pracuúba; Andrew Henderson, New York Botanical Garden; Michael Heckenberger, University of Florida, Gainesville; Marinus Hoogmoed, National Museum of Natural History, Leiden; Victoria Isaac, UFPA, Belém; Walter Judd, University of Florida, Gainesville; Alba Lins, Museu Goeldi, Belém; Pedro Lisboa, Museu Goeldi, Belém; Harry Luther, Selby Botanical Gardens, Sarasota, Florida; Marinaldo Machado, EMATER, Breves; Dennis Mahar, Gainesville, Florida; Harm Meelissen, Eco Logic Systems, Belém; Jorge Mesquita, Fazenda Memória, Rio Tauá, Marajó; Celeste Miralha, director, SEMSA, Breves; Manuel "Santana" Miranda, fisherman and musician, Vigia; Mãe Dulce Costa Moreira, healer, Macapá); Genésio Caetano de Oliveira, rancher, Breves; Elzemar da Silva Paes, mayor, Abaetetuba; Evaldo

Pamplona, store owner, Santa Cruz do Arari, Marajó; João Pamplona, EMATER, Cachoeira do Arari, Marajó; Raimundo "Galo" Pantoja, farmer, Igarapé-Miri; Rosalva Pantoja, farmer, Igarapé-Miri; Sir Ghillean Prance, Lyme Regis, England; Nelson de Figueiredo Ribeiro, former federal minister, Belém; James Ratter, Royal Botanic Gardens, Edinburgh; Joana Castelo Branco Rocha, Fazenda Paraíso, municipality of Cachoeira do Arari, Marajó; Denise Schaan, Museu Goeldi, Belém; Elias Sefer, former director, SUDAM, Belém; Luiz Afonso Sefer, state assemblyman, Belém; Adilson Serrão, director, EMBRAPA, Belém; Odete Fátima Machado da Silveira, IEPA, Macapá; Fátima Siqueira, homemaker, Vigia; Francisco "Soeiro" Siqueira, teacher and historian, Vigia; Marcos Moreira de Souza, Fabrica Jayrê near Afuá, Marajó; Bill Stern, University of Florida, Gainesville; José Teixeira Neto, EMBRAPA, Belém; Armando Acatauassú Teixeira, Fazenda Campo Limpo, Rio Anajás, Marajó; Raimundo Nonato Guimarães Teixeira, EMBRAPA, Belém; Rodolfo Monteiro Ferreira Teixeira, Fazenda Santo André, Rio Anabiju, Marajó; Ronaldo Teixeira, Fazenda Cajueiro, Marajó; Ricardo Tibery, rancher, Belém; Sue Ann De Miranda Tibery, rancher, Belém; Manuel Tourinho, director, FCAP, Belém; Jean-François Tourrand, CIRAD/EMBRAPA, Belém; Giorgini Venturieri, Universidade Federal de Santa Catarina, Florianópolis; Richard Vogt, INPA, Manaus.

Roy Duenas and Michael Goulding prepared the map.

None of the organizations or individuals I have collaborated with during the course of this study necessarily agrees with any of my findings or interpretations. The views and conclusions expressed here are entirely my own.

AMAZON SWEET SEA

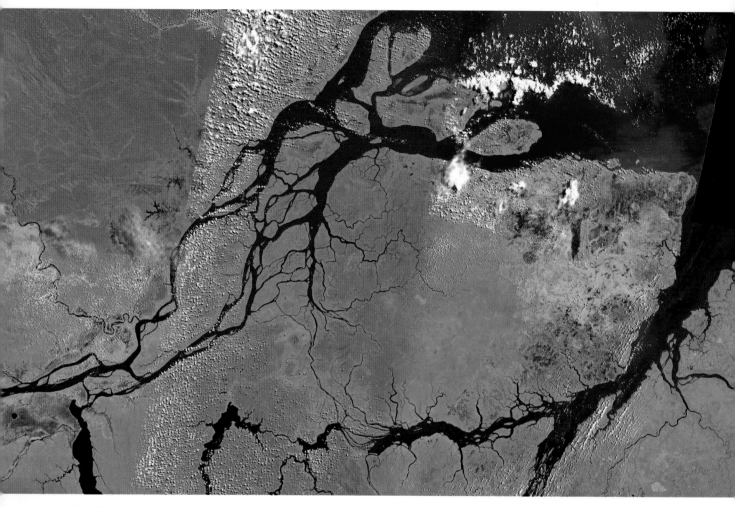

Satellite image of the Amazon estuary, which extends some 300 kilometers from southeast to northwest. The large island straddling most of the mouth of the Amazon is Marajó, which is about the size of Switzerland. Savanna areas are depicted in orange. Courtesy of INPE, *Brazil.*

CHAPTER 1

Where Titans Meet

The Amazon delta, the world's largest, has inspired awe among visitors for centuries because of the huge volume of freshwater it pours into the sea and its vast expanses of swamp forests, floating meadows, and mudflats. Locals respect its treacherous currents and white-capped waves, but they have also learned to adjust to its daily and seasonal rhythms and to tap its rich banquet of natural resources. The mouth of the Amazon, gaping some three hundred kilometers wide, embraces a mosaic of habitats that locals have long tapped for food and other goods and in many cases have transformed.

Born in the lofty, snow-clad Andes, the Amazon flows four thousand kilometers until it confronts the Atlantic at the equator. The Amazon is not only the world's longest river; it carries more water than any other river—more than ten times that of the Mississippi, for example. One-fifth of all the water flowing off the face of the earth passes through the Amazon's mouth. Such is the force of the Amazon as it clashes with the Atlantic that it pushes out a vast plume of freshwater for hundreds of kilometers into the sea. Five centuries ago a Spanish explorer traveling up the coast of Brazil noted that at a certain point the sea tasted fresh, even though his ship was out of sight of land. Pinzón dubbed that spot the sweet sea (*mar dulce*), which historians and geographers take to be the mouth of the river, named after women warriors in Greek mythology.

The battleground between the Amazon and the Atlantic never ceases to amaze travelers. While sailing up the Brazilian coast toward Belém in 1865, a zoological expedition from Harvard noted their approach to the Amazon estuary thus:

> Early yesterday morning, a few yellowish patches staining the ocean here and there gave us our first glimpse of the water of the Amazons. Presently the patches became broad streaks, the fresh waters encroaching gradually upon the sea, until, at about ten o'clock, we fairly entered the mouth of the river, though, as the shores are some hundred and fifty miles apart, we might have believed ourselves on the broad ocean.[1]

The Southern Equatorial Current pushes this turbid plume, which reaches some 400 kilometers long and between 100 and 200 kilometers wide, in a northwesterly direction up the coast of Amapá and the neighboring Guianas. Because it is lighter, the fresh-

A fisherman hauling in a drifting gill net at the mouth of the Amazon. Because the river pushes out into the Atlantic for hundreds of kilometers, the water is fresh at this distance from land. Near Mexiana Island, May 19, 2001.

water overrides the salty ocean and dilutes and muddies the surface for up to one million square miles. No wonder that Pinzón and his crew were amazed at being able to taste freshwater so far out at sea.

This plume of freshwater was a sure sign to European traders of the sixteenth and seventeenth centuries that they were on course to the Amazon. In 1604 Charles Leigh, an English captain on his way to the Amazon to trade for tobacco, remarked on the change in water color of the Atlantic still two days' sailing time from the mouth of the Amazon: "We passed over to the West Indies, and upon the tenth of May comming in change of water, which shewed thicke and white, by the next day we were in fresh water."[2] William Davies, an English surgeon on Captain Robert Thornton's trip to the Amazon in 1608, noted as their vessel was heading south from the West Indies, "[A]nd you shall see the Sea change to a ruddie colour, the water shall grow fresh, by these signes you may run boldly your course."[3]

MAJOR FEATURES OF THE DELTA

The main channel of the Amazon flows into the northern part of the estuary, hugging Amapá's southern coast. The river is so broad along the northern channel that the horizon seems to melt with the sky. The sheer volume of freshwater flowing through the northern channel prevents much salt water from penetrating upstream, so mangroves are rare. Only when the Amazon heads north as it mixes with the Atlantic do red mangroves, with their distinctive stilt roots, become common. Washed by fresh sediment from the Amazon, waters in the northern estuary are especially muddy and bathe the richest farmland on floodplains.

A small arm of the Amazon branches south and hooks around southern Marajó. This sideshow is barely distinguishable on a remote sensing overview of the estuary but is the main route for river traffic between Belém, Macapá, and cities upstream, such as Manaus. Boat traffic between Macapá and Belém takes the longer, inland route via western Marajó because the waters off eastern Marajó are too risky. Only fishing boats venture off the seaward coast of Marajó. The southern estuary is less rich in sediments than the northern channel because clear and black water rivers dilute the muddy Amazon. The first river to mix with the southern arm of the Amazon, the Anapú, flows into the southwestern estuary. In the rainy season the Anapú is almost black as rainwa-

Tossing a cast net into the sediment-rich waters of the Amazon. The boy is after freshwater shrimp, which he attracts to the muddy banks of the river with manioc flour. Vila Nascimento, Municipality of Chaves, Marajó, May 18, 2001.

Clear water mixed with tannin-rich waters along the lower Anapú a few kilometers from its confluence with the southern arm of the muddy Amazon near Marajó. During the summer, the Anapú runs almost clear, but during the rainy season, it takes on a darker color because rainwater has soaked through leaves and other vegetation in floodplain forests. The boys are on a kapok log that broke loose from a raft destined for a sawmill. Lower Anapú, May 13, 2000.

Xareu, one of several species of jack, all marine species, that move into brackish waters in the southern part of the estuary during the low water season. Vigia, November 14, 1998.

Bandeirado, with its distinctive long barbels, is one of several marine catfishes caught off the mouth of the Amazon. Ver-o-Pêso market, Belém, November 13, 1998.

ter picks up tannins from leaves and other organic debris in floodplain forest. In the dry season the river runs almost clear. The next major river that merges with the southern arm of the Amazon is the clear water Tocantins in the southeast corner of the estuary. Less freshwater flushes through the southern estuary, so these waters are more brackish, especially during the dry season.

The contact zone between fresh and salt water varies according to location within the estuary, the tide, and the season. The constantly changing interplay between the realm of fresh and salt waters has much to do with the availability of certain fish and other aquatic resources, the rhythm of economic activities, and the distribution of vegetation, especially mangroves. The shifting contours of fresh and salt waters allows some marine species to temporarily penetrate the estuary, such as certain jacks. During the low water season, therefore, a dozen or so catfish species are typically on display in local markets, ranging from those confined to freshwater, such as silvery dourada, to those adapted to saline conditions, such as olive gurijuba and steel gray bandeirado.

Gurijuba, a marine catfish, comes closer to shore during the dry season. The boy's father is a buyer who has just purchased the gurijuba from a fishing boat. The fish are about to be carried into Vigia's main market, May 11, 1999.

Geologic History of the River Mouth

To appreciate the diversity of environments in the Amazon estuary, the geologic footsteps that have led to the present landscape need to be traced. For most of South America's history, the Amazon has flowed west to the Pacific. The headwaters of the Amazon used to be in the east, probably in the vicinity of Óbidos, where rivers gnawed into broad granitic uplands, part of the original Gondwanaland before South America split off from Africa. As the South American plate began grinding over the Pacific plate some ninety million years ago, however, the Andes Mountains began to form. About thirty million years ago, the crumpling of the western edge of the South American plate combined with increased volcanic activity accelerated the formation of the Andes, eventually cutting off the Amazon's exit to the sea.

The history of the Amazon becomes a bit murky at this point, but it seems that the Amazon was dammed, at least for a while, forming a series of vast lakes and swamps. A number of marine ingressions also occurred as the Andes were forming, leading to brackish swamps and mangroves in what is now well-drained tropical rainforest.

In the meantime, however, the Amazon did not become a stagnant reservoir waiting to cut an exit to the Atlantic. It seems that the river turned north and flowed into the proto-Caribbean through what is now the Magdalena valley in Colombia. At present the Magdalena is completely cut off from the Amazon drainage, yet it shares many fish species, suggesting that they were once one and the same. As the South American plate continued to collide with the Pacific plate, various cordilleras formed offshoots to the backbone Andes in present-day Colombia and Venezuela, similar to ripples in a blanket as one pushes it across a bed. The Amazon was once again forced to find another exit, this time via the present-day Orinoco.

About eight million years ago, the Amazon broke through the granitic shield to the Atlantic. The itinerant Amazon forged its current route to the sea because of continental-scale forces at work. The massive granitic basement complex in northeastern South America had begun to split in half as far back as the Jurassic, forming the Guianan shield to the north and the Brazilian shield to the south. This split accelerated as the South American plate began to push against a spur of basaltic rocks that had solidified from magma spewed onto the surface along the eastern Andes in present-day Bolivia. As the two shields continued to separate, a deep trough formed along fault lines, leading to a down-dropped valley. The resulting gap made it easier for the headwaters of the Amazon to erode through the last impediment to the Atlantic.

Numerous islands dot the Amazon estuary, especially along the northern channel where most of the sediment-rich Amazon flows to the sea. Most of them are alluvial in origin, resulting from the Amazon dropping some of its silt load, especially at high tide when the current slows. The Amazon discharges close to a billion tons of sediment into the sea every year, and a vast underwater sediment cone has formed off the continental shelf that stretches ten degrees north of the equator. Not all the sediment is dumped on that underwater mountain; significant quantities of silt from the Amazon are also carried north as far as the Orinoco delta. Most of the Amazon's suspended sediment, at least 80 percent, comes ultimately from erosion in the Andes. With so much sediment to work with, it is little wonder that the river has sculpted numerous islands at its mouth. Only the Ganges and the Yellow River rival the Amazon with respect to the amount of suspended sediment, in part because their watersheds have witnessed massive deforestation, much of it on steep slopes. The yellow-brown tidal creeks in northern Marajó are so laden with silt that they stir complaints at bath time. The mother of a cowboy family living in the headwaters of the Cajueiro River remarked to me that her kids emerge dirtier than ever after plunging into the tidal creek in front of their home.

But not all islands owe their existence to alluvium dropped by the Amazon. As recognized by the French geographer Élisée Reclus a century ago, some are outliers of uplands that have been separated from the mainland and are now increasing in area with accretion of sediments along their shores. These upland islands—Marajó, Caviana, and Mexiana—were cut off from the mainland by tectonic movements and alternating sea levels during the Pleistocene ice ages.

Sea level dropped several times during the ice ages, falling by as much as one hundred meters off the coast of Brazil. While large amounts of freshwater were locked up in ice sheets in polar and temperate regions, the Amazon and its tributaries excavated their channels. Rivers also scoured deeper in their headwaters, and some of them eventually joined in their upper courses. As the ice sheets melted and sea levels rose, patches of upland then became isolated, forming islands.

Such is the case of Colares Island near Vigia in the southern estuary. During the last Ice Age, hunters and gatherers probably waded across a narrow stream to hunt, fish, and collect wild fruits on Colares. Now one can only reach the potato-shaped island by boat. Upland islands in the estuary can easily be distinguished from those formed by pure alluvium because they have patches of terra firma (*terra firme* in Brazil) forest with different plant species than are found on floodplains. Also, upland islands often contain seasonally flooded savannas and in some cases nonflooded scrub savanna.

Marajó, another island anchored to terra firma, was cut off from the mainland much earlier than Colares. The Tocantins River separated Marajó from the mainland long before the Amazon breached the granitic basement and began flowing into the Atlantic. The Tocantins is one of several sizable rivers that drain the Brazilian shield; it has always flowed north, and in its final stretch it turns north-northeast into the Atlantic. The Tocantins now enters Marajó Bay (Baía de Marajó), a challenging expanse of water where ceaseless trade winds during the summer months whip up foaming waves. Immediately to the north of Marajó are Mexiana and Caviana Islands, both continental outliers now largely ringed by alluvium from the muddy Amazon.

Unlike Colares, though, the Amazon has added substantially to Marajó because it brushes against the northern and western perimeter of the island. Much of western Marajó is built up alluvium quickly colonized by floodplain forests. Seasonally wet savannas, upland forest, riparian forests, and tracts of scrubby, nonflooded savanna characterize the eastern half of the island. Southern and eastern Marajó is nevertheless fringed with floodplain forests and mangroves. Micro-relief features, combined with a highly dynamic geologic history, have created a mosaic of habitats for plants and animals, and people, both local and urban based, extract resources from all of them.

Another distinguishing feature of the Amazon estuary is the presence of a couple of tributary rivers with unusually broad mouths. The Tocantins is the most impressive; it is so broad that standing on one shore, one can hardly discern the other side. During the ice ages, torrents dug the lower Tocantins, creating a riverbed deeper than could be formed under present conditions. Starting ten thousand years ago, waters backed up as the sea level rose, thereby forming a generous mouth that was once a flourishing fishery until overfishing and dam building undercut this important resource. Geomorphologists refer to such mouths as *rias*; they share features with the fjords of Norway, which were ground by glaciers rather than water. Another impressive ria mouth is found in the lower Anapú. The Anapú is a modest-sized river, which also drains the Brazilian shield and has a mouth disproportionate to the volume of water it carries. At one time the Anapú likely flowed north into the Amazon; now it has been captured by the seaward flow of the southern estuary.

THE SEASONAL PULSE OF FLOODWATERS

During the low water season, from June through November, underwater saltwater lenses can penetrate far into the southern estuary, thereby changing the mix of species available for local fishers. At Vigia, for example, several marine fish species come closer to shore and can be caught on day fishing trips. And siri crabs, which are locally appreciated and also are sold in markets, appear at this time from deeper waters and can be caught along shores.

The low water season coincides with the drier months, known locally as *verão*. In the interior of Marajó, lakes shrink dramatically, making it easier to catch fish. Seasonally wet savannas dry out, providing extensive grazing land for cattle and water buffalo. And at low water, farmers can take advantage of nutrient-rich alluvium to plant short cycle crops, such as rice, watermelons, and squash. The brisk Southeast Trades blow during the dry season, thereby helping to propel numerous sail-powered boats and canoes. During the colonial period, annual trading and supervisory missions up the Amazon were attempted only during the dry season to take advantage of the favorable winds. The trades blow so strongly during this season that homes on the open plains moan, fanning stories about haunted houses.

Soon after the rains begin in earnest in about December, the water level starts to rise. The difference between high and low water levels in the estuary is not nearly as dramatic as along the middle and upper stretches of the Amazon, where the seasonal amplitude in water level can exceed ten meters. At the mouth of the Amazon, the difference between high and low water seasons is about three to four meters but is sufficient to dramatically alter the landscape. Once dry grasslands become marshes and rivers and creeks back up, canoes can enter floodplain forest and cross over into adjacent river systems.

The rising waters trigger a shift in economic gears. The pace of timber extraction in floodplains quickens at this time because it is easier to float out logs. Although production of açaí palm fruits declines, the tempo of heart-of-palm extraction quickens. Crop farming all but ceases, except on the highest portion of the floodplain and on patches of upland within the delta. Ranchers generally sell off parts of their herds to compensate for the reduced grazing area. Fishing returns in floodplain lakes decline as the fish disperse into floodplain forest and into seasonally flooded savannas.

TIDES AND THE TEMPO OF LIFE

Superimposed on the annual variation in water level is the waxing and waning of the tides. This other leitmotiv determines the daily rhythm of activities for those eking out a living in the estuary. Whether it be fishing boats biding their time in midchannel for the incoming tide (*afundiado*) or passenger and cargo boats waiting for a favorable tide to shorten travel time, many economic activities are undertaken in synch with the daily flux of the water level. In the case of boats traveling from Afuá north to Macapá, for example, trips are usually planned for high tide, whereas river traffic moving upstream or downstream will often wait for an incoming or outgoing tide. High tide is the time to set up removable fences to cut off the retreat of fish that have entered creeks. At low tide fish are trapped behind the fence and can be easily drugged with piscicides and taken home for lunch or dinner.

Fish corrals are checked at low tide, and shipworm collectors have access to fallen red mangroves where the worms live. Crab hunters are also about at low tide, and people check gill nets that have been strung in aroid jungles growing on mudflats when the

High tide along a creek in the southern part of the Amazon estuary. Because it is a Sunday, the fishing boats are staying home. Mosqueiro, August 20, 2000.

Low tide along the same creek. The fishing boats will be stranded until the next incoming tide. Mosqueiro, August 20, 2000.

Juvenile dourada catfish caught in the Amazon estuary being offloaded for market. Young dourada spend their first few years in the estuary before moving upstream to continue feeding and eventually breed; larval fish are swept downstream from the upper Amazon to the river's mouth. Adult dourada reach almost 2 meters and can weigh over 30 kilograms. Ver-o-Pêso market, Belém, November 13, 1998.

water is out. On the incoming tide, shrimpers deploy beach seines along the muddy shores of the Amazon and tidal creeks.

The difference between high and low tide varies according to location, season, and phase of the moon but usually ranges from one to three meters. At the spring and autumn equinoxes, exceptionally high tides can occur, sometimes associated with a dangerous tidal bore. Known locally as *pororoca*, tidal bores occur along certain rivers in both the northern and southern parts of the estuary. A loud roar announces the approach of a tidal bore, which has a wave up to four meters high. Pororoca races upstream for several kilometers, flinging any canoes still in the water onto banks and into trees.

Surfers from Rio de Janeiro travel to the Amazon estuary to catch pororoca in March and April. São Domingo do Capim in the southern part of the estuary hosts an annual surfing competition sponsored by Bad Boy, a manufacturer of surfing apparel. As would be expected in Brazil, the event includes a competition for Miss Surfing Pororoca. Pororoca has also captured the imagination of some songwriters and musicians. It is the title of a *carimbó* song, a popular music tradition that arose along the brackish coast of Pará. Pororoca is included in the repertoire of a group called Raízes da Terra (Roots of the Earth), which hails from Marapanim:

> The sea is very treacherous, it's full of pororoca
> Crazy waves are passing by, terns are flying past
>
> Come here to see the terns land
> After the pororoca of the sea have passed.[4]

PLANT COMMUNITIES

The varied soils and relief of the estuary foster a mosaic of plant communities, all of which provide fruits as well as medicines, construction materials, and other useful products. Typically, conservation in the Amazon focuses on forests, but other types of vegetation, such as mangroves and grasslands, contain significant biodiversity and are important sources of income and subsistence. Many of the products obtained from the plant communities in the Amazon estuary never enter markets and therefore are not considered valuable by policy makers. They are nevertheless important because locals would have to substitute manufactured items—if available—or do without. Many of the plants have special cultural or spiritual significance, especially those used in healing, and therefore are priceless.

Many of the fish caught for subsistence and commerce depend directly or indirectly on the survival of aquatic plant communities, from floodplain forest to floating meadows and mangroves. Pressures are mounting on these estuarine environments, which if left unchecked could undercut food resources not only for local people but also for consumers hundreds or even thousands of kilometers away. Nurseries for some migratory fish are found in the estuary, so landscape changes at the mouth of the Amazon could affect catches upstream.

Dourada catfish, for example, spend the first few years of their lives in the Amazon estuary, where they depend on floodplain forest and other habitats for their nurture before migrating several thousand kilometers upstream to breed. And some of the fish caught in the estuary are salted and sun-dried for distribution by trade channels far inland.

Most of the forests of the Amazon estuary are flooded, either daily by the tide or seasonally when rains swell the Amazon and its tributaries. Species composition varies markedly according to whether the waters are brackish at certain times of the year, how long the area is flooded, and whether the water is silt-laden, clear, or stained dark brown by tannins. Floodplain forests on alluvial islands in the estuary are washed with the creamed-coffee waters of the sediment-rich Amazon. Headwater rivers and streams on larger islands, such as Marajó, are often clear or black water, and their floodplain

AMAZON SWEET SEA

Forest flooded by the silt-laden Amazon in the northern part of the estuary. Note the prominence of palms in the landscape, especially açaí on the left. Furo de Beija Flor, Ilha dos Porcos, municipality of Afuá, August 17, 1998.

Arumã in the shady interior of a floodplain forest. Leaf stems of arumã are employed to make baskets and sieves. Destruction of these forests not only endangers the productivity of many fisheries but also eliminates a host of plants used on the farm, in the kitchen, and to hunt and fish. Combu Island near Belém, November 20, 1998.

An arumã basket used for carrying manioc roots and cultivated and wild fruits. Rio Curupaxizinho near Afuá, Marajó, August 20, 1998.

forests contain a different mix of species than those under the influence of the muddy Amazon. The same applies to affluents of the Amazon, such as the Maracá River in Amapá, where tributary black water streams form extensive swamp forests during the rainy season, especially at high tide.

Although species diversity of floodplain forests is lower than at upland sites, they nevertheless contain a wealth of useful plants. In the northwestern part of Marajó Island, for example, extensive stands of buriti palm, used for fruit and fiber, occur in what are locally called *mondongo* swamps along the sinuous border between savanna and forest. Arumã is a particularly useful plant in the understory of floodplain forests, for its leaf stems are split to make baskets for carrying farm produce and forest fruits, to sieve manioc dough and açaí palm juice, and to make fish and shrimp traps. Floodplain forests dominate western Marajó and many of the islands in both the northern and southern parts of the estuary. Strips of forest finger their way across the savannas of Marajó, and these gallery forests bordering streams provide fruits, building materials, and medicines to locals. Islands of forest, or *ilhas*, also characterize the open grasslands of Marajó, particularly in the transition zone to dense forest.

Fleshy plants in the aroid family often form dense stands along the fringes of floodplain forests. Aroids are best known to North Americans and Europeans as indoor ornamental plants with broad, showy leaves, such as dieffenbachia. In the Amazon several species of this pantropical family are aquatic, including aninga (known as arum in English), which has large elephant ear–like leaves growing from the top of a stem that can attain three meters. Stands range in width from a few meters to dozens of meters and may extend along riverbanks for several kilometers. In some areas locals have cut narrow corridors through these aroid jungles to extend gill nets. Fish become entangled in the nets at high tide when they swim into the aroid jungles to feed.

UPLAND FOREST

Although not extensive, patches of upland forest are found on higher parts of Marajó, especially in the southeast. Because of their proximity to Belém, terra firma forests in the Amazon estuary have been essentially stripped of their valuable hardwoods. Nevertheless, locals still obtain wood from such forest patches to make fence posts and build their houses. Small patches of upland forest also provide a number of locally consumed fruits.

OPEN SAVANNAS

Expansive savannas (*campo*), stretching for dozens of kilometers without a single tree, characterize large portions of eastern Marajó. Savannas also cover much of Mexiana Island off Marajó's north coast as well as the interior of some other islands, such as

Colares in the southern estuary. On Marajó alone campos cover some twenty thousand square kilometers. Because they are so flat and low-lying, savannas are mostly underwater during the rainy season. They are flooded by rivers and streams backed up by the Amazon as well as by the torrential rains that unleash nearly three meters of water during the first few months of the year. At high water many roads and trails across the savannas are underwater, so travelers and cargo switch to boats.

The landscape changes dramatically during the dry season. Days pass without a drop of rain. Much of the forage is parched, and cattle and water buffalo become thin. Cattle fare better at the beginning and end of the rainy season. Fires often rage across

A gill net being extended through a stand of aninga at low tide. A family will typically cut several narrow corridors through these aroid thickets perpendicular to the shore. Fish become entangled in the nets at high tide. Ilha dos Porcos, municipality of Afuá, August 17, 1998.

A boat carrying passengers and their baggage across a savanna under 1.5 meters of water. The boat is navigating a channel through algodão bravo, considered a weed by ranchers because it is unpalatable to cattle. Near Igarapé Fundo en route to Cachoeira do Arari, Marajó Island, May 12, 1999.

the savannas, resulting in large, black smudges as seen from the air. Lightning-set fires have swept across the savannas of eastern Marajó and some other islands for millions of years, but when people arrived tens of thousands of years ago, fires undoubtedly became more common. Indigenous folk deliberately burned the savannas to facilitate hunting, and Portuguese landowners and Catholic missions also set fires to improve forage for cattle. In the mid-nineteenth century, the great English naturalist Alfred

Russel Wallace reported that ranchers on Mexiana Island set fire to the savannas in the dry season to promote fresh growth. Frequent fires set by people over millennia have helped to prevent the encroachment of trees on the savanna and have doubtless expanded the area occupied by treeless or "clean" plains (*campo limpo*).

SCRUB SAVANNAS

Some of the higher savannas are covered with scrub woodland, or *cerrado*. Patches of cerrado are found just inland from a belt of forest along the coast of southeastern Marajó; the landscape of gnarled trees interspersed with grasses gradually changes to open, seasonally flooded grassland as one travels to the interior of the island. Confined to uplands, cerrado grows on acidic and highly leached soils. Because of their low productivity, patches of scrub savanna are used mostly for extensive grazing of livestock. Cerrado is a good indicator of well-drained land now isolated from the mainland.

FLOATING MEADOWS

Floating meadows proliferate during the rainy season and are particularly well developed in the inland lakes of Marajó, especially Lake Arari. Floating meadows can form virtually impenetrable mats covering a square kilometer or more. Fishers and boat crews hack paths through them and often have to repeat the chore as the vegetation grows back so quickly. Winds can drive clumps of floating grasses, water hyacinth, and water lettuce across the entrances to channels, so regular waterways require constant maintenance. At ground level floating meadows are like a maze, but locals know which gaps lead to dead ends and which ones remain open to the other side.

Composed of several species of grass, rushes, and other aquatic plants, floating meadows are important habitat for many species of fish, especially in their juvenile stages, as well as numerous birds and mammals. Floating meadows are productive hunting grounds at high water because they provide food for large flocks of ducks and herons, as well as capybara, the world's largest rodent. Water buffalo munch through floating meadows, immersing themselves in the floating islands all day.

MANGROVE

Mangrove, known in the Brazilian Amazon as *manguezal*, is confined to tropical and subtropical waters and provides important habitat for coastal fisheries. Although widely distributed, mangroves are nearly everywhere threatened by a variety of forces, ranging from cutting down the trees to obtain the bark for the tanning industry to clearing for shrimp culture, agriculture, and urban growth. In the Amazon locals have selectively cut mangroves for generations to provide building material and limited supplies of fuelwood, but only recently have mangroves begun to suffer wholesale destruc-

tion for industrial needs. Along the coast of Pará from São Caetano de Odivelas to Bragança, for example, the Brazilian botanist Samuel Almeida reports increased pressure on red and black mangroves to supply fuel for brick factories and bakeries. On a floodplain island near Abaeté, the owner of a small sawmill reported to me that he occasionally processes red mangrove to provide rafters for local markets.

At Terra Amarela along Rio Tauá-Pará near Vigia, I saw a charcoal-making kiln with stacks of red mangrove. As urban areas continue to grow, mangroves could come under increasing pressure from the charcoal trade geared to households in the poorer sections of towns and cities. In the Amazon charcoal is still used by many households to cook their daily meals rather than for the occasional barbecue, as in North America.

Mangroves are found throughout the estuary, though the density and species composition vary according to the degree of salinity. Mangroves are often intermixed with species typical of freshwater floodplains, such as açaí palm, stilt-rooted mututí, gnarled aturiá, and ananí, the latter a valuable timber species. Red mangrove, known locally as *mangue*, occurs sporadically inland as far as the Furo de Breves and Afuá, but in the southern estuary it frequently lines islands and sloughs, with black mangrove (ciriúba) found immediately behind.

Mangroves are concentrated in the southern part of the estuary because less freshwater flushes around southern Marajó and along the Atlantic coast of Amapá, which is washed by the equatorial current blended with freshwater from the Amazon. Estimates on the area of mangroves in Pará range widely, from 900 to 2,900 square kilometers, so it is hard to determine the area of mangroves at the mouth of the Amazon. It is probably safe to assume that several hundred square kilometers of mangroves, mostly mixed with some freshwater floodplain species, are found in the estuary. Although they account for a relatively small area, mangroves are nevertheless critical habitat for the several species of shrimp and crab and a regional delicacy, shipworm.

(OPPOSITE PAGE)
Red mangrove at low tide along a slough in the southern estuary. At high tide, many species of fish, shrimp, and other aquatic organisms gather among the stilt roots to feed and reproduce. Near Vigia, November 15, 1998.

CHAPTER 2

Reinventing Pristine Nature

People have been deliberately and unconsciously reshaping "wilderness" at the mouth of the Amazon for a long time. When the first people stepped onto the shores of the great river-sea is not known and probably will never be known. Sea levels started rising at the close of the last Ice Age, thereby burying or erasing any vestiges of ancient settlements along coastal inlets. About five thousand years ago, the sea level rose temporarily at the mouth of the Amazon by one to two meters, further obliterating cultural footprints in the lower parts of the estuary. Moreover, the restless Amazon has shifted its course from time to time, wearing away some islands and forming new ones. Nevertheless, it seems likely that the first hunters and gatherers arrived at the mouth of the Amazon tens of thousands of years ago.

Early settlers soon began altering the landscape. Widely scattered shellmounds in the estuary attest to the long history of exploitation of aquatic resources. Sadly, most of the shellmounds have been destroyed to obtain lime for kilns; they were once particularly abundant along the Pará coast east of Belém. Relatively undisturbed shellmounds, often associated with anthropogenic black earth, still abound along the lower Anapú. At Fazenda Vitória near the mouth of the Anapú, for example, an extensive shellmound stretches for several hundred meters along the shores of Melgaço Bay. Neither the ranch's owner nor the cowboys on the property have any idea that the shellmound is anthropogenic, although it is interlaced with black earth containing potsherds. Locals call the shellmound "calcário" and consider it a natural formation. Curiously, the freshwater mussels, which are found in abundance in the shellmound and buried in the mud along the bay shore, have not been exploited for centuries or even millennia.

Even more curious is the fact that shellmounds are scattered across an island some five kilometers wide along the northern shores of Melgaço Bay. A circular shellmound two hundred meters inland on Fazenda Vitória was about one meter high with a diameter of about forty meters. Apparently these long gone residents preferred a dispersed settlement pattern to living in one large center. Mussels were evidently carried inland in baskets for consumption, and the ancient inhabitants built low mounds, partially built up with discarded shellmounds, to keep habitation sites dry during the rainy season.

When the current owner of Fazenda Vitória purchased the ranch in 1978, most of the property was in forest. The shellmounds have only been revealed in the last decade as the forest has been progressively cleared to establish cattle pasture.

Various cultures have thus modified the landscape to suit their needs. When the mussel eaters lived there, the landscape was probably mostly open. Crops were likely cultivated in cleared areas during the low water season. When the mound builders disappeared is not known, but they were probably gone before the arrival of Europeans. Floodplain forest reclaimed the cleared land, only to fall again to the ax in the last few decades. The abundance of native bamboo on the ranch, as well as other indicator species of disturbance, such as mucajá and inajá palms, suggest human-induced waxing and waning of forests for thousands of years. In tropical Asia, bamboos are also considered indicators of disturbance.

Pure stands of a native bamboo, known locally as taboka, occur throughout the estuary and are a sure sign that forest has been cleared. Stands of bamboo, of which there appear to be several species in the Amazon, are also found in some upland parts of the region, such as in the state of Acre and near Juruti and Marabá in Pará. Only one species of native bamboo is found in the estuary or at least is dominant there. It can be distinguished by its barbed-wire thorns growing from appendages at the base of the stem, an effective deterrent to browsers.

Taboka was likely present in the Amazon estuary before the arrival of people. But clearings in the forest by indigenous groups to make way for crops created openings for the bamboo to proliferate after fields were abandoned. And although the rural population is less dense in the estuary today, some river dwellers still clear riparian forest to grow food and market crops, thereby maintaining favorable conditions for bamboo. The thinning of floodplain forest by loggers has also undoubtedly favored populations of bamboo.

EARLY FARMERS AS LANDSCAPE ENGINEERS

Although much remains to be learned about the prehistory of the Amazon estuary, it is clear that at times populations were dense, with a relatively sophisticated social organization. Agriculture enabled people to amass food surpluses and permitted the development of craft specialization. And the early farmers in the estuary were not flash-in-the-pan civilizations. Some of the cultures endured for centuries and produced fine pottery with exquisite designs. The Marajoara culture on Marajó Island, for example, endured for more than a thousand years. During its long evolution from A.D. 350 to 1650, various distinct pottery styles emerged, such as the impressive urns of the Marajoara phase and Pacoval pottery from the shores of Lake Arari with its distinctive white slip etched with intricate designs.

Pacoval phase of Marajoara pottery, from Teso Pacoval in the southeastern part of Lake Arari. Fazenda Severino, Marajó, April 24, 2000.

A colorful Marajoara urn designed for burial, now part of a rancher's collection. Fazenda Campo Limpo, upper Anajás, Marajó, April 22, 2000.

A Marajoara urn, approximately one thousand years old, used for storing water under a home. The family knew that the urn is indigenous but not that it once contained a human corpse. Near Santa Cruz do Arari, Marajó, May 14, 1999.

An unpainted small Marajoara urn used for keeping drinking water cool through evaporation. Near Santa Cruz do Arari, Marajó, May 14, 1999.

Many of the ornate urns on Marajó have been dug up for private collections and museums. But some locals use them to store drinking water, a use for which the urns are well suited as the earthenware is slightly permeable and evaporation cools the water. Larger urns were formerly used for burying the elite; smaller pots without paint were likely used also for storing water or alcoholic beverages prepared from fermented manioc.

Although the Marajoara did not have stone readily available for building monuments, unlike other major civilizations of Latin America such as the Incas in the Andes and the Maya in the Yucatán Peninsula, their artistic achievements and landscape engineering skills were nonetheless impressive. The Marajoara built large earthen mounds, rather than masonry pyramids, to bury the society's elite and to build their homes. At least two hundred Marajoara burial mounds, which can be up to 210 meters long, 80 meters wide, and 20 meters high, are found scattered over twenty thousand square kilometers of forest and savanna. Some mounds are found in groups, such as along the upper Anajás and one of its tributaries, the Camutins. Other cultures in the estuary also built mounds, albeit smaller and now mostly covered by forest. Altogether over one thousand such mounds dot the forest and savannas of Marajó.

Little is known about the agricultural underpinnings of the Marajoara, or any of

A Marajoara mound about 15 meters high, 100 meters long, and 60 meters wide in seasonally flooded savanna in the Arari watershed. Potsherds can be seen throughout the profile on the northern part of the mound exposed by erosion. The mound is currently used by water buffalo and cattle for sleeping at night, hence its name the "island of the beasts." Ilha dos Bichos near Cachoeira do Arari, Marajó, May 17, 1999.

the other cultures that once inhabited the estuary, but their ornate pottery and huge burial urns suggest that the ancient cultures had their subsistence needs well in hand. Archaeological evidence indicates that a combination of farming, fishing, and the gathering of wild products from forest and savanna helped to maintain sizable populations at several locations for almost one thousand years. Anna Roosevelt, an archaeologist at the Field Museum in Chicago who has conducted digs on Marajó, suggests that as many as one million people lived on the island a thousand years ago. Marajó today has less than one hundred thousand inhabitants. Marajoara settlements in the savanna zone of Marajó would have been supported by crop production in forested areas to the west. Substantial portions of what is now forest in the western half of Marajó was most likely a patchwork quilt of cultivated fields, based mainly on manioc, fallow gardens with fruit and nut trees, and forest in various stages of succession after clearing. The Marajoara had satellite settlements in the forest and likely traded with other indigenous groups living there.

The better-known indigenous mounds are in the seasonally wet savanna zone of central Marajó, but indigenous folk who once inhabited the forested parts of the island also heaped mounds to live on and to bury the departed. On Fazenda Santa Agida along the lower Camutins near its confluence with the Anajás, for example, indigenous people built a large mound some thirty meters high and two hundred meters long; abundant potsherds scattered on the surface attest to its former occupation. At high water no other dry land can be found for dozens of kilometers, and açaí gatherers currently use the site to construct temporary huts during the rainy season. Denise Schaan, an archaeologist at the Goeldi Museum in Belém, has located dozens of Marajoara mounds in the forested portions of the Anajás watershed. Interestingly, she has also located some Marajoara sites not associated with mound building. Many less obvious sites likely dot the forest-clad portions of western Marajó.

Although the Marajoara dominated Marajó for more than one thousand years, other cultures thrived on the island and adjacent archipelagos. The relationships between the Marajoara and these other cultures are imperfectly understood; rather than wage constant war, it seems likely that they forged political alliances. Archaeological sites abound on the fringes of the Marajoara Empire, but their relationships with other sites on the island warrant further study. On the forested floodplain of the Curupaxizinho River about seven kilometers inland from Afuá in northwestern Marajó, a sinuous mound some 3 to 4 meters high, 10 meters wide, and 150 meters long was likely constructed long ago by an indigenous group. No potsherds have been found on the surface of the elongated mound, suggesting it was used for planting rather than as a village site. Now enveloped by forest, the mound was inhabited several decades ago by rubber tappers. Their huts have long since gone, but the exotic fruit trees planted on the mound by the rubber tappers, such as breadfruit, orange, and lime, survive, though all of them are gradually being shaded out by forest regrowth.

In addition to a few remnants of Marajoara culture in the interior of Marajó, a number of other indigenous cultures inhabited the Amazon estuary when Europeans arrived. In the northern part of the estuary, for example, the Aruã lived in longhouses on Mexiana, Caviana, and parts of northern Marajó. In 1597 John Levy, an English explorer and trader, described the Aruã as living in "greate and veerie longe howses." Indigenous longhouses (*malocas*) in other parts of the Amazon have accommodated as many as several hundred individuals. That Levy reports the houses were not only very long but numerous as well suggests that indigenous populations in parts of the northern estuary were still relatively dense until at least the close of the sixteenth century.

When the French explorer Daniel de la Touche investigated the southern estuary in 1613, he befriended the Tupinambá in the vicinity of present-day Belém, an indigenous group that had migrated along the coast from the northeast of Brazil in the century or so before the Europeans arrived. Along one river near Belém the Tupinambá inhabited twenty-six villages in 1616. As a favor to the hospitable Tupinambá, de la Touche attacked their enemies, the Camarapin Indians of the lower Tocantins, inflicting heavy losses. Clearly, then, the estuary was far from a pristine wilderness when the first Europeans arrived.

THE COLONIAL PERIOD

The colonial period witnessed a collapse of the indigenous population in the Amazon estuary within about one hundred fifty years after contact with Europeans. Indeed, the drop in both the number of cultures and their respective populations appears to have been especially dramatic at the mouth of the Amazon for two reasons: Europeans first settled the region there, and contacts with outsiders were more frequent than farther upstream.

With the precipitous decline of indigenous cultures, many areas in rotational fallow reverted to forest. Europeans introduced cattle, but they were raised mostly on the savannas of eastern Marajó. The Portuguese did not settle in large numbers; rather they were mostly interested in trade from urban bases and in establishing control over the region's natural resources. To that end, they finally rid the estuary of other Europeans who coveted the timber, drug plants, and crops, particularly tobacco, that could be grown after clearing the forest. By the mid-seventeenth century, Portuguese military expeditions had finally expelled the Dutch, British, and French from the mouth of the Amazon. Had the latter managed to stay, they likely would have colonized in greater numbers than the Portuguese.

Relatively small areas of forest were therefore cleared during the colonial period, mainly on floodplain islands and adjacent uplands to plant sugarcane, cacao, and rice. The Amazon was not permitted to compete with the northeast of Brazil in sugar production; thus most of the cane grown in the Amazon estuary was for distilling potent white rum, known as *aguardente*. Cacao was planted in the estuary in the mid-eighteenth century, but the Amazon has never been a significant exporter of cacao because of the depredations of witches' broom disease and the scarcity of labor. The fungal pathogen that causes witches' broom is native to the Amazon and attacks the crop when planted on a large scale. Until relatively recently, the northeastern state of Bahia has been free of the disease and has produced most of the cacao used to make chocolate in Brazil and for export. As the taste for chocolate grew in Europe, cacao planting increased in other parts of the tropics free of witches' broom, such as the Caribbean, Central America, West Africa, and parts of Southeast Asia.

The pace of environmental and cultural change began to quicken markedly from approximately the mid-nineteenth century and continues to accelerate in the new millennium. Improvements in transportation, urban growth, and the growing domestic and international appetite for natural resources, especially timber, are propelling landscape transformations and shifts in lifestyles.

TRANSPORT INNOVATIONS
AND THEIR ENVIRONMENTAL IMPLICATIONS

Indigenous cultures in the Amazon apparently did not use sails. Rather, they paddled dugout canoes, probably great distances along trade routes. Some of the dugouts were doubtless quite large and capable of carrying substantial loads. Evidently, the lack of sails did not retard the development of indigenous cultures.

The Portuguese brought sails of various designs into the region, but large sailing ships were deployed mostly on transatlantic trips, probably because their draft was too great for the numerous sand- and mud bars along the Amazon and its tributaries. Smaller craft proved easier to manage and had a shallower draft, so they were fitted with rectangular sails, fashioned from a native bamboo. Rectangular sails were about two and a half meters tall and were rigged to large dugout canoes, called *igarités*, which

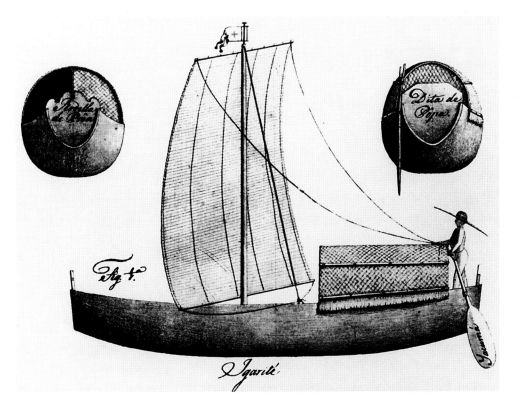

A late-eighteenth-century dugout rigged with a rectangular sail fashioned from taboka, a native bamboo. From Alexandre Rodrigues Ferreira, Viagem Filosófica pelas Capitanias do Grão Pará, Rio Negro, Mato Grosso, e Cuiabá, 1783-1792, vol. 1: Iconografia: Geografia-Antropologia (Rio de Janeiro: Conselho Federal de Cultura, 1971), pl. 35.

Paddle steamers operating on the Amazon at the beginning of the twentieth century. From Percy Lau, Tipos e Aspectos do Brasil *(Rio de Janeiro: Instituto Brasileiro de Geografia e Estatística, Conselho de Geografia, 1949), 15.*

were often fitted with a palm thatch shelter at the stern. A major disadvantage of such craft is that they can only run with the wind. The latine sail, in contrast, allows the boat to tack at an angle into the wind. The single triangular sail, made of fabric, is rapidly deployed and can be equally quickly wrapped up in a storm. The origins of the latine sail are obscure, but it may have been introduced to the Mediterranean from the Arab world in the Middle Ages. While square sails have disappeared in the Amazon estuary, the distinctive latine sail still graces fishing craft, although they are often fashioned from plastic rather than canvas.

Although sails allowed vessels to travel more quickly, they were still cumbersome by today's standards of motorized power. Most expeditions up the Amazon were confined to the dry season when brisk trades blow from the east. Even so, it would take months to reach trading posts upstream. In 1844 Manoel Paranhos da Silva Vellozo, governor of Pará, complained in a state of the union address that it often took two months to travel from Belém to Manaus. The steamship era was just beginning in Europe, and the governor was well aware of the economic benefits steamships could bring to the Amazon. Vellozo argued that they would greatly facilitate transportation and foster prosperity by "shortening distances, linking population clusters hitherto so isolated from each other, and as a consequence boosting agriculture, industry, and commerce."[1]

Almost a decade was to pass before Vellozo's dream was realized. In 1853 the Companhia de Navegação do Amazonas began regular steamship service with four lines along the Amazon and some of its tributaries. Freight charges and delivery times shrank dramatically. On the Belém-Manaus run, for example, the round-trip journey was completed in three weeks, down from several months by sail. Furthermore, service was at least monthly rather than seasonal. By 1862 steamships were plying several thousand kilometers up the Amazon as far as Yurimaguas in Peru. By 1870 nine steamship lines were operating in the Amazon. With approval from Brazilian authorities, the Companhia de Navegação do Amazonas was taken over by an English group in 1874 and renamed Amazon Steam Navigation Company. Flush with fresh capital, the number of steamships and routes multiplied quickly, and by 1898 the new company was operating dozens of steamships on regular runs along the Amazon and its main tributaries.

By cutting transportation costs and travel time, steamships provided a boost to cattle ranching along the middle Amazon, particularly near Monte Alegre. Cattle could be brought to the Belém market in reasonable condition after the four- or five-day trip

Cattle aboard the steamship Alagoas *making its way through a passage between some islands on the Amazon floodplain, circa 1900.*
From O Album do Amazonas *(Manaus, 1908).*

downstream. Although steamships likely accelerated the destruction of floodplain forest of the middle Amazon for cattle production, pressure on cattle producers in the estuary to supply the Belém market was reduced, thereby deflecting deforestation upstream.

The opening of the Amazon to international river traffic in 1866 provided a further boost to commerce. Within short order, steamship companies based in Europe—particularly in Liverpool and Hamburg—as well as the United States launched passenger and cargo service to the Amazon.

The advent of international steamship lines to the Amazon alarmed one nineteenth-century French traveler. Ahead of his time in terms of environmental consciousness, Paul Marcoy fretted one hundred forty years ago about the accelerated pace of forest destruction that steamship navigation would bring:

> The introduction of steamboats on the Amazon, by lessening distances and multiplying commercial relations, has only added to the means of destruction employed by man. Already we foresee the time when sarsaparilla will have disappeared from Brazil, or have been reduced to regular cultivation like cacao.[2]

Marcoy's concern stemmed from his observations on second growth in the vicinity of Manaus. He noted that forests often took a long time to heal after clearing:

> A freshly arrived European would have deceived himself with respect to these forests by mistaking the apparent luxuriousness of the vegetation for that of virgin forests; they were however capoueras, a Tupi word used in Brazil to designate forests which have grown up on land which has been formerly cleared and abandoned by cultivators. It is a fact of which European botanists are perhaps not aware, that a tropical forest which has once suffered by the hand of man never recovers its original splendour, even where it is left to itself for a century. Some will say that this indelible mark is the seal with which man, as king of creation, impresses his conquest; others will be inclined to think that this miserable biped has, like the fabled harpies, the sad faculty of soiling and withering whatever he touches.[3]

In spite of concern by early environmentalists, the arrival of steamships in the Amazon provoked little widespread deforestation beyond floodplain forests near Santarém and Monte Alegre. True, wood was gathered and stacked at ports to provide fuel for the iron ships, but much of it was garnered from slash-and-burn fields cleared for crops. The new, faster ships accelerated the extraction of forest products, especially rubber, rather than stimulate large-scale clearing for agriculture.

The introduction of steamships to the Amazon enabled the rubber boom, which lasted roughly from the 1860s to 1910, to take off. Steamships collapsed travel time

*The first foreign steamship on
the Amazon in 1866. From Paul
Marcoy,* A Journey across South
America from the Pacific Ocean
to the Atlantic Ocean *(London:
Blackie and Son, 1873), 4:491.*

from the Amazon to Europe from months to weeks. Although much of the rubber tapped in the region came from forests of the upper Amazon where the trees are more plentiful, enough of the latex-bearing trees were found in the estuarine forests to attract the attention of locals and refugees from droughts in the northeast of Brazil. By 1870 rubber gathering was so attractive that rural residents were abandoning agriculture. In 1875 Pedro Vicente de Azevedo, governor of Pará, noted that the rubber boom had knocked the sails out of crop production in southern Marajó and the municipality of Gurupá in the western edge of the estuary as early as 1870. In his outgoing address, Azevedo remarked: "There is absolutely no agriculture and no industry or jobs except for rubber production."[4]

The rubber boom, then, led to less forest clearing for crop production in the estuary. Following the collapse of the rubber boom, locals either returned to fishing and farming or migrated to cities. Rubber has not been tapped in the estuary for decades, and although the trees are still plentiful in some areas there, they exhibit ancient, rather than fresh, scars.

Steamships reigned along the main rivers of the Amazon for a relatively brief episode in the region's long history of human occupation. In the 1930s, after some eighty years of dominating navigation, steamships gave way to diesel-powered boats,

Rubber trees are relatively common in floodplain forests in the Amazon estuary but are no longer tapped because prices for rubber are too low and there are no buyers. Old rubber trees still bear the scars from tapping during bygone dry seasons. Rio dos Macacos near Breves, Marajó, May 17, 2000.

and by the 1950s virtually all steamships in the Amazon had been withdrawn from service. The major advantages of diesel-powered boats are that, unlike steam-operated machines, their engines are economical to operate and occupy less space, and the boats can operate for a month or so before taking on more fuel.

Many river dwellers own a small, covered boat with a 12- to 15-horsepower diesel engine, to take children to school or produce to market. Some canoes are fitted with even smaller, clutchless 7.5-horsepower diesel engines; such craft are called *botes* in northern Marajó, *igaratés* on Caviana, and *rabetas* in southern Marajó.

The flexibility and affordability of diesel engines has transformed river travel in the Amazon, allowing more people to penetrate remote areas in search of natural resources and to produce crops and livestock for sale to markets that were previously inaccessible. Rather than provoke massive deforestation, however, affordable diesel boats have spurred many river dwellers to plant açaí palms. Açaí fruits are highly perishable, and without access to rapid boat travel the palm would not dominate the landscapes of the estuary as it does in many parts today.

A river trader (regatão) *in the Amazon with a diesel-powered boat. From Percy Lau,* Tipos e Aspectos do Brasil *(Rio de Janeiro: Instituto Brasileiro de Geografia e Estatística, Conselho de Geografia, 1949), 19.*

The skyline of Belém is now punctuated by hundreds of apartment buildings and office towers, and more skyscrapers arise every year as the city of more than two million continues to grow. Two hundred years ago, when the population of Belém was only 11,000, churches dominated the skyline. Belém, May 12, 2000.

THE EXPLOSIVE GROWTH OF CITIES

The spectacular growth of cities and towns in the estuary, as indeed throughout the Amazon and much of Latin America, is transforming the culture and landscapes at the mouth of the Amazon. Urban growth has been almost exponential in the last several decades. For example, Belém, the largest city in the Amazon, grew slowly from its inception in 1616 until 1964 when the Belém-Brasília highway was inaugurated, thereby breaking the isolation of Pará's capital from the rest of the country. At the height of the rubber boom in 1900, Belém still had only one hundred thousand inhabitants; today some two million people live in the sweltering yet lively city.

Although the spotlight usually focuses on Belém, all the cities, towns, and villages in the Amazon estuary are burgeoning because of rural-urban migration, local population growth, and fortune seekers from other parts of Brazil. Breves, nestled in the southwest corner of Marajó, was little more than a cluster of huts in the 1866. Today Breves anchors a booming timber trade and has grown to more than forty thousand inhabitants. Similarly, Igarapé-Miri in the southern part of the estuary consisted of little more than a dozen buildings clustered near the main church in 1866. Now several rows of streets extend back from the waterfront, and the church is crowded by commercial houses and telecommunication and television towers. Youngsters in Igarapé-Miri, formerly known for its fine sugarcane alcohol, can now surf the Net. And merchants in Igarapé-Miri place orders with distributors in Belém by cell phone; a century ago, it would take the better part of a day for a message to reach the state capital one hundred kilometers away.

Each urban nucleus has its own orbit of suppliers, and many growers, fishers, and loggers supply more than one urban market. Indeed, today about two-thirds of the

Breves on the southwest tip of Marajó in 1866 when inhabitants of the village lived largely off the land and waters. From Paul Marcoy, A Journey across South America from the Pacific Ocean to the Atlantic Ocean *(London: Blackie and Son, 1873), 4:538.*

Breves is one of the many fast-growing towns in the Amazon estuary. Many of the town's 40,000 inhabitants are involved in the lumber industry and in commerce. This shot shortly after sunrise is relatively tranquil because it is a Sunday (November 5, 1995).

people living in the Amazon inhabit urban areas, contrary to the popular perception that the region is a green hell inhabited mostly by Indians and screeching macaws. When asked about the dangers of doing fieldwork in the Amazon, I point out that one is far more likely to be struck by a careening bus in Belém than pounced on by a jaguar or devoured by piranhas.

Urban growth creates ripple effects in the surrounding countryside as producers respond to market opportunities. Landscapes are resculpted to meet demands of expanding or emerging markets. Areas that were formerly planted in sugarcane are now occupied by açaí palm groves as competition from alcohol producers in southern Brazil has forced farmers to shift to other crops. Açaí is one such option, especially with growing markets for the pulp of the fruit in central and southern Brazil. The growing appetite for beef has prompted some river dwellers to clear forest for cattle pasture. The chapters that follow explore the ways in which locals have either safeguarded or altered habitats in response to market signals, both domestic and international.

Jungle Cowboys

For many people, Amazonia is synonymous with rainforest, but it also conjures up images of rampant deforestation, especially at the hands of ranchers. Television programs, newspaper accounts, and magazine articles depict the region going up in smoke, exacerbating global warming and destroying biodiversity. Almost invariably when I tell laypeople in the United States that I do fieldwork in the Amazon, they inquire whether there will soon be any forest left. Although some parts of the Amazon forest have been converted to pastureland, especially along pioneer highways torn through the uplands in the second half of the twentieth century, many areas have been largely spared the onslaught of the "grass rush." The Amazon estuary is one such area.

This chapter explores the paradoxical situation of cattle ranching juxtaposed with forest, with the latter largely holding its own. Most of the cattle in the estuary graze on seasonally flooded grassland rather than on planted pasture cleared from forest. For the most part, ranchers in the campos are clearing little if any *galeria* (gallery) forest along streams, nor are they encroaching much into the forest that dominates the western part of Marajó. On the contrary, in some areas of south-central Marajó, forest seems to be invading savanna. Yet in some areas historically dominated by floodplain forest, a few smallholders are adopting cattle and clearing forest to plant pasture. If that trend should accelerate, then habitat for fisheries and other economic wildlife will be threatened.

It is ironic that cattle were first introduced to the Amazon basin at the river's mouth yet the forests—both "natural" and modified to suit local people's needs—have largely survived. The explanation for this is both ecological and economic. Extensive savannas are found in parts of the estuary, especially on eastern Marajó, on much of Mexiana Island, and on the north side of the estuary in Amapá. Such seasonally wet savannas serve as convenient places for free-range cattle as they require little or no maintenance, other than burning in the dry season to encourage better forage at the onset of the rains. And forests that cloak western Marajó and penetrate savannas along streams have largely held their ground because many of them have been turned into semiwild orchards, brimming with economic plants that provide sufficient sustenance and income to warrant protection.

Another factor accounting for the survival of forests in the Amazon estuary is that demand for beef in Belém, the region's main city, is increasingly met from suppliers in upland areas. Bulldozers tore corridors deep into upland rainforest during the 1960s and 1970s, and with the help of generous fiscal incentives, many ranchers followed in their wake. In 1961 Marajó supplied 85 percent of the cattle slaughtered in Belém, but by 1972 that proportion had shrunk to a third. The cattle herd nurtured by artificial pastures eked from upland forest in the state of Pará now stands at about six million, about twenty times the number of cattle on Marajó. The focus of cattle ranching in the Amazon has clearly shifted to the uplands. Indeed, more and more ranchers on Marajó are selling calves for fattening on upland pastures.

Even before new highways rent the forest that once carpeted much of the uplands, Marajó was never the sole supplier of beef to Belém. Although it was the main supplier of meat to the city until the mid-twentieth century, cattle have been shipped to Belém from Óbidos and Monte Alegre along the middle Amazon since the early nineteenth century. In the early 1900s cattle were being brought to Belém by boat from as far afield as Maranhão, Ceará, and even Argentina to satisfy the city's appetite for fresh meat. It even paid to fly fresh beef to Belém from Goiás at the close of World War II when droves of DC3s, workhorse transport planes during the war, were put to civilian uses. By 1968 an estimated 40 percent of the beef consumed in Belém was being flown up from Goiás and placed in cold storage for distribution to butcher shops the next day. Several firms were involved in this aerial meat bridge linking slaughterhouses in Cristalândia, Pedro Afonso, and Porto Nacional in the cerrado region of central Brazil with the growing market of Belém. By 1970, however, the aerial beef shuttle to Belém collapsed as cattle pastures became established around Paragominas on the Belém-Brasília highway, thereby provisioning Belém with cheaper supplies.

INTRODUCTION OF CATTLE AND HERD GROWTH

English settlers brought the first cattle to the Amazon in the early 1620s to provision their ships and trading outposts in the northern part of the Amazon estuary, particularly at Macapá. The cattle apparently were kept on seasonally wet savannas along the southern coast of Amapá. The English had designs on establishing a large-scale beef and hide industry in the Amazon. In describing products from the lower Amazon in 1627, an English merchant, George Eveling, wrote: "Allsoe our cattle beeinge carried theather by reason of the continuall summer increase much more from which great proffitt will bee drawne."[1]

After the Portuguese chased the English out of the Amazon in 1636, Portuguese entrepreneurs and Catholic missions went on to establish sizable ranches in the Amazon estuary. Portuguese merchants brought cattle to Belém in 1644 from Cape Verde, but little suitable forage was available around the urban center, established twenty-eight years earlier. When forest was cleared around the outskirts of the town, second-growth herbs and bushes rather than lush grasses soon asserted themselves. Nutritious African grasses, standard issue today on upland pastures, had not yet been introduced to Brazil. Old World grasses, such as guinea grass (*colonião*), only became established in Brazil in the eighteenth century and in the Amazon only in the twentieth century, at least to any significant extent.

With no suitable grazing land in the vicinity of Belém, merchants looked across the bay to Marajó. In 1680 Francisco Rodrigues Pereira, a Portuguese carpenter, established a ranch along the Mauá, a left bank affluent of the Arari River a little above its mouth along the coast of southern Marajó. One of the largest rivers on the island, slicing across seemingly endless plains, the Arari provided an ideal penetration route for the cattle-laden sailing ships. The Mercedarians soon followed suit with a ranch on Marajó in 1696, followed in short order by Jesuits and Carmelites. Spurred by a desire to be self-sufficient in food and to generate income from the sale or barter of dried meat and hides, the fathers soon dominated cattle production in the Amazon estuary.

Cattle herds multiplied in their new Eden. By 1750 almost half a million cattle grazed on Marajó. The Jesuits alone had 134,475 head of cattle and 1,409 horses on various ranches on the island by 1759. After increasing for about one hundred fifty years, the cattle herd on Marajó dwindled as a result of shifts in landownership and social upheaval. In 1759 the Jesuits were expelled from the Amazon by royal edict because they were resisting efforts to enslave Indians; their ranches on Marajó were confiscated. Ranches of the other Catholic religious orders on Marajó were also mostly taken over by the crown by the close of the eighteenth century. Prosperous ranches fell into the hands of politically well-connected people, but they were often poor administrators. And in 1835, at the height of a regional peasant revolt in the Amazon called the *cabanagem*, about half of the ranches on Marajó were temporarily abandoned. The cattle herd declined precipitously as rural folk slaughtered the cattle at will. Cattle rustling, a perennial problem on the island, worsened. By 1875 the herd size had dropped to 300,000, slipping further to 250,000 in 1881. In the twentieth century, however, the herd rebounded, and by 1914 an estimated 750,000 head roamed the seasonally wet savannas and cerrado of Marajó.

CATTLE BREEDS AND NEW BLOOD

For centuries, hardy stock from Iberia dominated cattle production in Amazonia, as in other parts of the New World tropics. In the 1870s, however, larger Zebu cattle were introduced to Brazil from India, but they did not start making an impact on Amazonian herds until the 1930s. Humpless Iberian cattle were still relatively common in the

Amazon until about 1950. For example, pure Nelore and Nelore crossbreeds, which now account for most of the cattle on the Marajó, were not common there until the latter half of the twentieth century. Gir crosses, also encountered on Marajó, are derived from stock imported to Brazil in 1918 from India to improve milk production. Guzera, another dairy breed imported from India in the twentieth century, is also evident in the crossbreeds that dominate cattle production today on Marajó. No creole herds are left; they have been replaced or genetically swamped by Brahma cattle. Although smaller than Brahma, old Iberian stock was extremely resilient, and valuable genes have undoubtedly been lost as a result of their disappearance.

Cattle ranching on Marajó is commonly regarded as decadent. Marajó is seen as a tourist destination for locals and as a backward place suffused with traditional culture. In contrast, upland ranchers often hail from central and southern Brazil and have introduced modern management techniques. But Marajó ranchers are not backward. Although their cattle take longer to reach market weight, operating costs are lower. The prevailing attitude seems to be, take what nature gives rather than invest heavily in risky strategies to maximize production.

Yet a surprising number of ranchers on Marajó are intensifying their operations, albeit cautiously, mostly by upgrading the genetic stock of their herds. For example, the owner of Fazenda Paraíso near Cachoeira do Arari has introduced Santa Gertrudis, a breed developed in Texas, because it tolerates waterlogged conditions better than Nelore. Santa Gertrudis is already partly tropical because it is a cross between Brahma and Hereford, a beef breed developed in England. Periodic livestock auctions at Soure in southeastern Marajó provide ranchers with an opportunity to compare notes on the attributes of different breeds and crossbreeds. Crossbreeds predominate on Marajó because they are hardier; some ranchers keep purebreds just for breeding purposes. Among the crossbreeds common on Marajó are various tropical and temperate breeds such as Gir x Friesian (Girolandia), Simmental x Nelore, and Limousin x Nelore.

Water Buffalo Roundup

(OPPOSITE PAGE)
The Carabao breed of water buffalo, with distinctive large, upswept horns, on flooded savanna. Water buffalo are ridden by cowboys and are also used to pull carts. Near Cachoeira do Arari, Marajó, May 12, 2000.

Water buffalo are superbly adapted to wetlands, so it is not surprising that Marajó was the first place in Brazil where the animals were introduced. Water buffalo were brought to Marajó from India in 1899, and the island still contains the largest herd in Brazil. Precise numbers are not available, but hundreds of thousands of water buffalo roam the savannas of eastern Marajó. Although they are raised mainly for meat and milk, they also pull carts, and cowboys ride them across the grasslands, especially during the annual flood. Some ranches are dedicated almost exclusively to raising water buffalo, and others raise only cattle, but most have both. On the whole, though, water buffalo are overtaking cattle on Marajó because they gain weight faster and are hardier.

Cattle roundup on savanna at the end of an unusually long rainy season. The mixed coat colors and diverse horn shapes of the cattle indicate that the rancher has opted for crossbreeds, which are hardier than purebreds. The cattle will be picked up by boat for a two-day trip to Belém. Fazenda Cajueiro, municipality of Chaves, Marajó, August 18, 2000.

The Murrah and Mediterranean breeds of water buffalo predominate on Marajó, in part because they are more manageable than the irascible Carabao, also known as the swamp buffalo. The Mediterranean breed was developed in Italy for milk, whereas the Murrah is a dual-purpose breed. The imposing Carabao, known locally as Rosilho, sports massive upswept horns and is increasingly rare because of its temperament and propensity to wound other livestock when being shipped to market. Carabao are essentially feral and have historically been hunted and shot in the field rather than rounded up. On Caviana Island, a cowboy on Fazenda São Luis told of an encounter a companion of his had several years ago with an irate Carabao. The black beast, weighing almost a ton, gored his horse to death when the lasso broke. The cowboy escaped only because he was close to a forest island and managed to shimmy up an açaí palm. The

ranch still has about three hundred Carabao, a tiny fraction of the herd of thirty-five hundred water buffalo that roam the seasonally flooded savannas on the property.

A few ranches also stock the Jafarabadi breed, easily distinguished by its massive downswept horns that give it the appearance of an overgrown bloodhound. Water buffalo are usually black, but a lighter variant, the tan Baio, is found in some herds. The latter were brought to Marajó to upgrade herds because they are bigger than the Mediterranean. But some ranchers are dubious about Baio's virtues and see no advantage in paying a premium for Baio breeding stock at auction.

The exceptionally high butterfat content of water buffalo milk makes it ideal for making mozzarella cheese. Pizza is popular in Brazil, including the Amazon, and demand is growing for mozzarella cheese from Marajó. Consequently, some ranches on the island specialize in dairying with water buffalo, such as Fazenda Campo Limpo in the headwaters of the Anajás, which maintains a herd of fourteen hundred water buffalo and no cattle. Cheese making is a dry season operation. The whey by-product is ideal for pigs, kept on virtually every ranch. Cheese is also made from cattle milk, especially from Nelore x Gir crosses. The pale, rubbery cheese known as queijo de Marajó keeps well without refrigeration, an important consideration in predominantly rural Marajó. Marajó cheese and jam made from cupuaçu (doce de cupuaçu), a relative of cacao, is a favorite dessert of ranch families.

THE RHYTHM OF RANCH LIFE

The seasonal cycle of ranch life in the estuary is dictated by the rains, or more precisely by its effect on water levels, as is the case along the middle and upper Amazon. At the river's mouth, though, flooding regimes are quite different, and locals have responded accordingly. Unlike the other areas, where the Amazon rises some ten meters every year and spills sediment-rich waters over a sprawling floodplain along the central stretch of the river, flooding on Marajó is caused by a river's backing up and a deluge of rainwater that together form marshes and vast, shallow lakes in the island's savanna. Along the middle Amazon, livestock owners respond to the rising waters by taking their herds to upland pastures until the floods recede six months later and verdant meadows proliferate. Smaller operators along the middle Amazon may corral their cattle on floating platforms and feed them floating grasses gathered twice daily.

On Marajó, the rhythm of life is different. The coming of the rains produces a flush of fresh growth, albeit not especially nutritious. This is the season when cattle fatten, although weight gain on the savannas is slow compared to upland pastures. In fact, the low carrying capacity of savannas on Marajó is one of the reasons that the island's ranches are considered rather backward compared to those on the uplands. The carrying capacity of savannas on Marajó varies according to soil conditions but is generally in the range of one head per two to seven hectares, compared to about one head per hectare on planted upland pastures.

Cattle and water buffalo are sold year-round on Marajó and adjacent islands, but a slight peak occurs during the six-month rainy season. After a month or so of rains, conditions become increasingly soggy and difficult for cattle, now confined to patches of higher ground. As the heavy rains render conditions increasingly stressful (*apertar*), some ranchers thin their herds by dispatching some of the cattle to market. During the height of the rainy season, barges fitted with corrals (*boiadeiros*) can gain access to ranches along the margins of shallow lakes, creeks, and rivers, so cattle are often sold at this time. Water buffalo fare better at the height of the rains because they can stay in water all day up to their necks as they browse on diverse aquatic plants such as arumã-rana, a giant marantaceous shrub, and wild grasses, such as canarana, arroz bravo (wild rice), and andrequicé. The main drawback to water buffalo is their ability to swim far from the watchful eyes of cowboys: it makes them more vulnerable to poachers, a perennial problem on Marajó. Water buffalo are in peak condition as the rains taper off, so many of them are sold at this time.

In exceptionally rainy years, many cattle succumb to drowning or malnutrition. Some ranchers have used bulldozers to push up earthen mounds to help the cattle dry out and sleep at night, but forage is still a problem. Cattle and water buffalo also seek out indigenous mounds, once used for ceremonial purposes or habitation, for rest and refuge from the waters. During the day, the livestock leave the mounds to feed; locals use the expression *sai para mariscar*, "going off to fish." Cattle avoid prolonged periods in the water and are forced to feed in the shallows when the last patches of savanna are engulfed by rainwater. In poor condition and battered by ceaseless thunderstorms, the cattle are all "beat up" (*muito baqueado*), as the cowboys put it.

Some ranches have built corrals (*marombas*) on stilts, but these hold no more than about forty head so are used only for milking or sheltering cows and their calves at the height of the rains. To help prevent the cattle and water buffalo from slipping, the parquet floors of the elevated corrals are uneven and are fashioned from durable itaúba or maçaranduba. The supporting poles are also made of resistant hardwood from upland forest, especially charcoal-colored acapu. Fourteen-year-old acapu poles supporting a maromba at Fazenda Severino on the shores of Lake Arari show no signs of decay. And at Fazenda Campo Limpo in the headwater region of the Anabiju, a twenty-year-old maromba floor of acapu showed few signs of wear despite the pounding hooves of water buffalo and alternating seasons of baking sun and torrential rain.

The height of the dry season is a time of deprivation for both cattle and water buffalo. The dry season is particularly stressful for water buffalo, because they need to stay

A cattle buyer taking a consignment of sixteen head to the Portel slaughterhouse. The cattle were raised on pasture cleared from floodplain forest in the eastern part of the Amazon estuary. Melgaço Bay, lower Anapú, near its confluence with the Pacajá, May 14, 2000.

A large cattle boat on its way from Marajó to the Belém slaughterhouse. Near Jenipapo, Arari River, April 23, 2000.

close to mud hollows to keep cool and much of their favorite forage has withered under the bright blue skies and constant summer breeze. Unlike the middle Amazon, where livestock fatten on lush floodplain meadows at low water, unwavering easterly trade winds wither the tough grasses and herbs on estuarine savannas. As the dry season sears the campos, many ranchers opt to sell off part of their herd or send calves to upland pastures. Cattle and water buffalo also lose condition because they have to walk long distances to drink. In the eighteenth century, a Brazilian explorer, Alexandre Rodrigues Ferreira, noted that numerous cattle died on Marajó if the summer was unusually long and dry.

Driven by thirst only made worse after trudging several kilometers across virtually treeless plains, some cattle perish in deep mud along banks of streams in their haste to drink. At Fazenda Cajueiro in northern Marajó, I passed a cow stuck almost up to its shoulders in mud along a tidal stream at the beginning of the dry season. Three black vultures had already assembled on the stream bank waiting for the animal to perish in the heat of the rising sun. The cowboy escorting me on a tour of the savanna upstream seemed unconcerned. The incoming tide would buoy the exhausted animal out of the muck, he explained. Sure enough, on the return boat journey several hours later, the water had risen and the cow was gone. As the dry season progresses, however, the creek dries up and careless cattle are not so fortunate.

Faced with the risk of high herd mortality during the dry season, many ranches have dammed streams to form ponds. Streams are blocked by either of two means: a simple earthen ramp dam (barragem) or a wall dam made by erecting two parallel fences and then filling the space between them with earth (tapagem). Ramp dams became a common feature on savanna landscapes of Marajó starting in the 1930s when diesel tractors and bulldozers were introduced to the island. Tapagems have been around longer because they are constructed manually. A locally made earth carrier (bangué) is fashioned from water buffalo hide or cowhide strung between two poles. The 1.5-meter-long stretcher requires two men to carry the earth into the dam held in place by the pole fences. A patch of the stream bank is cleared and the earth loosened with a pickax. Hoes are then used to scoop the earth onto the stretcher laid on the ground. The parallel fences, about 2.5 meters apart, are made with poles of cecropia, a sun-loving plant that colonizes disturbed sites. Cecropia, known locally as embaúba, is used because it rots quickly; the idea is to have the wall dam hold up only during the dry season. When the floods come, the central part of the tapagem is dismantled to permit fish such as the torpedo-shaped pirarucu to migrate upstream and boats to pass unhindered.

In the absence of streams to dam, ranchers deploy bulldozers to gouge rectangular hollows in the otherwise almost flat landscape to store rainwater. Bulldozed ponds are called rampas (ramps) because the water depth increases gradually. Small ponds

Cowboys filling leather stretchers (bangués) with earth to fill in a dam (tapagem) across a small stream. Igarapé Mandioca, Fazenda Cajueiro, municipality of Chaves, Marajó, August 17, 2000.

Cowboys carrying a cowhide stretcher loaded with dirt into a dam at the beginning of the dry season. The dam will provide drinking water for cattle and water buffalo until the onset of the rains, when it will be dismantled. Igarapé Mandioca, Fazenda Cajueiro, Municipality of Chaves, Marajó, August 17, 2000.

The main house of a cattle ranch on Marajó. House styles vary but usually incorporate a veranda and wooden shutters rather than glass windows. Few ranch houses are air-conditioned, and the generator is usually turned on only for a few hours in the evening for lighting and to run the refrigerator or freezer. Fazenda Severino, Lago Arari, Marajó, April 24, 2000.

(açudes) dug by hand close to the homes on ranches are often stocked with fish such as pirarucu, apaíari (known as oscar in the aquarium trade and acará-açu farther up the Amazon), and armor-plated tamoatá.

These artificial impoundments provide a haven for many aquatic birds, particularly the great egret, and are testament to the fact that not all human tinkering on the landscape is detrimental to wildlife. Ranchers on Marajó are carrying on a long tradition of molding the land to fit their needs, just as indigenous groups did before them.

LIFESTYLES AND CUISINE

The owners of large ranches live in Belém and make only periodic appearances on Marajó. The main house (*casa grande, casa do dono*) often remains unoccupied for most of the year. One ranch I visited along the shores of Lake Arari had not received a visit from its owner in more than two years. And on a large ranch in northern Marajó, a cowboy family thought I was the owner. After I explained that I was just a professor gathering information for a book, the atmosphere relaxed considerably.

All ranchers have a head cowboy (*encarregado, feitor*) who lives in a modest home close to the main ranch house. On exceptionally large ranches, such as Fazenda Cajueiro, a professional manager with a small staff runs the day-to-day operations. Such managers, however, are not usually graduates fresh out of business school; rather, they are typically owners of smaller ranches who are moonlighting for extra income.

A head cowboy in charge of day-to-day ranch operations. Most ranch owners live in cities and visit their properties infrequently. Fazenda Zebulandia, Lago Arari, Marajó, May 15, 1999.

The head cowboy or manager typically makes daily contact with the owner in Belém via a radio located in the main ranch house, usually shortly after dawn or at sunset, when reception is better (storms are more frequent in the afternoon) and the owner is more likely to be at home. The two-way radios are powered by electric generators or, on a few ranches, by photovoltaic panels. On ranches with no radio, the head cowboy may travel to the nearest town to make a telephone call once a month or so to relay news and receive instructions.

Depending on the size of the ranch, as many as eighty cowboys and their families may be employed. The constant threat of cattle theft has led to a dispersed pattern of settlement on ranches, so that the cowboys' homes are scattered at different points (*retiros*) on the property. A few ranchers have resorted to gunslingers (*pistoleiros*) to keep trespassers at bay. Some cattle thieves are thought to penetrate ranches under the guise of fishing expeditions or to hunt or gather forest products. Others make nocturnal raids along the remoter perimeters of the property.

The term "retiro" aptly describes the isolated existence of cowboys, who are retired from view and much social interaction. To help counteract loneliness and boredom, some ranchers promote periodic parties (*festas*) for employees and invited guests. At Fazenda Santo André along the Anabiju, for example, a festa in honor of Saint Sebastian, the patron saint of the savannas, is held on the second Saturday in January. In addition to copious amounts of barbecued beef, the two-day event includes horse races, soccer matches, and a dance contest. *Cachaça* (sugarcane alcohol) is not allowed in the interest of maintaining peace; only beer is available to help cowboys overcome their shyness when asking someone to dance. Soft drinks are sold to the ladies. At Fazenda Santa Teresa near Breves in southwestern Marajó, the annual festival is held on December 8 in honor of Our Lady of Conception (Nossa Senhora da Conceição). The two-day festival celebrates the day in 1946 when the ranch's owner, Genésio Caetano de Oliveira, arrived in Breves from a rural part of the estuary where he was brought up. Genésio, now in his seventies, donates a couple of cattle for the barbecue and supplies all the rice, beans, and manioc flour for the partygoers. He also contracts a band and a deejay, who takes over when the musicians take periodic breaks. Participants sleep wherever they can find a place to sling their hammocks and pay only for soft drinks and beer.

Brazilians love to dance and listen to loud music, so even in the remote headwaters tavern owners have learned that it pays to put on periodic dances in a specially constructed hall adjacent to the store. Large banners stretching across storefronts and at the entrance to busy boat passages advertise forthcoming dances. Loudspeakers (*som*) and a deejay are brought in by boat from the nearest town. Partygoers make their way by small boats and canoes to the dance, which typically starts around midnight and lasts until dawn. Old-timers remember dancing to live music played on guitars (*banjos*) and selecting partners for lundum, a traditional dance introduced by descendants of African slaves. Now ranch hands, fishers, hunters, and woodsmen shuffle to the imploring beat of country music (*brega*), the lilting rhythm of Brazilian reggae recorded by African-Brazilians in São Luis, or the frantic pace of American rock, all blaring out of speakers taller than the average man. Again, cachaça is not sold. Canned beer sells briskly and is considered less risky than bottled beer because people are less likely to be cut in the event of a misunderstanding. Both men and women consume beer at tavern dances and when interested in getting better acquainted may negotiate rickety plank walkways to find seclusion in dark açaí groves.

Other opportunities for amorous encounters arise when cowboys and their families make their way to Catholic festivals celebrating the local patron saint in nearby towns. Such events usually last several days, and if the town is large enough, such as Abaetetuba or Belém, kids and young adults can enjoy carnival rides. The largest festival of this kind is Belém's *círio*, held in October, which draws a million faithful from the surrounding countryside. Ranch owners sometimes give long-term employees a holiday bonus so that they can enjoy these events.

The isolation of ranch life poses a problem for educating children. In the past some ranches set up schools for their employees and families, but the Ministry of Education has since promoted primary schools in rural areas. Yet rural schools function precariously if at all and only offer instruction for the first few grades. Furthermore, many ranch children as well as those from farming and fishing families do not have ready access to schools even when they do function. More than one mother has expressed consternation that her eleven- and twelve-year-old children cannot read or write their names.

In an effort to give their children greater opportunities in life, some cowboy families send one or more of their youngsters to live with relatives in towns to study. But it is a tough decision. The parents miss their children, and with the children gone they have fewer helping hands around the house and on the ranch. A ten-year-old boy on a ranch on Caviana Island refuses to live in Macapá with an aunt in order to study because he is so devoted to his father. Furthermore, parents must provide a subsidy for their children because relatives in urban areas are typically poor. Alternatively, the wife may leave the ranch to live in town so that the children can receive an education. Children aspiring to study in high school must go to Belém and Macapá. During Easter weekend in April 2000, I encountered some teenage girls visiting their parents who work on the Tres Marias ranch in the upper Anajás watershed. The young ladies study or work in Belém, and none of them expressed any intention of living on a ranch again, much to the consternation of some young cowboys who were quaffing beer below the veranda.

Salted beef hanging out to dry in the sun on the back porch of a cowboy's home. The slabs of dried beef, known as charque, *can be stored without refrigeration for months; sections are periodically cut off to be fried, boiled, or added to bean stews. Retiro Santa Quiteria, Fazenda Ilha Nova, Anabiju headwaters, Marajó, April 22, 2000.*

Not all cowboys are married. Some have separated from their wives and live alone, without as much as a radio for evening entertainment. A few are gay. I was surprised to learn that some cowboys are openly gay, given what I thought was a conservative or "traditional" culture in the rural parts of the Amazon. In the case of a ranch along the Anabiju River on Marajó, a couple of gay cowboys are well liked and participate in social events on the ranch. They are the targets of some ribbing, however, which they apparently take good-naturedly. One rancher on Marajó is reputedly gay, not entirely surprising considering that the island has some eight hundred ranches.

As in the cities, people are relatively tolerant of diverse approaches to sexuality in the backwaters of the estuary. In Breves, for example, the annual beauty contest at the end of the summer holidays (the last Sunday in July) has expanded during the last five years to include various age groups and sexual orientations. In addition to the traditional Miss Summer (Miss Verão), little girls now parade for the honor of being crowned Miss Miri (*miri* means "small," derived from an indigenous tongue), young boys compete for the Mister Miri award, and gays in imaginative attire display onstage for the title of Mister Gay. A female table server in a hotel in Breves recounted the 2000 beauty pageant to me. Somewhat scandalized but nevertheless wearing a broad grin, the young woman, in her early twenties, recalled that one of the contestants for Mister Gay wore a thong swimsuit so skimpy that it could have passed for dental floss. It is doubtful, however, that gay cowboys enter such competitions. Nevertheless, an old-timer on a ranch along the Anabiju explained that there have always been gay cowboys on Marajó. Only now they live together and make little or no attempt to keep the nature of their relationship secret.

Head cowboys are typically paid about twice the minimum wage (U.S. $180/month), whereas auxiliary cowboys usually receive half that amount. Sometimes food and medical supplies are discounted from the salary; in other cases the salary is paid in full and the cowboys purchase their own food and medicines. Given the modest salaries, it is not surprising that game, fish, and wild fruits supplement the cowboys' fare. *Vaqueiros* on Marajó and neighboring Mexiana and Caviana are woodsmen in every sense of the word.

Although cowboys are surrounded by cattle, fresh beef is not often on the menu. And when cowboys and their families do eat fresh meat, it is more likely to be game or small livestock. Beef is more commonly consumed in salted and sun-dried form, similar to jerky (*charque*). Cattle are for generating income for the owner, not for feeding employees. Nevertheless, ranchers permit the periodic slaughter of a cow to feed personnel, usually once a week or every two weeks, depending on the number of cowboys. This event, known as *matalotagem*, provides one of the rare opportunities for families to get together and catch up on gossip. Old cows, between ten and twelve years old, are typically selected for matalotagem, because they are tough and less valuable than young bulls, which typically go to market when they are four years old.

On fresh meat day, cowboys and their families typically consume copious amounts of fried or boiled beef. But cowboys do not own refrigerators, so they preserve the remaining meat by several means. For short-term preservation, meat is diced and fried in lard, a dish called *frito de vaqueiro* or *frito Marajoara*. This artery-clogging repast would be anathema to sedentary urban folk but is highly suitable for active cowboys and their families. Cowboy's fried beef can be stored in the pan for several days and is typically eaten with gritty manioc flour. Occasionally, cowboys take frito de vaqueiro with them for lunch in the field in a leather pouch called a *surrão*. Some cowboy wives prepare sausages from the fatty cuts; the chopped up meat is mixed with salt, garlic, lime juice, and cumin seeds. After drying in the sun for a day or two, the sausages can be hung from the ceiling of the kitchen for another few days before they begin to spoil. For consumption over a period of weeks or months, meat is cut into one-inch-thick slabs, rubbed with salt, and hung on racks to dry. When drying charque on the back porch, family members must be vigilant lest black vultures swoop down and devour the stiffening meat.

Although cattle ranching on the savannas of Marajó is commonly perceived as the domain of large landholders, small-scale operators are also increasingly adopting cattle and especially water buffalo. While some ranches on Marajó are indeed large—such as the 124,000-hectare Fazenda Cajueiro near Chaves—none of them rival the vast ranches found in some upland areas, such as in northern Mato Grosso and southern Pará. In those areas corporations own ranches approaching 400,000 hectares. On Marajó, ranches typically shrink over the generations because property is frequently divided up among heirs after the owner dies, especially if they cannot agree on how to manage it jointly. For example, Fazenda Anabiju in southern Marajó once sprawled over 54,000 hectares until its owner, José Ferreira Teixeira, died in 1944. Since then the property has been divided into a dozen ranches, ranging in size from 5,000 to 10,000 hectares. Some of the mini-ranches belong to an extended family; others have been sold to investors.

Some river dwellers occupying interstices between ranches, usually along streams flanked by galeria forest, also own cattle or water buffalo. One such community is Vila do Rosario near the Camará River; several villagers own a few cattle or water buffalo that graze on nearby savannas. Another is the village of Jabuti near Retiro Grande, located along the watershed divide between the Camará and Arari Rivers, where households typically own a dozen or so cattle that graze on small, individually owned properties in the 15- to 50-hectare range. Inhabitants of Jabuti are reputed to make fine cheese, a logical specialization for those with small herds.

The pathways to cattle adoption by smallholders are many, and only a few examples are given here. In the Lavrado community in the watershed divide between the Arari and Anabiju Rivers, a zone characterized by a patchwork quilt of savannas and forest, one former cowboy has acquired a small property on which he raises twenty water buffalo. He was able to amass the necessary capital to buy the land and livestock when the owner of the ranch on which he worked died and left him some cattle. He sold the cattle, invested in a small store, and after several profitable years was able to buy his mini-ranch. And near Santa Cruz do Arari, the owner of a property slightly under three hectares maintains a herd of one hundred twenty cattle and sixty water buffalo. The property, Fazenda Sete Irmãos (Seven Brothers Ranch), is not fenced, and the livestock range freely on the savanna of neighboring farms and ranches. If the owner of the ranch, an eighty-seven-year-old lady who came from Lebanon as a girl, had to confine her livestock to her property, she could maintain at most one cow or water buffalo. Landowners, both large and small, have a relaxed attitude about cattle and water buffalo grazing on their land because they know that their cattle do the same. Only at roundup, when cattle are brought to boats for delivery to market, do cowboys pay attention to the branding mark.

In Nazaré village at the mouth of the Ganhoão River along the northern coast of Marajó, fifty-three-year-old "Tibi" (many locals go by nicknames in the estuary) decided to sell his fishing boat and buy water buffalo. He now has fifteen animals, which he grazes in the village and on a nearby ranch belonging to a friend. Tibi is also the village butcher. Profits from this enterprise and the selling of water buffalo have enabled him to buy an electric generator and a parabolic antenna for his television set. His wife now prepares açaí juice with an electric beater, and the entire family watches soap operas at night. Tibi enjoys one of the highest standards of living in the village; no wonder others are also beginning to adopt water buffalo, or would like to.

On some of the smaller ranches, cowboys have acquired cattle of their own that they graze on the property with the permission of the owner. Such is the case on Fazenda São Sebastião along the Ganhoão River in northern Marajó. Amadeu, a fifty-two-year-old vaqueiro with six children, began acquiring cattle nine years ago and now has thirty-five head. Last year he started buying water buffalo and already has thirteen. Amadeu's livestock blend in with the landowner's herd of two hundred twenty cattle; he sees it as a sound investment and requests payment in cattle or water buffalo whenever possible.

HOOFPRINTS IN THE FOREST

While upland forests are thought to contain greater biodiversity than floodplain forests because the latter are stressed by annual and in many areas daily floods, they nevertheless are species-rich and are no less important ecologically. Floodplain forests play a critical role in the productivity of many fisheries as they serve as nurseries and provide feeding grounds for fish and turtles. Furthermore, floodplain forests are the favored nesting grounds for several species of caimans and turtles, all of which are hunted. The fate of the forests in the Amazon estuary, as elsewhere in the basin, is tied largely to the dynamics of cattle ranching. And here the tide seems to be turning, albeit slowly, toward cattle ranching, as it has in upland areas that have been opened for settlement. The forested areas of Marajó have long been considered inappropriate for cattle ranching because of seasonal and tidal flooding and are therefore safe from the grass rush. But landowners—both large and small—in forested portions of the island are responding to some of the same incentives as property owners on uplands: cattle and water buffalo are good investments, so some have decided to fell estuarine forests to create pastures.

Cattle pasture cleared in flood-plain forest in northwestern Marajó. The logs in the water were cut on Caviana Island. Near Afuá, August 19, 1998.

The scale of deforestation in the estuary for cattle production pales compared to the huge swaths of forest cleared in upland areas for ranches over the last few decades. But a few meters' difference in elevation means that some patches of estuarine forest may be covered with water only during exceptionally high tides for a couple of months in the rainy season, so the land is dry for most of the year and suitable for planting pasture. Thus it is no longer true that cattle ranching in the Amazon estuary is confined to savannas and that the forests are safe.

Various indigenous and exotic grasses are planted in cleared estuarine forest, including canarana and canarana erecta lisa, both native grasses of sediment-rich floodplains. Capim arroz (rice grass), also native to the coffee-and-cream waters of the Amazon, has been planted by a smallholder on Colares Island in a former mangrove. Of the introduced African grasses so commonly planted on the uplands, quicuio is the best adapted to wetlands. One rancher near Melgaço has cleared 585 hectares of estuarine forest to plant quicuio, brachiarão, and Tanzania, the latter a variety of guinea grass. Given the low-lying nature of his land, however, the rancher has opted mostly for quicuio. And on Ilha do Nazaré in the western part of the estuary, the Superintendência de Desenvolvimento da Amazônia (SUDAM) is financing the clearing of floodplain forest for water buffalo. In 2000, the Agropecuária Ilha de Nazaré ranch had eighty water buffalo on 300 hectares of pasture. The ranch plans to clear an additional 700 hectares of floodplain forest to accommodate a projected herd of three thousand water buffalo.

Upland rainforest cleared for a ranch of 150 hectares, small by Amazon standards. The boys are crouched inside the charred remains of a giant angelim vermelho tree. This canopy emergent can soar for 50 meters and was probably several centuries old until it succumbed to the fire set to clear the brush for planting quicuio pasture. If cattle ranching spreads farther into the forest, timber resources will be further diminished. Fazenda Santa Luz, kilometer 14 of the PA 159 highway near Breves, Marajó, August 9, 2000.

Clearing of hitherto forested areas for cattle production is noticeable in other parts of the estuary, particularly near Afuá, Anajás, and Breves on Marajó. One of the reasons that pasture is gradually spreading into estuarine forests is that some smallholders are beginning to adopt cattle, albeit at a slower pace than those along the floodplain of the middle Amazon and in upland areas. Valdemar, a smallholder along the Pararijós River near Breves, for example, recently acquired three head of cattle as a result of selling posts to ranches along the upper Anajás. Ranchers often prefer to make payment in cattle rather than cash. Hitherto, most of Valdemar's income had come from the sale of manioc flour and açaí fruits. Recently, however, Valdemar cleared three hectares of forest to plant quicuio for his livestock, and he plans to expand his nascent herd. Al-

*Home-fried dumplings filled with ground beef (*cochinha de carne*). The vendor's mother made the dumplings, whereas the popsicles in the Styrofoam container were purchased from a local family for resale. Boys have traditionally sold street snacks, but now girls are beginning to enter the trade to supplement family income. Portel, May 14, 2000.*

though only about one hectare of the cleared area is on a floodplain, Valdemar has pioneered cattle raising in his village and others may soon follow his example. Another factor in Valdemar's decision to experiment with cattle production is health: now in his early fifties, he has back problems from carrying produce and timber for several decades. Valdemar thinks diversifying into cattle will make life easier.

In the predominantly forested portion of western Marajó, ranches are little more than isolated pockets of artificial grassland in a sea of forest. When small operators take on cattle or water buffalo, they are almost always involved in other economic activities such as fishing, lumbering, and extraction of nontimber forest products such as açaí fruits and palmito. Management of mixed farming operations requires a hands-on approach, and for this reason it is rare to find a small ranch with an absentee landlord.

Urban markets in the estuary are pushing the adoption of cattle ranching by river dwellers. Most of the cattle and water buffalo on Marajó are destined for consumers in Belém, where some one thousand head of cattle are slaughtered every day. Actual consumption rates are higher, because about one-fourth of the beef consumed in Belém comes from clandestine sources. Furthermore, slaughterhouses in Castanhal, Santa Isabel, and Paragominas also supply the Belém market. As Belém has grown, particularly after 1960, so has beef consumption. In 1850, only thirty cattle were slaughtered daily to supply the town, which then had 16,000 inhabitants. By 1875, when Belém's population had reached 40,000, the slaughter rate had risen to eighty head. Around 1900, when the city's population stood at 96,000, about one hundred head a day were being butchered.

Other urban centers in the estuary, although smaller, are also growing rapidly and therefore expanding local markets for beef. The 6,000 inhabitants of Muaná on Marajó, for example, consume about ten cattle a day, although that number drops a little in the dry season when shrimp and fish abound. About a dozen cattle are slaughtered every day to supply the twenty-two butcher shops in Portel, a town of 25,000 inhabitants at the mouth of the Pacajá. Breves, on the other hand, with 40,000 inhabitants, consumes close to two dozen cattle a day. Beef is not just the domain of the well-to-do in such towns; cheaper cuts are avidly purchased by the majority of the population, and ground beef in fried dumplings or pastries is a popular street snack.

Cattle merchants and ranchers generally regard chicken as the main competition for beef. Frozen chicken sells for about U.S. $0.82 per kilogram, nearly half the price of the cheapest cuts of beef. The cost of chicken meat is determined largely by the price of feed; when maize prices are low, chicken is a bargain and beef sales slump. Frozen chickens turn up in even the remotest villages of Marajó, where local entrepreneurs keep them from spoiling by packing them with ice in Styrofoam containers. The abundance of fishing boats loaded with ice in the region helps to make such marketing possible. Many of the chickens consumed in urban areas of the Amazon are brought from southern Brazil or are raised on commercial farms located near highways, using feed from central and southern Brazil. Although chicken will likely increase its market share in the Amazon, beef demand will continue to accompany population growth and increased purchasing power in urban areas. Pressure will therefore mount on the floodplain forests for beef production.

HORSE HAVEN

Without horses there would be no true cowboys. Vaqueiros on Marajó ride bullocks and water buffalo, but when rounding up herds nothing matches the speed and agility of equines. Horses were introduced to Marajó about the same time as cattle and quickly became feral. In the early 1800s some of the wild horses were rounded up for sale in the British West Indies, especially Barbados. Still, complaints came in that the feral horses were causing overgrazing, so an Englishman applied for a license to harvest some of the horses for their hides. At least five thousand were thus killed in 1826. Many of the corpses were left to rot, causing a widespread foul odor. Shortly thereafter, an epidemic, called *quebra-bunda* (lit. "broken backside"), swept through the horse population, killing many of them. Whether the fetid carcasses had anything to do with the disease outbreak is not known. The quick-acting disease was aptly named: the horses collapsed as their rear legs became paralyzed. Unable to feed, they soon perished. The virulent disease nearly wiped out the horse population on Marajó, and as late as 1875 ranch owners complained that there were not enough horses to round up cattle.

To address the shortage of horses and introduce fresh genetic stock, new breeds, such as the quarter horse (known locally as *quarto de milha*), were introduced to Marajó in the late nineteenth century. The main advantage of the stocky quarter horse is that it accelerates quickly, a valuable asset when rounding up recalcitrant cattle and water buffalo.

Two other breeds, Marajoara and Puruca, are also common on Marajó. Both are homegrown and well adapted to the rigors of life on the island, which is pounded by torrential rains for half the year and seared by easterly trades in the dry season. The medium-statured Marajoara is a Creole breed. Marajoara horses sport highly variable coat colors, ranging from chestnut to gray or white. Descendants of horses that survived the 1826 carnage and subsequent outbreak of quebra-bunda, the Marajoara breed is much sought after by upland ranchers as well because they are so hardy and therefore require minimal veterinary care. The diminutive Puruca was developed by crossbreeding the venerable Marajoara with Shetland ponies, introduced to Marajó in 1894 by Pedro Leite Chermont at his Fazenda Santo Antônio along the Anabiju. Although they look a little underpowered, Purucas are nevertheless good sprinters and tireless workers. Ranchers and cowboys like them because they are especially docile and obedient.

When donkeys made their appearance on Marajó is not clear, but they have been used for at least a century for breeding mules. Donkeys serve no other purpose; they are never used as beasts of burden. Mules account for about one-fifth of the equine herd on the island. As is the case with the Marajoara and Puruca horses, mules are hardy and useful for rounding up cattle in soggy or dry conditions; but they are not as nimble as the horses. Mules are also reputedly less manageable, yet their toughness makes up for their shortcomings in other areas.

The contribution of horses and mules as well as pigs, sheep, and goats is often overlooked when discussing livestock on Marajó. All have long been an integral part of ranch life in the estuary and a significant source of income. Horses and mules account for about 15 percent of large livestock on Marajó and doubtless exert appreciable grazing pressure on forage resources. For example, Fazenda Paraíso near Cachoeira do Arari on Marajó keeps 120 horses to manage a herd of 800 water buffalo and about 100 head of cattle.

Although cowboys sometimes ride bareback, locally made saddles are standard issue. In the village of Rosário near the Camará River, for example, a leatherworker

A Marajoara horse rounding up water buffalo in flooded savanna. The Marajoara breed is well adapted to the equatorial climate at the mouth of the Amazon. Near Santa Cruz do Arari, Marajó, May 16, 2001.

makes saddles for about $80 from locally produced hides. Cowhides stretched to dry are a common sight on ranches and are used to make saddles, twine, pouches, and stretchers for carrying earth. Soft drink bottles are used to smooth the leather, while the saddle's frame (arção) is made of caroba wood, obtained from the nearby non-flooded scrub savanna. At the largest ranch on Marajó, Fazenda Cajueiro, a full-time saddle maker produces about seventy saddles a year. The leather for making the saddles is treated in concrete tanks containing the tannin-rich bark of red mangrove, obtained from the nearby shoreline. No caroba for making saddle frames grows on this ranch, so employees are dispatched to nearby Mexiana Island. On Fazenda Campo Limpo along the upper Anajás, which is characterized by a mosaic of low-lying grassland and forest, saddle frames are fashioned from the wood of the calabash tree (cuiá), a regular fixture of home gardens, or cedar (cedro), a timber tree of upland forests.

Saddle pads are fashioned from junco, a reed that abounds on tidal mudflats. The reeds are gathered and hung like curtains to dry. The dried, yellow reeds are trimmed to the desired length, then tied together with twine. In some areas where junco is difficult to find, such as the seasonally flooded savannas at Lavrado between the Arari and Anabiju Rivers, small-scale ranchers plant junco near their houses so that they have material for saddle pads readily at hand. Plant domestication in the Amazon estuary thus covers a wide range of end uses, from food to medicines and livery supplies.

Horses are not native to the Amazon, so no indigenous groups had myths or tales that incorporated the Old World animals. Horses have been on Marajó long enough, however, to appear in the lore of the current rural population, an ethnic mix of indigenous, African, and European peoples. On Fazenda Cajueiro, for example, a ghost horse and rider have been making seasonal appearances on moonlit nights for some fifty years. According to the head boatman, a fifty-three-year-old who has spent his entire life on the ranch, an enchanted man (homem encantado) appears twice a year: just before the dry season and at the onset of the rains. In early August the ghostly cowboy appears from the west on a white horse and rides past the chapel and a row of nearby houses at an easy gait. In January, when the rains begin in earnest, he appears from the opposite direction, sporting his usual broad-rimmed hat.

One year, a cowboy took it on himself to chase the apparition. But as the foolhardy vaqueiro galloped toward the phantom horse and its rider, he fainted and fell. When the dazed cowboy got up, he was disoriented. Even after several hours, he was still not right in the head ("ele ficou variado da cabeça"). He only recovered his senses after receiving treatment from a curer in Belém.

PIGS GALORE

It is not known when pigs were introduced to the Amazon, but they have been in the region as long as cattle, perhaps even longer. When a Portuguese military force wrested two wooden forts from the Dutch on the lower Xingu in 1622, they encountered pigs in the stockade. The Dutch forts of Orange and Nassau on the Xingu were established by 1616, and pigs likely supplied the garrisons with meat and fat for cooking. Given their fondness for pork chops and bacon, the English most likely kept pigs in their forts along the Amazon in the early 1600s.

No cultural checks restrict pork consumption in the estuary because Jews and Muslims account for less than 1 percent of the region's population and are essentially absent in rural areas. Consequently, pork is popular in both rural and urban areas and is cheaper than beef. Pigs are a significant source of income for many *ribeirinhos* (river dwellers). On Combu Island near Belém, for example, pigs account for up to one-fifth of their monthly income.

Pigs are loaded on to boats to be taken to urban markets, where they are trussed dockside before delivery to butchers. Some entrepreneurs have converted their boats so that the holds can carry forty to fifty pigs at a time. When ribeirinhos wish to sell pigs directly in urban markets, they usually butcher the animal at home in the early hours of the morning and arrive around daybreak in town to sell the meat at dockside.

Pigs in the estuary are mostly free range and get much of their sustenance by rooting in forests and home gardens. Such practices were once common in North America and Europe but have now been supplanted largely by industrial-scale operations in which pigs of the Large White breed are crammed in small pens to save on food consumption and usually do not venture outside because they are susceptible to sunburn. In the estuary, perennially hungry pigs, mostly dark-skinned and therefore immune to sunburn, feed on a wide range of wild foods, including ceru nuts and forest fruits such as parápará and caxinguba. Palm fruits, particularly those of açaí, buriti, buçú, murumuru, and jupatí, figure prominently in their diet. Ribeirinhos collect the fruits of buçú for sale to urban pig raisers, such as in Afuá. People dining on pork in urban centers in the estuary are thus linked to the floodplain forests, although most are probably unaware of the connection.

Pigs are partial to leafy vegetables, so it is not surprising that ribeirinhos have devised several strategies to thwart the voracious animals. Vegetable and herb beds are on stilts or are protected by a stockade. Pigs can wander uninvited into houses in search of snacks, so some ribeirinhos have nailed a plank or two across the bottom of doorways, thus requiring people to step over the barrier. In the vicinity of Santa Cruz do Arari on Marajó, locals fashion a specialized whip to punish transgressing pigs. Called a

A boat with its hold converted for carrying pigs. This boat belongs to a rancher who supplements his income by buying pigs from river dwellers and selling them in Macapá. Near Afuá, Marajó, August 19, 1998.

muxinga, the lash consists of a leather strand with three knots to increase the pain level; it is also unleashed on other trespassing animals, such as chickens and dogs.

On ranches, most pigs are feral and fend for themselves. Because of their irascible nature and suspicion of people, feral pigs are shot, like game animals. Many ranches derive income from their feral pigs, which have to be rounded up by cowboys with the aid of dogs. Pigs can be quite pugnacious at such times, and both cowboys and the dogs must take care when trying to persuade indignant boars and sows to move in the desired direction. Feral pigs display a wide variety of coat colors, indicating a varied genetic heritage. Tame pigs kept by cowboy families often wander off into the woods and breed with feral individuals, and this gene flow undoubtedly improves the hardiness of the confined stock.

JUNGLE COWBOYS

A knotted leather whip (muxinga), *used to discourage pigs and dogs from wandering into homes. Santa Cruz do Arari, Marajó, May 14, 1999.*

A jaguar skin nailed to the wall of a cowboy home. The female jaguar was shot while feeding on a feral pig. The cowboy's nine-year-old son has been snacking on yellow tucumã fruit. Mexiana Island, May 20, 2001.

Feral pigs abound in floodplain forests on Marajó, including riparian woods in savannas, and are an important item in the diet of jaguars, which still prowl the remoter sections of the island, even though they are shot at every opportunity. The thriving populations of feral pigs have doubtless helped jaguars to survive pelt hunters and attempts by ranchers to stem livestock losses. Poachers are a far greater source of cattle losses, however, than the powerful spotted cat.

A ranch that makes significant quantities of cheese for market, Fazenda Mironga near Soure on Marajó, has intensified pig production by taking advantage of whey, a by-product of cheese making. Penned pigs are fed whey mixed with wheat bran, maize, and sweet manioc. To increase weight gain, Large White has been crossed with local landraces and the rusty-colored Sorocoba. Pure Large White would not fare well in the hot and humid conditions of Amazonia, but crosses incorporate some of the hardy traits of tropical breeds.

On most ranches, though, pigs wander at will, as is the case in villages and around the homes of river dwellers. And their occasionally aggressive nature has been captured in lore. It is not uncommon for a sow with piglets to surprise a person with a mock charge if she feels that her offspring are threatened. Yet certain pigs, those that are unusually feisty and all but impossible to kill, are deemed supernatural. Supernatural pig stories are told in large cities, such as Belém, as well as smaller towns up the Amazon and along its tributaries.

Lindalva, the wife of a native son of Portel who operates a sawmill along an affluent of the lower Pacajá, told a story of a supernatural pig with repugnant habits. Lindalva, a vivacious seamstress in her thirties, recounted the tale, while her teenage son and nephew eagerly added details. In 1989 a pig was discovered digging up graves in the cemetery of Portel, a small town nestled at the juncture of the Pacajá and Anapú Rivers. Because most people in the town are relatively poor, the deceased is often wrapped in a hammock and lowered into a shallow grave, without a coffin. Only a simple wooden cross that soon disintegrates marks the spot; few can afford a gravestone or a stone slab. The pig was reportedly rooting open the graves to dine on the bones of the departed. Residents were disgusted, so three hunters resolved to check out the graveyard at night and try to dispose of the macabre pig. Sure enough, the pig made another appearance at the graveyard, so the closest hunter took a shot. But when the hunters went to investigate, there was no sign of the pig or any blood. Undaunted, the pig approached again, and even though several more volleys were released, it simply disappeared. The empty-handed hunters deemed the pig a supernatural entity and gave up.

Raimundo, a fifty-six-year-old lumberjack and longtime resident of Portel, recounted another story about a feisty, supernatural pig that used to scare people late at night. It would lunge at partygoers without warning when they were returning home from dances. One night in 1993, a bewildered partygoer managed to locate a piece of wood and club the aggressive pig. The next day a man who operates a small store out of the front room of his modest home on the edge of town was seen with an ugly gash on his head. The store owner, José Castelo, is still in business, even though people's suspicions were aroused when the pig attacks stopped the day he was seen with a head wound. The eleven-year-old grandson of the storyteller, Washington, listened intently as the story was told. Washington happens to live next door to the alleged pig-person and volunteered that there is something odd about Mr. Castelo.

Curious about the alleged ability of supernatural pigs to slip into the guise of humans, I asked ranch hands at Fazenda Cajueiro whether similar incidents had happened

71

in their isolated, sparsely settled parts. On most ranches, cowboy families maintain free-range pigs for their own consumption. Sure enough, several cowboys recounted being chased late at night by extraordinarily agile and belligerent pigs. For some reason, such attacks stopped in 1974. When I pressed Alfredo, head boatman on Fazenda Cajueiro, about the ability of people to transform into pigs, he recounted the following story. Returning from work around eleven o'clock one night in 1969, Alfredo headed for the wooden jetty across a stream where he customarily bathed. The stream, Igarapé do Guarda, cuts through the administrative center of the ranch and is also used to load and unload passengers and cargo. As Alfredo approached the stream, he noticed a man sitting on the jetty and a pig lolling in the mud exposed by the low tide. Before he reached the jetty, the pig got out of the mud and transformed into a woman; she then left hastily with the man who had been sitting down and headed for a row of cowboy residences. The mysterious woman was deemed responsible for several incidences of pigs chasing people on the ranch; these alarming events occurred on Thursdays or Fridays, days close to the crucifixion of Christ when the devil is deemed to be loose.

GOATS AND SHEEP

When goats and sheep arrived in Amazonia is uncertain, but William Smyth and Frederick Lowe, British naval officers, noted them at Gurupá in 1835. Periodic droughts in the northeast of Brazil have sent waves of settlers into the Amazon, and some of them have brought goats and sheep. One of the largest influxes of Nordestinos occurred in 1877 when a severe drought seared the backlands of Ceará and adjacent states.

Goat meat is gaining converts in Belém, especially as a barbecue item on weekends. Consequently, landowners on uplands as well as some floodplain areas in the estuary are investing in goats. Compared to cattle or water buffalo, startup costs for goat production are much lower. The animals are cheaper to acquire, and they thrive in poorly maintained pastures because they browse on weeds.

Sheep in the estuary are not as plentiful as goats, but some ranchers, such as near Soure, raise small flocks for meat. Villagers also sometimes keep a few sheep, as long as there is a grassy commons, used on weekends for football games, where the sheep can graze. Sheep are more demanding with regard to pasture than goats, and they do not fare well in grazing areas overrun by second growth.

The main sheep breed in the estuary is deslanado, which means "without wool." Deslanado sheep have thin, short coats and look like they have just been sheared. The climate in the Amazon is too hot and humid for sheep breeds developed for wool production. Because the sheep in the estuary have thin coats, at a distance they can be confused with goats. Although deslanado is the most common breed encountered, other

breeds and crossbreeds are sometimes seen, such as Pele de Boi (Cattle Hide), with its distinctive black coat with brown patches and a white belly, seen on a floodplain island near Abaetetuba.

Sheep grazing in a tidal marsh planted in coconuts near Soure, Marajó, September 7, 1997.

CHAPTER 4

Pillars of Life

Diverse palms along the Ucayali River in the Peruvian Amazon. From Paul Marcoy, A Journey across South America from the Pacific Ocean to the Atlantic Ocean *(London: Blackie and Son, 1866), 3:258.*

More than any other trees, palms provide character to the landscapes of the Amazon estuary. Some two dozen palm species adorn the forests and meadows of Amazonia, and about a dozen of them thrive in the estuary, where they furnish food, utensils, and income to hundreds of thousands of people. The varied architecture and diverse leaf forms of palms in the Amazon impressed early naturalists, including Paul Marcoy. They also caught the attention of Nikolai Vavilov, the great Russian biogeographer and plant geneticist, during his visit to the mouth of the Amazon in 1933: "But most amazing are the banks of the Amazon with their splendid vegetation and, most of all, the variety of palms. This is, in the fullest sense of the word, a kingdom of palms."[1]

The most important palm of the Amazon estuary, both nutritionally and economically, is the graceful açaí. Because of its abundance, the slender-trunked açaí symbolizes the estuary; indeed, it has saved large stretches of forest from conversion to cattle

Açaí palm with immature fruit. When ripe, the fruits will turn purple. Ilha dos Porcos near Afuá,
August 18, 1998.

Açaí fruits in a thimble-shaped basket (rasa) on the front porch of a river dweller's home. The fruits will soon be taken to a nearby market; in the meantime, a twelve-year-old boy who helped to gather them cannot resist a snack. Near Igarapé-Miri, December 10, 1999.

ranching. Other palms also make valuable contributions to the diet and provision of household supplies. Massive buriti palms, with their light gray trunks resembling Roman columns, provide a cornucopia of nutritious fruits. Although not as economically important as açaí, buriti fruits are nevertheless richer in vitamins and are widely appreciated. A diminutive relative of buriti, the caraná palm, is also a denizen of swamps and seasonally flooded savannas. Although the caraná's fruits are smaller than those of buriti, they are also rich in vitamin A.

A host of other palms are used locally in the estuary, underscoring the importance of conserving forests and wetlands. Only a few are sampled here. Some are relatively widespread, such as murumuru, with its menacing spines; others, such as the broad-leaved buçu, are confined to the mouth of the great river. Although these palms may appear to blend in naturally with the forest vegetation, many have been planted or have arisen spontaneously from discarded seeds in backyards.

Açaí

As a staff of life, few palms around the world rival açaí. Southeast Asia's sago palm, felled to obtain starch from its pithy trunk, probably comes closest. For certain extinct indigenous groups, particularly in Costa Rica, the farinaceous fruits of peach palm were a major source of calories. And in towns and cities of Costa Rica today, vendors with pushcarts sell boiled peach palm fruits on street corners. But for rural folk in the Amazon estuary, the marble-sized fruits of açaí are, next to manioc flour, the most important source of energy. The purple fruits, which resemble large blueberries, would seem an implausible pillar of life for so many. Yet they are rich in oil. Indeed, the high oil content imparts a smooth texture to açaí juice, which may help to explain its popularity.

Açaí fruits have been consumed for millennia, as attested by açaí seeds in archaeological sites on Marajó Island. When the Portuguese started settling the Amazon in the early seventeenth century, they soon acquired many of the local food habits, perhaps as much out of necessity as from desire, as most of the crops grown in temperate Portugal cannot be cultivated in the tropics. According to Francisco Sampaio, a traveling judge in the Amazon, all classes were consuming açaí fruit juice with gusto by the late eighteenth century. And José Verissimo, an astute Brazilian observer of Amazonian culture, noted that by the latter part of the nineteenth century locals joked that if one visits Pará and drinks açaí juice, one stays (*quem vai ao Pará, parou; quem bebe açaí, ficou*).

The American naturalist Herbert H. Smith noted how foreign visitors to Belém could be easily seduced by açaí juice. In describing an açaí stand at the main market in 1874, Smith remarked:

Yes, the Americanos will have assaí, com assucar; so the little shirtless son scampers off after sugar. Ordinary customers at the stand are of the lower classes, who drink their two cents' worth of assaí with only a little mandioca meal by way of seasoning. In the forest, where sugar was scarce and the fruit plenty, I learned to like it quite as well so myself; its brisk, nutty flavor is rather spoiled by the sweetening. However, our new-comers may prefer the civilized side; so the sugar is added, and we dip our moustaches into the rich liquid. Even the squeamish ones empty their bowls, and begin to suggest to themselves the possibility of entertaining another half-pint.[2]

Not all newcomers succumb to the delights of açaí, however. In December 1999 I talked with a taxi driver in Belém who hails from Fortaleza, capital of the dry northeastern state of Ceará. The ill-shaven driver volunteered that he had tried açaí when he first came to Belém seven years ago. That night he experienced violent stomach cramps and never touched the drink again. I offered that it might have been contaminated water used in the açaí juice that upset his constitution, but he remained unconvinced.

An açaí stand in Belém in 1874. The vendor is mashing the fruits by hand while customers sip the juice from bowls. A sieve for removing the seeds can be seen hanging from the wall on the left; such sieves, usually made from arumã, are still in use today. The clay pots in the foreground probably contain water for mixing with the pulp. From H. H. Smith, Brazil, the Amazons and the Coast *(New York: Charles Scribner's Sons, 1879), 44.*

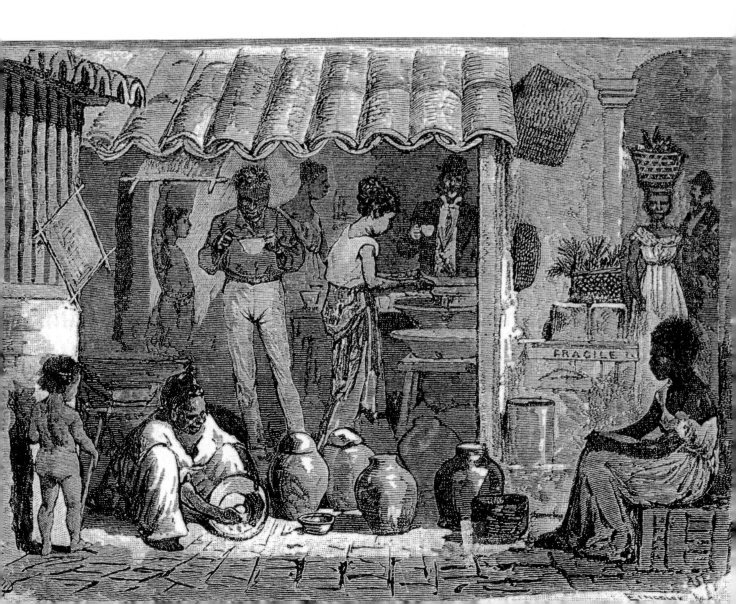

Boy descending an açaí palm next to his home with fruit in hand. The açaí will be prepared for dinner and served with manioc flour. Fazenda Santa Luz, 14 kilometers north of Breves on PA 159 highway, Marajó, August 9, 2000.

Some well-to-do mothers in Belém insist that to protect their families and guests, they send their maids only to those açaí stores that claim to use bottled mineral water for making the juice.

   In the drier months when açaí is in high season, fruits are gathered once a day, usually in the afternoon. Youngsters, including teenage girls, are typically dispatched up the palms, which can soar to twenty meters or more. Men in their twenties and thirties also climb the polelike palms, especially if they have no children or their kids are too young. Women will also climb açaí trees if their husbands are off on a prolonged fishing trip or have taken outside employment, such as work on a timber crew. Instead of repeatedly ascending and descending the trees, expert climbers will pass from one açaí

*Foot sling used for gathering açaí fruits fashioned from the fibrous material (*tururí*) that covers the fruit bunches of buçú palm. The boy has taken a break from helping his mother and sisters make manioc flour, hence the smudges of white manioc dough. Nossa Senhora da Luz, Rio Tauaú, near Breves, Marajó, August 11, 2000.*

tree to the next by tugging on a frond of a neighboring tree to pull it closer. Falls are rare, but from twenty meters up, they can be fatal. An açaí tree snapping under the weight of the climber causes most falls, and this typically occurs with older palms.

A foot sling (*peconha*), formerly made from the young fronds of açaí palm but now usually fashioned from polypropylene sacking, is used to help climbers shimmy up and down the narrow trunks. In the community of Nossa Senhora da Lua along the Rio Tauaú near Breves, youngsters fashion foot slings from the fibrous material covering the fruit stalks of buçú palm. Technically a nonopening peduncular bract but known locally as *turirí*, the tough brown fibers are also gathered for sale in Belém, where they are fashioned into handbags and baseball caps for the tourist trade.

If the fruits are for home consumption, one or two fruit bunches suffice. The stalks are cut with a knife or short machete that the climber holds between the teeth or tucks into the back of the shorts. The adept youngster then slides back down the trunk with fruit stalk in hand. An açaí palm can have several fruit stalks ripening at one time, each containing a thousand fruits or more. If fruits are also being collected for sale, the fruit bunches, which are about 1.5 meters long, are cut loose and allowed to fall to the ground, where the fruits are stripped into a basket. If only one or two stalks are involved, the fruits are often removed at home. One family near Afuá had stacked the stripped fruit stalks into a compost pile about two meters square and almost two meters high. As the stalks break down, the resulting compost is placed around young co-

Children stripping açaí fruits into a ceramic bowl on the floor of their living room. The bowl (alguidar) is made of local clay mixed with the ash derived from burning the silica-rich bark of the caraipé tree. Vila Jurupari, municipality of Afuá, August 16, 1998.

conut palms in the home garden. More commonly, stripped açaí stalks are fashioned into brooms.

To make juice, the stripped fruits are first soaked in heated water for about half an hour to soften the pulp. Various containers are used for soaking the fruits, ranging from small wooden troughs to aluminum bowls, cut-off kerosene tins, and specialized earthenware basins (*alguidar*). Alguidars are usually sold in pairs for about U.S. $8, with the smaller one fitting inside the larger. The large bowl is used for soaking; the smaller one collects the juice after sieving. The bowl's color tells whether the alguidar is a local product or was made elsewhere and purchased in a nearby town.

Açaí soaking bowls are a cottage industry, especially in the Abaetetuba area, and itinerant merchants dispatch the naturally orange bowls throughout the estuary. Some potters, as on Jurupari Island near Afuá and Rio Paráijó near Breves, still employ indigenous techniques such as mixing silica-rich ash from burned caraipé bark with clay to render it more plastic. Caraipé is a tree of upland forests, and bowls made with its ash are gray rather than orange.

While açaí fruits soak, children often become impatient and fish out some of the softened fruits for a snack. The warm, slightly mushy fruits are sometimes mixed with manioc flour in a cup and greatly appreciated as predinner morsels. At Vila Jurupari near Afuá, young and old sit down on the wooden walkways and verandas of their homes in the late afternoon and chew on softened açaí fruits between mouthfuls of manioc flour scooped from a separate dish. While enjoying the respite from the day's heat and relishing the mushy fruits along with crunchy manioc flour, families and friends chat and observe what their neighbors are up to.

After the açaí fruits have finished soaking, the water is drained off. Açaí juice can be prepared in one of three ways: the fruits may be kneaded by hand, placed in a homemade churn, or poured into a purchased aluminum blender powered by electricity (*batideira eletrica*). All three methods can be seen in houses relatively close to each other along a tidal creek or small village. Such is the cultural importance of açaí that some households have installed backyard electric generators solely for making açaí juice. The flickering yellow light of tabletop kerosene lamps brightens the otherwise gloomy interior of homes after nightfall.

In households without manual or electric batideiras, fruits are mashed by hand, as one would knead bread dough. Or a stubby wooden pestle or the bottom of a glass bottle may be used to remove the pulp from the seeds. Small amounts of the water used for soaking the fruits are added to obtain the right consistency. When all of the flesh has been removed from the seeds, the açaí pulp is passed through two sieves placed on top of each other. The first sieve (*caroçeira*) catches the seeds, while the finer sieve (*paneira*) immediately below filters out bits of skin. The sieves are usually fashioned from arumã, one of the plants used to make baskets to carry açaí fruits, but the seed-catching sieve is also fashioned from the midribs of jacitara palm fronds. The dark purple juice collects in a plastic bowl or a rectangular wooden container with sides that slope out at a forty-five-degree angle. The receptacle is roughly half a meter long at its base, and the sides are about ten centimeters high. The juice may then be transferred to another bowl for serving.

A milder version of açaí juice, açaí *sem tinta* (without ink), is prepared for the elderly and infirm. Stain-free açaí is prepared by rubbing the unsoaked fruits, some of which are not yet ripe, with a little water to wash off the skin. The skinless fruits are then soaked in warm water and prepared like regular açaí. The resulting juice, however, looks like liquid guacamole instead of grape juice. Inhabitants of Arapaxi village near Chaves in northern Marajó claim that açaí sem tinta is easier to digest and is especially indicated for those suffering from liver ailments. Because of the extra labor involved, stain-free açaí is not an everyday dietary item.

Families with lots of mouths to feed sometimes make or purchase a wooden cylinder to extract açaí pulp, much like a butter churn but narrower and taller. Açaí churns (*maquinas de bater açaí*) are about 1.5 meters tall. A handle at the top turns a vertical shaft with wooden paddles. The opening at the bottom is only large enough to let the juice pass through to a pan underneath. Periodically, a small trapdoor is opened to remove the seeds. The advantage of this device is that it is relatively cheap to make as it uses locally available materials and can process açaí fruits faster than mashing by hand. Durable woods are preferred for the manual açaí churns. A homemade açaí churn that I saw in operation at Vila Jurupari was fashioned from macacaúba, a rot-resistant timber tree of floodplain forests. In Abaetetuba, a hardware store was selling açaí churns chiseled from acapu, a hardwood from upland forests; the churns, complete with four splayed legs for stability, were selling for only a dollar apiece.

Most households in rural areas lack refrigerators, so açaí kept overnight is usually rancid the next day. *Açaí azedo* (sour açaí) may be an acquired taste, but locals in the interior are accustomed to eating it for lunch. A housewife noted half in jest that the family has to put up with sour açaí because her young husband and son are too lazy to gather (*apanhar*) the fruits in the morning as well as in the afternoon. Slightly fermented açaí may be nutritionally more beneficial than the fresh product because it probably contains yeast. On the other hand, pathogenic bacteria have plenty of time to multiply when the juice is stored overnight at room temperature. A secretary in Abaetetuba, who was born in a small village nearby, told me that she counters the unpleasant taste of sour açaí by preparing a porridge of the fermenting solution with boiled rice and salt. Açaí porridge (*mingau de açaí*) is more typically made with fresh açaí juice and sold by street vendors in the morning in blackened bowls fashioned from cal-

Dinner in a river dweller's home consisting of açaí juice mixed with manioc flour, accompanied by fried fish. Ilha dos Porcos near Afuá, August 17, 1998.

abash gourds. Açaí porridge is a satisfying breakfast and, at 25 cents a bowl, relatively cheap. Some stalls sell a more substantial breakfast of reheated fried fish, manioc flour, and a bowl of açaí.

Açaí juice may also be thickened with manioc flour or crunchy tapioca, sometimes accompanied by a pinch of salt. Many consider açaí a fine balance to salty food, such as sun-dried and salted shrimp. A taxi driver in Belém, a native of Pará state, claimed that açaí helps one sleep at night; he likes a bowl of açaí juice shortly before retiring. Unlike hot milk, açaí probably does not contain any ingredients that promote sleep, but the satiated feeling after imbibing açaí certainly thwarts hunger pangs.

The importance of açaí in the regional diet may go unnoticed during a cursory visit to Belém and Macapá, the major cities of the Amazon estuary, where the middle and upper classes consume it more as an occasional dessert, especially as ice cream. Indeed, the wealthy are typically weight conscious and worry about getting fat from seductive açaí. Yet a stroll in the poorer sections of cities or in villages reveals another story. There açaí is part of daily life, eaten with every meal. Among the less affluent, a rotund figure is associated with well-being. It is common to see kids in crowded neighborhoods and in rural areas with purple lips and smudges around their faces from drinking açaí. An expression has even arisen to describe the condition: "black mouth" (*boca preta*). A Brazilian geographer, Mário Hiraoka, has made the interesting observation that the booming market for açaí is driven in part by rural-urban migration; people who have left the floodplain to seek a better life in the cities bring with them their passion for açaí.

Stores dedicated to the sale of açaí juice are called *batideiras de açaí* or *amassadeiras de açaí*. Red flags posted outside the small stores alert consumers that açaí juice is available. At night some açaí stores cover an outside light with a red plastic bucket to signal they are open for business. At the height of the açaí season in Breves, dozens of such lights can be glowing along a single street. With backyard and street fires ablaze to burn garbage and yard waste, the hazy streets of Breves take on a surreal ambience. A visitor unaccustomed to the region might think he had stumbled into a red-light district.

A pile of discarded seeds (*caroços*) spilling out into the street or ditch is another telltale sign of an açaí store. The garbanzo bean–sized seeds of açaí are sometimes mixed with soil for herb and spice gardens, either in individual pots or in raised vegetable beds. In the community of Nossa Senhora da Luz, one family mulches açaí seed at the base of peach palm trees. And in Belém, people in middle- and lower-income areas commonly compost açaí seeds for their home gardens.

A now-defunct kiln near Mojú once burned the seeds along with wood to fire bricks and roof tiles. Piles of açaí seeds also accumulate near the kitchen of many rural homes. Children have gained a healthy respect for them, because they are favored haunts of tiny mites. If one lingers on the pile, the mites soon crawl onboard and burrow into the skin of their unwitting host. The resulting itching is intense, the more so if the mites have reached delicate parts of one's anatomy. Many of the seeds in the mound sprout, and some of them are transplanted in backyards and in cultivated plots away from home.

A steady stream of customers make their way to açaí stores, especially in the late afternoon and early evening. Most of the açaí juice is sold in one- or two-liter plastic bags to be taken home and consumed, but some customers enjoy the smooth-textured juice at the store. While waiting in line to buy açaí, men, women, and children chat and exchange gossip. Most açaí stores specialize in just that product, but a few are associated with popular restaurants that also serve takeout food.

Customers can buy açaí juice in various concentrations depending on price. The thicker the mixture, the higher the price. Two or three grades are typically sold: *especial* or *grossa* (the more concentrated), *medio*, and *fino* or *comum* (the most diluted). In season, the thicker concentration typically sells for as much as $2.75 a liter, so most customers opt for the common grade, which sells for about $1.00 a liter. Some kiosks sell an even cheaper grade obtained from the water used to wash off the seeds in the container after the pulp has been removed. The pale liquid, known variously as *churamba* in Breves and

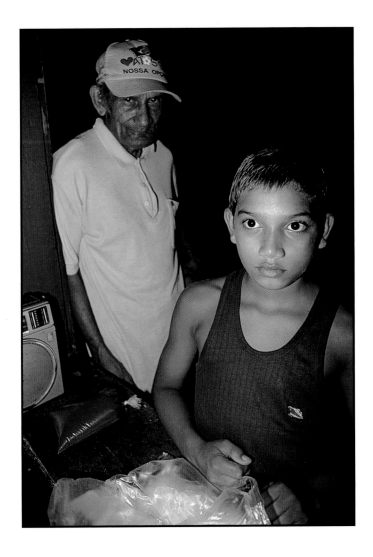

Customers lining up in the early evening at a small açaí store to buy juice in plastic bags. Açaí juice often accompanies lunch and dinner in towns as well as in the countryside. Breves, Marajó, August 8, 2000.

Pai Luis (Father Louis) in northern Marajó, sells for as little as 25 cents a liter. In spite of its weak consistency, the bottom grade still finds a market. An açaí store owner in Breves remarked with a smile that some of his customers fret more about the price than the quality.

With açaí playing such a prominent role in the diet and commerce of the estuary, it is not surprising that some small-scale industrial technology has arisen to facilitate the processing of the fruits. The first electrically operated açaí beaters probably date to the 1930s. The main difference from wooden churns is that the industrial ones are made mostly of shiny aluminum. Metal açaí churns, similar in design to the wooden ones fashioned in rural areas, are an urban cottage industry, made exclusively in Belém, where they cost between $220 and $320. Although most of the metal açaí churns are employed in açaí shops, a fair number find their way into the homes of river dwellers.

The Feira do Açaí in the Ver-o-Pêso district of Belém, November 13, 1998. This open-air market is one of several for açaí fruit. The stone wall in the background is part of a fort built by the Portuguese in the early seventeenth century. It is 7:30 A.M., and the market will close within an hour.

An impressive distribution and marketing system has developed to satisfy demand for açaí fruits in towns and cities. In the largest market, Belém, açaí is sold portside at several locations, especially at the Feira do Açaí (Açaí Market), adjacent to the stone fort built by the Portuguese in 1616. On the cobbled streets laid out almost four centuries ago, wholesalers (*atravessadores*) haggle with buyers supplying the hundreds of açaí stores scattered around the city as well as supermarkets and restaurants. Action begins early, an hour or so before sunrise, and continues daily until about 9:00 A.M. during the height of the season. In the rainy months, the market closes within an hour or so of sunrise. In the relative cool of the morning, the açaí markets in Belém are hives of activity as workers offload baskets (rasas) of açaí from the numerous boats huddled together along the dock and take the empty baskets back as the market winds down.

Rural folk make açaí baskets from the leaf stems of arumã, an understory plant in floodplain forests, as well as the fronds of two palms: the majestic buriti and the diminutive jacitara. Women make most of the baskets, and in any given area one or two housewives are known to be particularly skillful at this craft. The baskets sell locally for the equivalent of 85 cents, relatively inexpensive considering that it takes about forty minutes to make each one. One day such baskets may fetch handsome prices as decorative items for apartments in New York, London, and Paris. At the moment, though, basketry is not a significant source of income for households in the Amazon estuary. Locals nevertheless take pride in their artistry. A mother of three on Ilha dos Porcos near Afuá, for example, creates attractive bands on her açaí baskets by alternating dark and light arumã strands; this effect is achieved by flipping over the strands, as one side is darker. Spindly jacitara palm is another denizen of floodplain forests and also survives in isolated clumps of trees in wet savannas. The fronds of jacitara must be harvested carefully because of the punishing spines that adorn the spindly trunk. Açaí baskets come in two basic designs: thimble shaped with slightly deflecting sides and straight sided. Both types hold about eighteen liters of fruit.

After the açaí market closes, the boats begin fanning out across the estuary. Some may head to the lower Tocantins and its affluents while others set course for Marajó. Boats serving the Belém market obtain fruits as far up the Tocantins as Cametá. On returning to their ports of origin, the boats soon start making the rounds along winding creeks to pick up consignments of açaí fruit. Although traveling merchants may buy fruit at any time, they usually prefer to buy açaí in the afternoon so that they can travel overnight to Belém. Most açaí-laden boats arrive in Belém in the early hours of the morning before the market is in full swing. Depending on the season, river dwellers in the Amazon estuary receive between $0.75 and $1.50 per kilogram for their fruits sold at their "ports." The exact time of departure of boats heading for urban markets depends on the tide; boat owners have built up a healthy respect for the waves in the expansive bays that separate some estuarine islands. On the incoming tide waves are more danger-ous, so the preferred time to head out is at high tide or as the tide begins to withdraw.

Açaí fruits start to go rancid after about twenty-four hours, depending on ambient temperatures and whether the fruits have been soaked by rain, so merchants have lim-ited flexibility once they have the fruits onboard. If the fruits are wet, they deteriorate faster; customers can tell when açaí fruit is beginning to pass its prime because it de-velops a blue-gray sheen, similar to the pale gray film that coats stale chocolate.

The booming market for açaí in Belém has spurred some entrepreneurs to place açaí on ice during transport, thereby extending the range of commercial açaí gathering. Traditionally, only fish have been iced for urban markets, but now a small but growing proportion of açaí fruits warrant similar handling. A sawmill operator on Serraria Pe-quena Island near Afuá, for example, has recently begun dispatching açaí fruits chilled on ice by boat to Belém. He does this during the height of the season, when local mar-kets are saturated and he can purchase the fruits at a good price. The journey to Belém from Serraria Pequena takes some forty-eight to seventy-two hours, depending on the horsepower of the diesel engine and the tides. And the main buyer serving the commu-nity of Aruã in northern Marajó puts açaí in polypropylene sacks rather than tradi-tional baskets so that they are in closer contact with the ice needed to keep the fruits fresh for their long journey to Belém via the man-made Tartaruga Canal and Arari River. Açaí fruits reach Belém in the afternoon of the day following departure and must remain onboard for another twelve hours until the market opens. Without ice, fruits from northern Marajó and adjacent islands would not make it to Belém in ac-ceptable condition. Ice-making factories were first built in the Amazon at the turn of the twentieth century, and consumers in Belém were consuming açaí ice cream by 1925. But fishing boats have only been operating with iceboxes on a significant scale for the last half century.

Technological changes in transportation and refrigeration have thus created new opportunities for marketing açaí. The introduction of steamboats to the Amazon in the mid-eighteenth century extended the marketing radius of açaí fruits, but at that time steamboats stopped only at the larger urban centers. River dwellers still depended largely on paddling or sails. The arrival of diesel-powered boats after World War II, however, greatly increased marketing possibilities for açaí gatherers. Many river dwellers can afford small diesel engines that are easily bolted to locally made boats. Now itinerant merchants and river dwellers alike can reach small islands and remote streams in their quest for açaí fruit.

Although açaí fruit is marketed year round, the summer months—from June to October—are the main harvest season. In most areas fruit production falls off dra-matically during the rainy season, and prices for fresh fruit rise accordingly. During the off-season, people are so eager for açaí that they often resort to mixing green fruits with ripe ones, even though the resulting olive-colored juice is not as tasty. The green fruits are called parol and fetch a lower price. Açaí parol nevertheless finds grateful customers in urban centers, including São Miguel de Pracuúba, as I observed at the close of the rainy season in May 1999, and Abaetetuba, which I visited in December 1999 as a disappointing harvest season was winding down.

Although most açaí palms produce fruits that turn purple when ripe, a few, called *açaí branco* (white açaí), bear only green fruits. This trait has been selected for and maintained by rural folk because they appreciate its creamy fruits, which one farmer described as akin to avocado. White açaí is rare, and locals take care to separate the fruits from regular açaí when they are destined for market. White açaí was fetching a 15 percent premium on the Belém market in November 1998.

Another interesting genetic trait is the variability in the peaks of fruit production. According to river dwellers near Igarapé-Miri, some açaí groves along the Mojú, which flows into the estuary near Belém after joining the Acará, fruit more heavily during the rainy months. River dwellers have obtained planting material from various parts of the estuary, so current patterns of fruit production may have little to do with local ecological conditions. Another area of apparent anomalous fruit production is the upper reaches of the Anajás, Mocoões, and Pracuúba Rivers. Locals are able to cash in on the high prices, which can soar to five times those obtained in the dry season. Because the headwaters of those rivers are sparsely inhabited, some of the buyers bring along açaí gatherers, known locally as footslingers (*peconheiros*), who set up temporary camp on high ground, often indigenous mounds, such as along the Camutins. During the annual flood, small diesel-powered boats can travel up the Anabjiu and Pracuúba and reach the Anajás because the headwaters of those rivers blend into a vast flooded forest and savanna. Fruit from this area is taken to Ponta de Pedras, a major entrepôt for açaí on the southern coast of Marajó, for transshipment to Belém within a couple of days. If fruit had to travel down the Anajás and around the southwestern tip of Marajó it would not reach Belém in marketable condition.

A century ago, Jacques Huber, a Swiss botanist, noted that river dwellers were planting açaí along the lower Amazon. Now the pace of planting has quickened as urban areas have grown and the value of açaí fruit has risen. Açaí fruits are such an attractive proposition that many rural inhabitants in the estuary have abandoned slash-and-burn agriculture altogether and derive most of their income and sustenance from the ubiquitous palm. River dwellers are deflecting the normal trajectory after slash-and-burn fields are abandoned; instead of reverting to second growth, areas formerly farmed with annuals are being transformed into agroforests stocked with useful perennials. Even ranchers are getting into the act. Along the Anabiju on Marajó, for example, one *fazendeiro* has recently hired a ribeirinho to collect açaí from his forests and to plant the lucrative palm along streams by first thinning out "undesirable" species, such as jupatí palm, because it casts too much shade.

The tempo of açaí planting has accelerated to the point that many of the forests in the estuary are cultural artifacts. The transformation of "wilderness" into cultural woodlands enriched with economic trees has helped to save the estuary from being turned into a sea of pasture and second growth, so typical of settled uplands. Floodplain forests in the estuary pay for themselves by producing valuable nontimber forest products. On Combu Island opposite Belém, for example, families generate an annual income of a little over $4,000, most of it from açaí. Although low by U.S. standards, this income is quite high for rural Amazonia. Residents of Belém consume about one hundred eighty tons of açaí fruits a day, and this voracious and growing appetite has rippled through the landscapes of the estuary.

The virtues of açaí have recently been discovered in other parts of Brazil and in the United States. In the early 1970s it was virtually impossible to find açaí juice or ice cream for sale in Rio de Janeiro or São Paulo. Now residents of Rio are consuming

A cultural forest dominated by açaí palm. The taller fan-leaved palms in the background are buriti, also likely planted or at least protected when they were spontaneous seedlings. Rio Parauaú near Breves, Marajó, May 16, 2000.

about five hundred tons of açaí a month, and more cariocas are becoming aficionados of the fruit juice every day. Health clubs (*acadêmias de esporte*) in Rio serve milkshakes containing açaí, caffeine-rich guaraná—a fruit-bearing vine domesticated in the Amazon—and granola to recoup the energy and revive the spirits of those who have just finished working out. Rio's surfing crowd is particularly fond of mixing açaí with guaraná powder; recharged *surfistas* can thus keep going all day. In southern Brazil, açaí is touted as a "fortifier" (*fortificante*). When I ran that by a family on Ilha dos Porcos (Pig Island) in the northern part of the Amazon estuary, everyone laughed. The lady of the house (*dona da casa*) remarked wryly that those who eat a lot of açaí get fat, not strong.

In Porto Seguro, Bahia, a popular tourist resort in northeastern Brazil, locals and visitors enjoy açaí mixed with lime juice. One store in the vibrant town where the Portuguese seafarer Cabral first made landfall in the New World five centuries ago touts açaí as "nutritious and an energy booster." In the last five years, açaí ice cream and juice have also made their appearance farther up the coast in Ilheus, Bahia's main port for exporting cacao. Ice cream stores and health clubs in the laid-back seaside town now serve açaí, trucked from Pará in frozen plastic bags. And in Los Angeles, California, where people are constantly reinventing lifestyles, açaí is now served in certain upscale cafés and health clubs.

Although açaí juice is sometimes called *vinho de açaí* (literally, "açaí wine"), the fruit juice is generally consumed fresh rather than fermented into an alcoholic brew. As is the case with many of the world's fruits, however, a few enterprising individuals always seem to find a way to make booze out of fresh fruit. Açaí liqueur (*licor de açaí*) is not common, however, and is produced mostly for tourists. The liqueur is prepared by soaking the blueberry-like fruits in cachaça until they disintegrate, which usually takes about a year. The purple-tinted liquid is then passed through a cloth sieve and mixed with molasses. The resulting smooth-tasting beverage has the consistency of Kahlua, a coffee-flavored liqueur made in Mexico. A longtime resident of Abaetetuba explained to me why açaí liqueur is rare. It is related to the system of food taboos prevalent in the region. Locals believe it unwise to mix certain foods or drinks, including açaí and cachaça. The two are thought not to "combine" well in the stomach.

PALMITO FACTORIES: FRIEND OR FOE OF THE RIBEIRINHO?

Fueled by growing national and international markets, a boom in the extraction of heart-of-palm (*palmito*) started in the Amazon estuary in the late 1960s. Previously, açaí had been exploited only sporadically for palmito. But after a related species in southern Brazil, jussara, was virtually wiped out by predatory harvesting, the industry shifted north. Today virtually all of the heart-of-palm produced in Brazil comes from açaí gathered in the Amazonian state of Pará. Premium-grade palmito is exported, mainly to France and the United States, where it is mostly consumed in salads. Poorer-quality product is placed on the Brazilian market and is served as an hors d'oeuvre, in pastry snacks, in salads, and on pizza. The value of the açaí heart-of-palm trade is hard to determine because of underreporting to evade taxes, but it is probably in the tens of millions of dollars annually.

The first palmito factory in the estuary was built in 1968 at Barcarena near Belém. Other palmito factories were soon established in other parts of the Amazon estuary, such as Emprêsa de Palmito (EMPASA), which was founded in 1971 at Afuá. Many of the larger palmito factories that started operation at the beginning of the boom have closed, such as in Vigia and São Miguel de Pracuúba, because untended açaí stands were leveled. Now locals are more vigilant about cutting açaí for palmito and exercise more control over the harvesting rate. Numerous smaller palmito operations, called *fabriquetas*, have sprung up in many parts of the estuary. Often little more than backyard cottage industries, fabriquetas have the advantage of being cheap to set up and run.

Although the heart-of-palm industry suffers from a predatory image, the factories nevertheless generate jobs in rural areas where employment opportunities are limited. Palmito gatherers receive about 50 cents for each "baton," a tidy supplement to their annual income, which rarely exceeds a few thousand dollars. Heart-of-palm processing is a labor-intensive affair, and many plant owners contract workers among river as well as urban dwellers. Fabrica Jayrê near Afuá, for example, provides free transportation in the company boat for employees living in town.

Heart-of-palm is gathered by full-time cutters (palmiteiros) and by locals who also sell açaí fruit, fish, hunt, and farm. Palmiteiros either work for a factory or form independent teams selling the product to a number of factories. Palmiteiros tend to cut açaí in the interior of islands and along creeks with few or no settlers. Sometimes they contract with large landholders to harvest palmito on their properties for a percentage, but oversight is usually lacking. The owner of a pharmacy in Afuá complained that a team of palmiteiros deceived him in 1998 by harvesting some 70,000 açaí on his floodplain property rather than the 10,000 allowed in the verbal agreement.

Smallholders are much more wary because they live on their properties. Although clandestine teams may hit the açaí at the back of properties, which can extend for a kilometer or two inland, few palmiteiros would risk a confrontation with a river dweller by going after the dense grove of açaí around his house.

As the açaí fruit harvest tapers off during the rainy season, farmers turn to selling more palmito. Smallholders use the off-season to cull the taller trees that pose greater risk of a fatal fall or remove trees that bear little fruit. River dwellers may stack palmito on their docks to alert buyers or take the heart-of-palm directly to the factory. Many

A river dweller culling an old açaí tree from his grove to obtain heart-of-palm. The heart-of-palm will probably be eaten in Paris or São Paulo. Ilha dos Porcos, municipality of Afuá, August 18, 1998.

A worker in a palmito factory removing the outer husk of heart-of-palm. Fabrica Jayrê, Rio Marajozinho near Afuá, Marajó, August 20, 1998.

river dwellers thus manage their açaí stands for fruit and palmito; the heart-of-palm trade therefore boosts their income rather than undercuts their natural resource base.

When the palmito arrives at a factory, the first step is to remove the outer layers from the baseball bat–sized batons. Males are generally employed for this task, which is often performed at the port. Stacks of discarded outer layers of palmito typically litter the threshold of the factory. In some cases, such as the Jayrê plant, cattle and pigs are kept on the premises so that they can feed on the palmito trimmings. In Afuá, some residents pay workers to dig deep into the piles of palmito peelings to obtain a rich mulch for vegetable and flower gardens.

Placing palmito sections into jars that will be filled with salt water and citric acid, then sterilized. Fabrica Jayrê, Rio Marajozinho near Afuá, Marajó, August 20, 1998.

After the outer layers have been peeled off, the now more slender cylinders of palmito, about the thickness of a large carrot, are cut into fifteen-centimeter sections with the aid of a wooden retainer notched at the desired section length. The palmito sections are then placed in cans or bottles containing water mixed with salt and citric acid to retard browning. If the palmito cylinders are too thin, they are chopped manually into small pieces, known as picado. Similar in appearance to sliced string cheese, picado finds a market as a pizza topping. In São Paulo, picado is also used as a filling for fried pastry (pastel de palmito). Few residents of that giant industrial city are aware that the palmito they are eating comes from estuarine forests some three thousand kilometers away. Once the palmito sections or picado are in jars or cans, the lids are sealed and the containers are placed in shallow tanks for sterilization. Most palmito factories opt for wood-fired boilers to keep costs down. Many of the boilers were imported into the Amazon a century ago from the United States and Europe. Fuel is no problem, thanks to the timber boom in the estuary, which generates plenty of scrap wood. Only the larger factories use tin cans to preserve palmito; the others prefer working with glass jars because it is cheaper than investing in canning equipment.

After the cans or jars have been boiled, they are packed in cardboard boxes and dispatched by boat to warehouses in the larger cities. Labels are often glued on jars or cans in the larger factories, whereas the smaller operations ship a generic product to warehouses for labeling by their respective owners.

THE PUSH TO "MANAGE" AÇAÍ

The palmito boom in the Amazon provoked large-scale cutting of açaí stands in parts of the estuary. Newspaper reports and concerned citizens decried the imminent "destruction" of açaí and the elimination of an important source of food and livelihood for locals. Yet another boom-and-bust scenario appeared to be unfolding, generating wealth for the few and leaving an impoverished landscape in its wake. In response to outcries for action, the Brazilian government instigated policies addressing "reforestation" and "management" issues. But for the most part, the fuss was not grounded on ecological realities, and the prescribed cures are largely window dressing and have had perverse impacts on landownership.

Some argue that the narrow diameter of heart-of-palm sections reaching the U.S. market is an indication that very young palms are now being harvested. Thicker palmito fetches a premium price, but the diameter of the harvested product is not necessarily a reliable indicator of whether the resource is being exhausted. In some areas açaí is being cut for palmito after only five years, as opposed to the ten to fifteen years required for thicker palmito, but that does not mean the groves are being eliminated.

In response to media and political pressure, the Brazilian agency responsible for regulating the trade in timber and nontimber forest products and protecting wildlife—Instituto Brasileiro do Meio Ambiente e dos Recursos Naturais Renováveis (IBAMA)—requires owners of palmito factories to set aside areas for "sustainable management" of açaí. To obtain a license to operate, owners of palmito factories are supposed to draw up a management plan. This entails acquiring some land, either by purchase or lease, to plant açaí according to the volume of palmito production. For example, the Jayrê palmito factory, a relatively small plant near Afuá with an annual production of 120,000 kilograms (gross weight) of canned palmito, has addressed the IBAMA requirement by establishing a four-hundred-hectare açaí plantation on Caviana Island. A consultant was hired to devise the "management" plan and to facilitate its approval by IBAMA authorities in Belém. Most palmito factory owners buy land, which is relatively cheap in the estuary. Inadvertently, then, government regulations are encouraging the concentration of landownership. Plantations linked to palmito factories are set up primarily to satisfy a bureaucratic requirement rather than to promote "sustainable" development. Given the shortage of IBAMA personnel in the field, supervisory visits to "managed" açaí plantings appear to be irregular at best.

In contrast, river dwellers have managed açaí successfully for a long time. Locals often plant and selectively cull açaí stands to promote optimal production of fruit and heart-of-palm. I was impressed by one farmer on Ilha dos Porcos who seemed to be familiar with the fruiting behavior of almost all the hundreds of açaí palms in his extensive home garden-cum-cultural forest. He had a mental map with less productive trees earmarked for harvesting palmito in the upcoming rainy season. Some lore has even arisen concerning açaí management. In a home garden on Colares Island in the southern estuary, I noticed some young açaí with the terminal leaflets of each frond tied together. The owner explained that this makes the palms precocious fruiters; they apparently produce their first crop six years after planting rather than the usual eight. Other local management practices include regular weeding and felling of trees of little or no economic value. On Ilha dos Porcos, locals even have an expression for a poorly kept açaí grove: "açaí in the scrub" (*açaízal no cerrado*).

Overall, then, the palmito trade has not wiped out açaí. Açaí readily sprouts when cut down at its base. It dies only if the top is lopped off. To save time and trouble, açaí is simply felled with a machete at its base, and a replacement palm soon sprouts from the roots, producing fruit in as little as three years. After producing fruit for some five years, açaí can be cut for palmito again on an eight-year cutting cycle. Indeed, more açaí palms sway in the afternoon breeze today than ever before.

Açaí is a living pharmacy and hardware store, provisioning rural folk with building supplies, brooms, and medicines. Once stripped of fruit, the stalks are used widely as brooms for sweeping yards and houses; in fact, the local name for the fruit stalk is vassoura, which means "broom." Some households also mulch the fruit stalks for eventual distribution around fruit trees, especially coconuts, as I observed near Afuá on Marajó. In the last century, açaí trunks were burned to smoke latex balls in huts scattered throughout the estuary. Today the trunks are no longer burned to help coagulate latex, but in the vicinity of Abaetetuba they are used to fire brick-making kilns. Açaí trunks are still used for corrugated flooring in homes and huts at temporary camps, as well as elevated walkways when the ground is mushy during the rainy season.

BURITI

Buriti is relatively common in wetlands throughout the Amazon basin, from the sediment-rich waters of the Amazon floodplain to clear and black water rivers. Buriti, known as miriti in the Amazon estuary, is second only to açaí as a standout palm at the mouth of the Amazon. It is easily the tallest palm in the region, soaring thirty meters, and like açaí sometimes occurs in dense stands. The scaly fruits, slightly larger than golf balls, are relished for snacks; children gather them from the forest floor or fish them out of the water.

Some buriti groves (*miritizal, buritizal*) may be vestiges of artificial enrichment by indigenous peoples and their successors. In Caxiuanã bay along the lower Anapú, for example, a dense stand of buriti is found adjacent to an indigenous shellmound. The shellmound appears to have been more than just a temporary camp for harvesting freshwater mussels: extensive black earth full of potsherds surrounding the shellmound suggests that a village occupied the site for a long time. While indigenous groups occupied the site, they undoubtedly harvested buriti fruits and discarded the seeds nearby. On Marajó, extensive stands of buriti are particularly noticeable where savanna grades into forest, suggesting such transition environments may have been settlements in the past, perhaps villages on stilts. Although these areas are virtually deserted today, several villages on Marajó are built entirely on stilts, including Jenipapo along the upper Arari and Afuá in the northwestern part of the island. Indeed, Afuá is the only municipal capital in Pará without a single motor vehicle.

People have good reason to plant buriti, or at least protect spontaneous seedlings that germinate in trash piles. The creamy orange pulp of buriti fruits is relished in town and country alike. On Marajó, locals typically soak the fruits for about an hour

Silhouette of a buriti along a misty river at dawn. Rio Anabiju, Marajó, April 24, 2000.

Buriti fruits scooped out of the water during an early morning trip to check gill nets for fish. The fruits will be taken home for a family snack. Ilha dos Porcos near Afuá, September 18, 1998.

to soften them before eating. In the Peruvian Amazon, buriti is cut down on some parts of the floodplain to cater to the Iquitos market, but this destructive practice is absent or at least rare in the estuary. In towns and cities, red buriti fruits are consumed fresh, or the pulp is removed from the large seeds and mixed with water and sold in one-liter plastic bags for about 50 cents. In town, buriti juice is sweetened to make ice cream or blended with boiled rice and salt to make porridge (*mingau de miriti*) for a hearty repast at daybreak. In rural areas, a different buriti porridge is prepared by mixing the pulp with sugar and manioc flour. Far healthier than candy, buriti fruits contain more vitamin A than carrots and as much vitamin C as oranges.

The anthropogenic nature of dense buriti stands is also suggested by early European accounts of indigenous life at the mouth of the Amazon. In describing the Aruã who inhabited islands in the northern channel of the Amazon estuary and parts of ad-

Afuá in 1879, depicting the arrival of the monthly steamer from Belém. Afuá, on the northwestern tip of Marajó, has grown to a small town but is still entirely built on stilts. From M. Mauris, *At the mouth of the Amazons,* Harpers 58 (1879): 365–79.

jacent Marajó, an English trader, John Levy, noted in 1597 that "they make bread of a great tree called anarola and drink of the juice thereof, which they doe by poundeinge and seetheinge."[3] While the fruits of several palms are mashed and sieved, only buriti yields starch from its pithy trunk. The now-extinct Aruã evidently obtained starch from buriti and made a drink from its fruit. With buriti serving as a staff of life, the Aruã and other indigenous groups in the estuary likely planted the useful palm.

Today only the fruits of the towering palm are consumed in the estuary, though buriti contributes indirectly to people's diets when pigs are let loose in floodplain forests to feed on fallen fruits. A single stalk typically contains hundreds of the fruits, and since buriti sports as many as ten fruit stalks at one time, several thousand fruits typically adorn the palm. Although a tree does not produce fruits year-round, some buriti are always in fruit, especially during the rainy season from December to May.

Buriti also provides a host of other useful products. On Marajó, a tough fiber is obtained from the unopened fronds that is used to weave hammocks that are durable if a little scratchy. Buriti hammocks are also fashioned in other parts of the Amazon basin, such as among the Waimiri Atroari near Manaus, Amazonas. On Marajó, this craft is gradually dying out as people increasingly purchase cotton hammocks made in the northeast of Brazil, make their own hammocks from recycled polypropylene sacks, or opt for beds. Palmate buriti fronds are still cut to fashion baskets. Light green buriti baskets vary in shape and tightness of the weave, depending on whether they will hold fish, shrimp, chickens, or fruit. The midribs of buriti fronds are also fashioned into tipitis, cylindrical presses used for squeezing manioc dough in preparation for making flour.

In the late nineteenth and early twentieth century, buriti wood was burned in smoky fires to cure latex tapped from rubber trees. Although rubber trees are relatively abundant in parts of the estuary, they have only been tapped sporadically since the collapse of the rubber boom in the 1920s. Buriti trunks still find a variety of other uses, however. Because of their relative abundance, locals think nothing of felling the occasional buriti to provide a walkway from home to the water's edge. If the bank is steep, locals notch the log to create steps. Buriti trunks float readily, so loggers fell them to make rafts to buoy timber harvested from floodplain forests. As the tempo of timber harvesting quickens, these practices may reduce the availability of buriti fruit in some areas.

Mother weaving a basket with the split midribs of buriti palm fronds. Behind her is a storage area for maize, used to feed chickens and pigs. Lower Maracá, Amapá, May 4, 1996.

Boys returning home on a buriti palm log after fetching water from the river's edge. The poles stuck in the mud are for securing canoes. Lower Rio Anauera, Amapá, May 3, 1996.

Caraná palms with their distinctive studded trunks partially covered with lichens. Caraná fruits are gathered from the ground and eaten fresh as a snack or made into juice. Fazenda Memória, Rio Tauá, Marajó, May 22, 1999.

In the distant past, indigenous groups in the estuary may have had cultural checks in place to prevent the wanton destruction of buriti and other useful palms. In the upper Essequibo in Guyana, for example, the Waiwai believe that spirits inhabit buriti palms and that they will harm anyone attempting to damage or even mock the trees. Today buriti stands are vulnerable to the growing appetite for hardwoods and beef in Brazil and throughout the world.

CARANÁ

A near relative of buriti, caraná has similar fan-shaped fronds but is shorter and has fewer and smaller fruits. Unlike buriti, the slender trunk is studded with stubby thorns and is often partially covered with orange lichen. Caraná is another of the estuary's water-loving palms, found in clumps in marshes and seasonally flooded savannas, especially on sandy soils. Organic matter from fallen fronds tends to build up at the base of the palms, thereby providing a dryer platform for other plants to colonize wetlands. In this manner, caraná is a pioneer species in savannas, eventually giving way to forest provided that fires are not too intense.

Locals gather scaly caraná fruits from the ground and after peeling off the ocher-colored skin, nibble on the thin layer of pale yellow pulp. The olive-sized fruits do not enter urban markets, but rural folk enjoy snacking on the fruits and mashing them to make fresh juice. The midribs of caraná palm are split and loosely woven into small baskets, which are then lined with flat, fleshy leaves of heliconia to prevent produce from spilling out. Near Joannes along the southeastern coast of Marajó, for example, caraná baskets are used to take mangaba fruits, gathered from nearby scrub savanna, to market.

Buçú palm with its distinctive broad, drooping leaflets (center), flanked by açaí palms. In the Amazon, buçú is confined to the estuary, where its fronds are widely used to thatch houses and canoes. Ilha dos Porcos near Afuá, August 17, 1998.

BUÇÚ

Another floodplain palm with multiple uses is buçú, distinguished by its long, showy fronds that resemble torn banana leaves. In the Amazon, buçú is confined to the estuary. Locals cut its generous fronds to thatch their houses and cover their canoes. Buçú fronds endure for a decade or so, much longer than other palms also used for thatching. Consequently, buçú fronds are also in demand in urban centers to cover sheds and homes in low-income areas.

Sun-dried buçú fronds are used as covers on canoes to protect people and produce from the elements. Two thatch designs are commonly used: a tunnel or a peaked roof. In the former design, the fronds are carefully pleated or layered loosely over a super-

Buçú palm fronds drying on the dock of a river dweller's home. Nossa Senhora da Luz, Rio Tauaú near Breves, Marajó, August 11, 2000.

A diesel-powered canoe covered with plastic near the bow and a tunnel of layered buçú fronds. The rudder at the side of the craft near the rear is controlled by a rope from the front. Lower Pacajá near Portel, May 14, 2000.

structure of arumã leaf stems. In the latter, the fronds are layered on a peaked roof and held in place against storm gusts with a couple of long planks and twine. In the Breves market, charcoal is sold in open-weave baskets made with the midribs of buriti palm and lined with buçú fronds.

Buçú fronds are in demand as far inland as the lower Anapú, several hundred kilometers from the mouth of the Amazon. Stacks of buçú fronds are a common sight in street markets in the estuary, such as in Macapá, Muaná, and Breves. Palms that produce fronds suitable for thatching are often generically called *palheira* or *palha*, and in Belém, one of the ports serving the ever-expanding city is called Porto de Palha, so named for the large number of buçú fronds brought there.

Strong demand for the durable fronds of buçu has led to overharvesting in some areas, such as in the vicinity of Abaetetuba. Along the Rio Xingu on a floodplain island near Abaetetuba, locals have resorted to clearing plants around buçu seedlings in an effort to boost their survival rate. However, it is unlikely that buçu will be fully domesticated; other palms can be used for thatching, and manufactured materials can be purchased for covering houses. For example, plastic is replacing the buçú "cabin" on many canoes and small boats.

Other useful products from buçú include its rust-colored fruits, which contain an "emergency" supply of potable water for people working in the floodplain forest. The billiard ball–sized fruits contain only a thin layer of pulp, but the nuts are sliced open to liberate the clear liquid, like a miniature coconut, except that the pulp lining the inside of the nut is not eaten. Pigs relish buçú fruits, however, so rural residents and villagers dispatch youngsters along streams and rivers to scoop up the reddish brown

Buçú palm fruits are gathered as they drift on the surface of rivers. The fruits are fed to pigs. Afuá, Marajó, August 15, 1998.

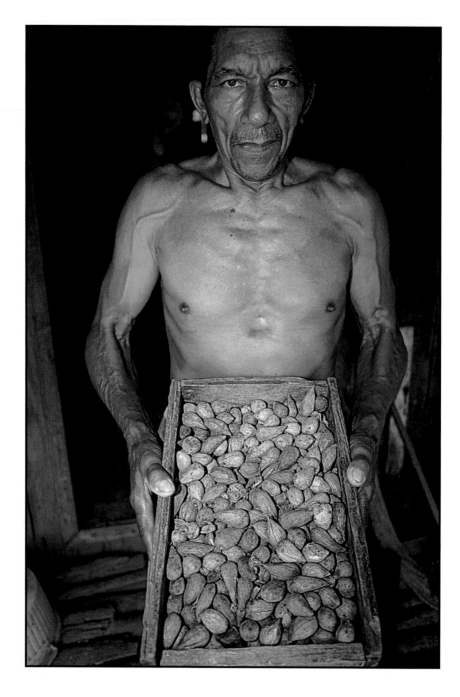

*Nuts of the murumuru palm
are rich in oil and were once
used for making soap. Today
they are gathered to feed pigs.
Fazenda Boa Morte,
Rio Ganhoão, municipality
of Chaves, Marajó,
May 18, 2001.*

fruits from the water's surface. The fruits are then dumped in backyards where the pigs' tough teeth and strong jaws make short work of the nuts. Hunters are aware that collared peccaries are fond of the fruits, so they amass them on the forest floor and wait for their prey. Large numbers of water-dispersed buçú fruits bob on the surface of estuarine rivers during the rainy season and, along with floating buriti fruits, produce a characteristic thunk on the underside of outboard-powered aluminum boats.

MURUMURU

Murumuru is arguably the most forbidding tree of the Amazon floodplain. Festooned with long, black spines the length of an adult's hand, the porcupine palm can inflict excruciating wounds on the unwary traveler. Even locals, who have learned to give its trunk wide berth, still step on the fallen spines hidden by leaves. And many a hunting dog has lost an eye to murumuru.

With such formidable armament, it is surprising that anyone would tamper with a tree that has clearly evolved an unfriendly disposition to mammals. Yet the nuts are so high in oil, and therefore calories, as well as protein that rural folk, such as along the Ganhoão River in northern Marajó, gather them to feed to their pigs and Muscovy ducks. The nuts are cracked open with a machete or large kitchen knife to access the milky white kernel; the sound of the cracking nuts elicits expectant grunts from pigs awakened from a snooze under the house. Even townspeople get into the act: children in Afuá go into the forest to gather murumuru fruits from the forest floor to feed pigs penned in their backyards.

At one time a small-scale industry grew up in the northern estuary to process the nuts for oil to make soap. Old-timers along the lower Pedreira, an affluent of the Amazon in the northern part of the estuary, remember buyers coming by boat from Macapá in the early twentieth century to buy murumuru nuts. The market for murumuru oil subsequently evaporated with the widespread arrival of soaps manufactured in southern Brazil. The construction of the Belém-Brasília highway in 1964 greatly increased the flow of manufactured goods into the Amazon estuary.

MARAJÁ

Another prickly palm in the understory of forest along the banks of streams and rivers in the estuary is the slender marajá. However, its short, black spines do not prevent locals from cutting off the fruit bunches with a machete. The dark brown to purple fruits, which grow in bunches containing about one hundred marble-sized fruits, are often lopped off by standing in a canoe. The tendency of the palm to lean over the water facilitates the harvesting of the fruits. Only a meager amount of pulp is sandwiched between the tough skin and the single, large black seed. Yet the gooseberry-like flesh has a pleasant tangy taste, similar to the bite of mamoncillo in the Caribbean and on the northern coast of South America. On Caviana Island, locals gather the fruit bunches and take them home for the family to snack on or to feed to their pigs.

Marajá palm fruits gathered in floodplain forest. The cowboy will take the fruits home as a treat for his family. Rio Pacajá, Caviana Island, May 22, 2001.

A Banquet of Wild Fruits

In developed countries, just about all the fruit that consumers eat comes from plantations. The same applies to people living in large cities in the industrial heartland of Brazil, especially São Paulo. In regions where many people still live off the land, however, wild fruits are gathered throughout the year and provide a welcome addition to the diet. The edible portion of wild fruits is typically small—one of the first aspects that is improved if the plant is domesticated—yet the exquisite flavors, unusual texture, or copious juice is reward enough for the effort of gathering them. Certain indigenous groups in the Amazon put on festivals celebrating the seasons of certain fruits. In the estuary, fruits are gathered in both the dry and rainy seasons from a variety of habitats, ranging from savanna to forest.

Forests are normally regarded as inimical to food production. With the advent of farming thousands of years ago, huge tracts of woodland both in tropical and in temperate regions were cleared for crops. In the nineteenth century, the pioneer American environmentalist George Perkins Marsh expressed the idea that forests cannot meet the food needs of people thus:

> In a region absolutely covered with trees, human life could not long be sustained, for want of animal and vegetable food. The depths of the forest seldom furnish either bulb or fruit suited to the nourishment of man; and the fowls and beasts on which he feeds are scarcely seen except upon the margin of the wood, for here only grow the shrubs and grasses, and here only are found the seeds and insects, which form the sustenance of the non-carnivorous birds and quadrapeds.[1]

Today that perception persists, at least among development planners and government policy makers. Forests are often viewed as impediments to progress, a "jungle" to be scraped away for more rational cultivation. The push to open pioneer highways in the Amazon in the 1960s and 1970s is testament to that distorted vision.

My purpose here is not to argue that the forests of the Amazon estuary can meet all the food needs of the region's population, especially given their current food tastes. Rather it is to point out that they provide important dietary supplements and income

A boy peeling a ceru nut with
his teeth. A relative of the
Brazil nut, ceru nuts are
fished out of the water
with cans tied to poles or by
hand. Muaná, Marajó,
May 20, 1999.

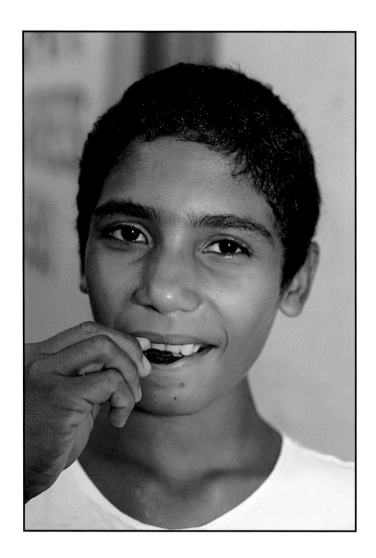

and contain a genetic treasure trove that could enrich agriculture, especially agro-forestry, in generations to come. Today's "minor" fruits could eventually emerge as important crops in their own right, provided that forests and other habitats do not perish. Roger Leakey, a British agroecologist, aptly calls such fruits with unsung virtues "Cinderella" fruits.

The contribution of palms to diet and income was discussed in the previous chapter. Here we embark on a tour of some of the other delectables gathered from forest and field in the Amazon estuary. They range from the almost effervescent yellow mombim to tart pitomba and the seductively smooth, sweet pulp of cacau jacaré, a near relative of cacao. The Amazon estuary is a mosaic of habitats—upland and periodically flooded forest, seasonally wet grasslands, lakes, marshes, and mangrove—and people gather fruits, nuts, and seeds from all of them. Some higher portions of eastern Marajó are covered with a woody, upland savanna, which contains various stunted trees normally associated with the expansive savannas of south-central Brazil over one thousand kilometers away. The fruit of one tree found in this habitat, mangaba, is gathered during the rainy season for local markets.

FLOODPLAIN FORESTS

Estuarine forests abound in tasty fruits and nuts, most of which never appear in urban markets and therefore are largely invisible to development planners and organizations charged with recommending areas for biodiversity conservation. The value of these phantom fruits lies more in their cultural significance to locals than in a tally sheet of calories consumed or an estimated dollar value for a number-crunching economic model of valuation. The tang of a forest fruit just coming into season brings joy to youngsters and parents alike.

The floodplain forests are a familiar larder to locals. To the adventurous and inquisitive visitor, they present a smorgasbord of gustatory surprises. For example, the diminutive ceru nut never finds its way into markets but is nevertheless highly appreciated by locals in the estuary because of its savory flavor.

THE CERU NUT

Ask shoppers in the fruit and nut section of a supermarket in Belém, "Do you know ceru?" and most customers will have no idea what you are talking about. I have been going to the Amazon for thirty years, but I came across this curious nut only recently. It was in Muaná, a sleepy town in southern Marajó. I noticed a bunch of kids along the waterfront talking excitedly and dividing what looked like small, black nails among themselves. Intrigued, I approached and asked what the items were. "Ceru!" was the amused reply, called out in unison, as if the answer was obvious. Such experiences serve to keep Amazon "experts" humble.

Reminiscent of almonds, ceru nuts are about five centimeters long and are covered by a blackish brown skin that has to be painstakingly peeled off to expose the edible portion. Although gaining access to the ivory-colored flesh takes some effort, the rich, creamy taste of ceru is reward enough. A relative of the Brazil nut, ceru nuts do not enter commerce.

Ceru illustrates the fact that many species have patchy distributions in the Amazon. Although ceru has been recorded as far inland as the upper Negro, it is most common in the floodplain forests of the southern estuary, where it also occurs occasionally in upland forest adjacent to water. It is a medium-sized tree and produces fruits, technically capsules, that ripen in April and May. Fruit maturation coincides with the high water season, thus facilitating dispersal of the buoyant seeds. The ten- to fifteen-centimeter-long capsule looks like a narrow bell with a lid on the bottom; when ripe, the lid falls off, scattering the nuts into the water. If the nuts fall on the ground and manage to escape detection by feral pigs, peccaries, agoutis, and opossums, they are picked up by the next high tide and carried off.

Children harvest ceru by one of two means. The most common method is to scoop the nuts out of the water with a pole. A plastic bottle is cut in half and the bottom part attached to the end of a pole so that the nuts can be fished out of the water from a dock. Ceru nuts are also picked out of the water by hand from canoes. If the children have been diligent enough, or have enough left over after snacking on the job, some of the nuts are stored at home for the rest of the family.

PITOMBA

Glistening pitomba fruits, like most wild fruits of the estuary, are a rainy season treat. Not to be confused with an upland fruit of the same name[2] that is widely cultivated in Brazil and some neighboring countries, the floodplain pitomba is a short tree that

A pitomba tree in fruit. The lustrous fruits, typically harvested from a canoe, resemble tart cherries. Near Cachoeira do Arari, Marajó, May 17, 1999.

grows along the banks and creeks of Marajó. The floodplain pitomba is one of the many Cinderella fruits that have escaped the attention of scientists and development planners.

The reddish purple fruits likely evolved for dispersal by birds such as toucans and guans and may have been planted around indigenous camps and villages thousands of years ago. It is especially common in the Arari watershed, where the Marajoara culture reigned supreme for so long. The refreshing pulp of floodplain pitomba bursts with flavor and could one day emerge as an agroforestry crop for wetlands. Because of its slightly tart taste, some locals prepare a thick treacle from the fruits that they serve as a dessert (*doce de pitomba*). Others take advantage of the fruit's tartness to prepare home-made vinegar by adding salt to the juice squeezed from the mashed pulp. Pitomba vinegar is poured on fish and other dishes as a condiment. A fishing family in Ca-choeira do Arari mashes the pitomba fruits and mixes them with manioc flour and sugar.

Pitomba trees along the banks of a creek during the annual flood. The trees have been partially submersed for months, and as the fruits ripen some of them drop into the water where they are eaten by fish and turtles. Near Cachoeira do Arari, Marajó, May 17, 1999.

As in the case of pitomba, both bacuri and bacupari are adapted to withstand months with wet feet. Bacuri can soar to twenty-five meters and drops copious tennis ball–sized fruits during the rainy season. Along the banks of Pacajá Creek on Caviana, a bacuri tree that is flooded only at high tide in the wet season was still producing fruit in late May, the tail end of the rainy season. Locals on the island retain mental maps of tree locations and check on them periodically during the rainy months. In the event that a forest animal, such as a paca, has beaten them to it, an adventurous soul may climb up the tree to dislodge more fruits by shaking the branches. The yellow fruits travel well back home because they are thick-skinned.

Bacupari is a small tree of disturbed forest and old second growth in low-lying areas where floodwaters lap almost to the lower branches when the plum-sized fruits are in season. Children canoe underneath the canopy and pluck the lime green fruits. Many youngsters are too impatient to wait until bacuripari fruits mature; they pick them when green, relishing their tartness. Another reason that kids pick bacuripari fruits when they are green is to make sure no one else beats them to the reward. Parents, on the other hand, prefer mature fruits because they taste like sweet custard. The outer skin is peeled off to reveal a slippery, almost jelly-like pulp surrounding a single flattened seed. The pulp is sucked off the black seed, which is then discarded.

Bacuri fruit gathered from floodplain forest. Rio Pacajá, Caviana Island, May 22, 2001.

(OPPOSITE PAGE)
Boy returning home with bacuripari fruit. The boy was gathering the fruit standing up in the canoe until interrupted by a thunderstorm. Lavrado, municipality of Ponta de Pedras, Marajó, April 24, 2000.

Another denizen of river- and stream banks in the estuary, camutim is a small tree bearing grape-sized yellow fruits. Never encountered in markets, the succulent fruits are nevertheless appreciated by locals, especially youngsters who can easily clamber up the tree and along the branches to pluck the fruit clusters. Camutim fruits in the rainy season, presumably because the seeds have an easier time germinating in the moist soil. While youngsters in Amazonian cities head to the candy aisle when supermarket shopping with their parents, rural kids check out their home gardens or wander into the forest in search of fruits.

Boys snacking on camutim fruit gathered in floodplain forest. Lower Maracá, Amapá, May 4, 1996.

The caiman cacao, known locally as cacau-jacaré, is aptly named for the fruit's corrugated skin. A relative of cacao, the well-known source of chocolate, caiman cacao is not sold in markets, nor are the seeds fermented and roasted to make a version of chocolate. Locals gather the green pods from the understory tree and break them open to enjoy the sweet pulp surrounding the dozen or so seeds.

For the moment at least, caiman cacao lingers as one of the many lesser-known, localized fruits of the region. But it could emerge as a trendy new rainforest chocolate a decade or so from now. Or its sweet, tangy pulp may eventually find its way into the

A BANQUET OF

WILD FRUITS

Fruits of cacau-jacaré, a wild relative of cacao, are gathered in floodplain forests throughout the Amazon estuary. The corrugated pods of the caiman cacao (as the fruit is referred to in English) are broken open to reach the sweet, white pulp surrounding the seeds. Lower Maracá, Amapá, May 4, 1996.

*Yellow mombim fruits scooped
out of a river to make juice.
Near Igarapé-Miri,
December 10, 1999.*

freezer cases of upscale supermarkets where tropical sherbets and novelty ice creams tantalize customers. Cupuaçu, another cacao relative, has already made this transition. Cupuaçu is native to the forests of eastern Amazonia and has long been gathered in the wild and cultivated in backyards for its exquisite-tasting pulp, used to make juices, jams, and ice cream. Spurred by increased demand from urban customers in the Amazon, as well as growing markets for frozen pulp from central and southern Brazil, farmers recently began planting cupuaçu in commercial agroforestry fields. Cupuaçu illustrates nicely the connections among forests, home gardens, and income-generating agriculture. Without the forest, future options for agricultural development in the region could stall. Caiman cacao has not yet been domesticated, but its turn may come.

The oval to oblong fruits of yellow mombim, known locally as tapereбá and as cajá in other parts of Brazil, are a bit too tart to eat fresh but when mixed with sugar and water make a delightful drink. The bright yellow fruits, sometimes tinged orange, are gathered off the ground along the banks of rivers and streams or are plucked out of the water from canoes. Yellow mombim grows spontaneously in disturbed sites in upland and floodplain areas of Amazonia but is particularly abundant along the Amazon, including its mouth.

Yellow mombim fruits in the dry season, and at the height of the season in November and December, some fruits end up in urban markets. Vendors also hawk yellow mombim fruits at ferry crossings and at speed bumps along major roads. The powerful, intriguing perfume of yellow mombim fruits wafts for several meters and often wins over customers if they have their car windows open. The delicately skinned fruits are sold in lots weighing about two kilograms, either in tall plastic bags or in slender, makeshift baskets (*paneiro*). The fruits are relatively inexpensive; in November 1998, for example, yellow mombim was selling for 40 cents a kilogram in Belém's bustling Ver-o-Pêso market. In addition to making juice, urban residents often put the fruits into a blender to make milkshakes or ice cream.

Yellow mombim is never encountered in mature forests and is a good indicator that people have been in the area. It arises spontaneously from discarded seeds and needs abundant sunlight to germinate and become established. Because the fruits are so widely appreciated, yellow mombim is usually spared from the ax or machete when encountered in backyard gardens and cultivated fields. Yellow mombim is also planted in home gardens.

Theodore Roosevelt, the former U.S. president, recognized the virtues of yellow mombim nearly a century ago. During his adventures along the River of Doubt in southern Amazonia in 1914, he noted:

> The vast still forest was almost empty of life. We found old Indian signs. There were very few birds, and these in the tops of the tall trees. We saw a recent tapir-track; and under a cajazeira-tree by the bank there were tracks of capybaras which had been eating the fallen fruit. This fruit is delicious and would make a valuable addition to our orchards. The tree although tropical is hardy, thrives when domesticated, and propagates rapidly from shoots. The Department of Agriculture should try whether it would not grow in southern California and Florida.[3]

Yellow mombim tree in a home garden. Because of its age, this tree is festooned with creepers and epiphytic aroids. Vila Jurupari, municipality of Afuá, August 16, 1998.

*Fruits of caju-açu for sale in
an open-air market. The red
caju-açu fruits are being sold
in bags of ten; underneath, the
vendor also has yellow
mombim fruits for sale.
Ver-o-Pêso market, Belém,
November 13, 1998.*

UPLAND FORESTS AND SECOND GROWTH

Although floodplain forests predominate at the mouth of the Amazon, some forest survives on upland bluffs that overlook the estuary, especially in the south. Furthermore, patches of well-drained soils occur sporadically in southern Marajó and have been colonized by upland species. Islands of nonflooded forest provide welcome variety to the diet because they contain a diverse assortment of fruits and nuts, one of which is profiled briefly here: the little-known but intriguing caju-açu.

The fiery red fruits of caju-açu, a relative of the cultivated cashew tree, are a welcome treat in the dry season when they fall to the ground. Caju-açu, which means "big cashew," refers to the size of the tree, not the fruit. The trunk soars to the rainforest canopy some thirty meters above ground and is much too tall for anyone to climb and pluck the kiwi-sized fruits from its branches. Rather, young and old alike gather the waxy fruits from the forest floor toward the end of the dry season. The other name for the tree, cajuí, means "diminutive cashew" and refers to the fruit that is about one-third the size of the cultivated cashew fruit.

Those fruits not taken by canopy dispersal agents eventually fall off. Most survive the long drop to the forest floor because they are compact and light. When ripe, the delicate fruits emit a pervasive, sweet odor, evidently to attract seed dispersal agents. The seed is an appendage to the fruit, and birds such as toucans and monkeys are careful to discard the single seed covered with a protective skin impregnated with a burning acid.

In addition to being eaten as a snack, caju-açu fruits are used as an accompaniment to cachaça. A bite of succulent caju-açu is a refreshing chaser after a shot of harsh sugarcane spirits. The yellow pulp of the fruits is also mashed to make juice for mixing with cachaça (*batida de caju-açu*). A few vendors in Belém's Ver-o-Pêso market carry the fruits in season, usually in plastic bags of ten. These vendors are strategically located close to stalls that sell cachaça and other hard liquor by the shot.

SAVANNA

When the current use and economic potential of wild fruits are discussed in the Amazon, attention naturally turns to the forest. Yet savannas cover nearly half of Marajó Island, and cowboys and river dwellers gather a number of useful products from them, including caroba wood for saddles. Although not as biodiverse as forests, savannas nevertheless produce several much-appreciated fruits, including cajuí do campo and mangaba. Only the latter is discussed here.

MANGABA

The soft, thin-skinned fruits of mangaba are gathered from contorted, often fire-blackened trees on savannas. The pale yellow skin is peeled to reach the sweet, white pulp. Some locals gather the fruits for markets in Marajó as well as Belém. The fruits are generally sold in lots of about twenty, contained in baskets woven from the midribs of caraná palm fronds lined with the banana-like leaves of heliconia gathered in the forest. Mangaba fruits are especially welcome, because few other wild fruits suitable for snacking are available during the dry months.

Mangaba fruits gathered on a scrub savanna. Near Joanes, Marajó, September 7, 1997.

Mangaba is relatively widespread in the savannas of Brazil and has served a variety of uses. During the rubber boom in the late nineteenth and early twentieth century, wild mangaba was tapped for its latex, known on world markets as Pernambuco rubber. Europe and North America purchased mangaba rubber again during World War II when Japanese forces cut off supplies of plantation rubber from Southeast Asia. Today the tree is no longer tapped because Southeast Asia has once again flooded world markets with relatively cheap, high-grade natural rubber.

ARUMÃ-RANA

On low-lying parts of the savanna that are flooded for several months of the year, locals gather the stems of arumã-rana, a marantaceous herb that grows to a height of almost two meters. The seeds of arumã-rana, also known as patazana or pariri along the central Amazon, are fed to chickens, especially when stocks of dried maize are low. The gathering of arumã-rana is not especially time-consuming because it grows in dense stands, often covering several hectares. Arumã-rana produces seeds toward the end of the rains and into the early dry season. Today people on Marajó do not eat the seeds directly, but indigenous groups most likely did so long ago.

Arumã-rana gathered in seasonally flooded savanna to feed the family's chickens. The girl is a daughter of a cowboy. Like most cowboy families, this one maintains small livestock around its home. Fazenda Cajueiro, municipality of Chaves, Marajó, August 15, 2000.

(OPPOSITE PAGE) *A feral cashew on a relict sand dune that produces abundant fruit in the dry season. Fazenda Cajueiro, municipality of Chaves, Marajó, August 18, 2000.*

Sandy Islands in Savanna

Relict sand dunes, vestiges of ancient shorelines, occur sporadically in the northern and eastern parts of Marajó. Most likely formed some five thousand years ago when the shoreline migrated inland a few kilometers as the sea levels rose by about one meter, the dunes are found in both savanna and forest. In both instances, the vegetation on the ancient dunes is distinctive, in part because of the moisture stress and the paucity of nutrients characteristic of sandy soils. But these sites make ideal places to set up camp or a village, and people have added plants to the sandy archipelagos over the last few thousand years.

On Fazenda Cajueiro in northern Marajó, for example, the large number of economic plants in relict dunes is striking. Indigenous people likely cultivated some of these plants long ago, and although they have since vanished, their handiwork survives in the form of feral crops. Some of the dunes have patches of darkened soil containing potsherds, evidently ancient village or campsites. On one such dune, the ash-stained soil covering about half a hectare is adjacent to a stream, an ideal location for a village. The inhabitants of that archaeological site likely shaped the plant communities around them, both deliberately and inadvertently. The list of economic plants on one sand dune near the headquarters of the ranch included cashew, pineapple, several other edi-

ble bromeliads, tarumã (an edible fruit also used for fish bait), jacitara palm (used for weaving baskets; fruits used for fish bait and eaten by people after cooking), tucumã palm (edible fruit and also used as twine), and jutaí (a leguminous tree with edible fruits).

On Mexiana Island, across some straits from northern Marajó, a relict sand dune known locally as Ilha dos Ananás is likewise stocked with economic plants, some of which are surely descendants of seedlings planted long ago by indigenous people. Among the economic plants on Ilha dos Ananás are tucumã palm, jacitara palm, baleira (wood for boats), tarumã (wood for boats, fruit for fish bait), yellow mombim (edible fruit), and tento (seeds used for necklace beads).

CASHEW

Ranchers, cowboys, and river dwellers have planted cashew seedlings all over Marajó, but it was indigenous folk who originally brought the trees to the island. After indigenous groups vanished, their cultural imprint on the landscape was not entirely erased. Such is the case with cashew, which was planted on relict sand dunes and subsequently became feral. Toucans and monkeys spread the fruits to other dunes and, after feasting on the succulent pulp, dropped the seed, which is covered by a lip-burning skin. Cashew has thus arisen spontaneously on many relict beaches on Marajó and is now part of the "natural" landscape.

Many of the feral cashew trees are ancient. Their branches are so thick and heavy that they bend to the ground and twist like giant serpents. The dome-shaped trees flush with waxy leaves flower in the rainy season and produce yellow to red fruits in the dry months. Locals pluck the juice-laden fruits from the low-lying branches and after pulling off the seed, suck out liquid, which is rich in vitamin C. Cashew nuts are roasted over open fires in the backyard to avoid inhaling the toxic fumes that emanate from the scorched skin.

PINEAPPLE AND RELATIVES

The inland "beaches" of Marajó also support at least three species of edible bromeliads, all of which were likely introduced by indigenous groups thousands of years ago. Feral pineapple, known locally as ananás, can be distinguished from the most common commercial cultivar—Cayenne smooth—by its toothed leaves. Backyard cultivars of pineapple also retain this primitive feature, which has been eliminated on commercial plantations to facilitate harvesting. Ananás also refers to traditional selections of pineapple in the Amazon, and the fact that feral populations go by the same name suggests that locals recognize it is the same species.

Ananás grows in clumps in the understory of stunted forest that cloaks relict sand

A BANQUET OF
WILD FRUITS

dunes. Locals on Marajó, such as on Fazenda Cajueiro near Chaves, gather the fruits for domestic consumption but make no effort to replant. Feral ananás populations are evidently self-maintaining. Fazenda Reicom on Mexiana also has wild pineapple, a small population growing in sandy soil just inland from Limão beach along the southern shore of the island. Water buffalo destroyed the only other population of wild pineapple on the ranch, and possibly on Mexiana. The understory of Ilha dos Ananás, a relict sand dune about ten kilometers inland, is now virtually bare; water buffalo like to cool off in the shade and sleep there, especially in the rainy season. They have eaten, trampled, or squashed virtually all of the herbs and young plants that formerly grew

Ananaí, a wild relative of pineapple, produces small but succulent fruits that are gathered by locals on Marajó and several other islands in the Amazon estuary. Fazenda Cajueiro, municipality of Chaves, Marajó, August 19, 2000.

Coatá, a terrestrial bromeliad with armed leaves, forms understory thickets on relict sand dunes. Locals have to carefully push aside the leaves to reach the fruits at the base of the plant. Fazenda Cajueiro, municipality of Chaves, Marajó, August 18, 2000.

on the island, which is surrounded by a soggy savanna during the annual flood. The cowboy who has his home at one end of the island has collected some ananás from the Limão site and is cultivating a few of the wild pineapple in his home garden, protected by a sturdy fence. It would be a pity if the last pockets of wild pineapple in the estuary disappeared; they might contain some interesting genes for the future improvement of the crop.

A BANQUET OF WILD FRUITS

Coatá fruits resemble red-skinned bananas, except the flesh is crunchy and tart. The fruits are gathered as a fresh snack or taken home and boiled with salt before eating. Fazenda Cajueiro, municipality of Chaves, Marajó, August 18, 2000.

Ananaí, meaning "small pineapple," produces miniature pineapples—no larger than tennis balls—at the end of long stems. The other common name for the wild fruit, ananás do miúdo, means "tiny pineapple." The sweet-tasting yellow fruits are gathered for local consumption and never enter markets. This diminutive relative of pineapple also occurs sporadically in the transition zone between savanna and forest, such as on Colares Island near Vigia. Even if ananaí never made it as a commercial fruit, it would be an attractive garden plant in warmer climates. The outermost leaves turn a copper-orange, making a nice contrast with the light green leaves underneath, and the fruit, although edible, may have more value for its beauty.

Coatá, another wild bromeliad found on sand dunes, also has edible fruits. But harvesting the fruits takes dexterity: the arching leaves, which can exceed three meters, are armed with thorns shaped like cat's claws. The spines lining the edges of the sword-shaped leaves have presumably evolved to keep mammals, such as peccary, at bay. Most rodents, on the other hand, are small enough to reach the fruits without being raked by the backward-curving spines. Perhaps they swallow some of the seeds and later defecate them, thereby dispersing the plant. Coatá forms virtually impenetrable thickets under the diffuse shade of the canopy. The fruits look like miniature red bananas, except the tart flesh is white and contains small black seeds the size of peppercorns. The crunchy pulp is eaten fresh and also boiled with salt.

CHAPTER 6

In the Shadow of the Forest

An examination of the farming history of an area is essential if one is to understand the current mosaic of habitats and their relevance for agricultural development and conservation. Only by probing into ways that people have altered landscapes to suit their needs can one appreciate how intimately nature and culture are tied together. The distinction between "wild" and cultivated areas in the estuary is often hard to make. Where do home gardens end and the forest begin? And the "forest" is often a cultural arrangement, because people constantly add and remove plants. Many areas now in forest were once farmed or open savanna. It is more useful, then, to view landscapes along a spectrum of land use intensity, from highly to little disturbed. In the estuary at least, few if any areas can be designated pristine, that is, never touched or altered by human activities. Hunters, fishers, and farmers are all agents of landscape change, and here I focus on the changing face of agriculture and how it has impacted the landscape.

Too often, judgments are made about the agricultural potential of an area or its human carrying capacity based on the current scene. Agriculture in the Amazon estuary today is not a significant economic activity, at least in terms of field crops. The rubber boom in the late nineteenth century took the wind out of agriculture's sails. River dwellers simply spent more time tapping and smoking latex from wild rubber (seringa) than cultivating crops because it paid more. In describing economic activities in the estuary in 1875, the outgoing governor of Pará, Pedro Vicente de Azevedo, remarked that "there is no agriculture of any kind and no other occupation other than the rubber industry."[1] The rubber boom collapsed by 1920, yet farming has barely recovered. A larger area was under field crops in the early eighteenth century than today, even though the urban population has increased severalfold over the past two hundred years.

In the distant past, indigenous peoples cleared substantial areas of forest in the estuary to plant food crops, especially manioc. Both floodplain and upland forests were cleared to support the relatively dense settlements. The banks of many rivers in the estuary are suitable for farming, especially at low water, even though today trees have reclaimed them. The dense upland forests that now cloak southwestern Marajó near Breves were likely dominated by cultivated plots and second growth in precontact times.

The perception that the estuary is largely unsuited to farming is understandable given the relatively small area devoted to field crops today. Furthermore, most of the food consumed in the estuary is produced on the mainland, in other parts of Brazil, and even abroad. Urban centers in the estuary have typically tripled in size over the last thirty years or so, but much of the food consumed in Belém, Macapá, and even rural villages in the estuary is imported. The Brazilian geographer Hilgard Sternberg has noted a similar process on the Amazon floodplain farther upstream near Manaus. The spectacular growth of Manaus since the creation of the free port three decades ago has hardly benefited farmers on the nearby Amazon floodplain.

Staples, such as manioc flour, rice, and beans, consumed in urban centers come mostly from uplands outside of the estuary, including central and southern Brazil. Even chickens marketed in the estuary are fed commercial feed produced in southern Brazil. Manioc flour in thirty-kilogram plastic bags is a common sight in markets and boats throughout the estuary; most of the flour comes from upland farms in the Bragantina Zone east of Belém and along the Pacajá River. Improved transportation links within the Amazon and between the region and the rest of Brazil have kept the cost of food down and allowed cities such as Belém to grow.

Debates about the agricultural potential of an area hinge on how agriculture is defined. For many policy makers, agriculture is synonymous with field crops, particularly cereals and pulses. But if one considers açaí a crop—and at least half of the fruits reaching markets likely come from planted palms—then the estuary is a significant agricultural zone. The Brazilian anthropologist Eduardo Brondizio points out that socioeconomic surveys typically treat açaí fruits as an extractive product when in reality the palm is an integral part of agroforests. Such perceptions can bias agricultural development policies. For many, agricultural intensification conjures up images of heavy machinery that triggers soil erosion and wanton application of fertilizers, pesticides, and herbicides that pollute groundwater and destroy beneficial organisms. Farmers in the estuary already manage their land intensively while minimizing off-farm environmental impacts because they do not deploy agricultural chemicals or use tractors.

Agriculture in the estuary today is based mainly on tree crops, usually intercropped. Indeed, agroforestry is one of the most promising avenues for agricultural development in much of the Amazon and other areas of the humid tropics because it is more environmentally friendly than monocropping and helps to diversify income, thereby providing stability for small farmers. A sound start for any attempt to formulate agricultural development policy would be to better understand the existing farming patterns. The importance of açaí in the lives of people at the mouth of the Amazon and its prominence in agroforests were the subject of Chapter 4. Here I highlight some other perennials and annuals cultivated in the estuary, many in successional agroforestry systems.

Several themes underpin this foray into a small sample of the rich assemblage of crops grown by farmers in the estuary: the impact of market integration on the choice of crops and varieties; how technological change prompts growers to adopt new agronomic practices or switch to other crops; and how such changes play out on the landscape. The texture and colors of the countryside are in constant flux in part because of shifts in agricultural practices.

In a survey of crops in two distinct environments, fields cut from forest and home gardens, two features are immediately striking. First, growers plant a mix of indigenous and exotic crops. Plants domesticated in tropical Africa and Asia play important roles in boosting food production and income. Future progress in agriculture will continue to hinge on encouraging international exchanges of plants and varieties. Second, people are recruiting wild fruits and nuts from the forest to plant in their home gardens. Such proto-domesticates sometimes take off and become crops in their own right. The forest is important, then, as a reservoir for tomorrow's crops as well as valuable genes for enriching plants already under cultivation.

FIELD CROPS

Both upland and floodplain forests are cleared and burned to raise crops for subsistence and to generate income. Crops raised on cleared floodplains and uplands range from short-cycle plants, such as squash and rice, to perennials, such as fruit trees. In floodplain areas, many such fields are planted to açaí or other fruit trees after the annuals have been harvested, thereby transforming the plots into multispecies fruit orchards.

In most parts of the estuary, the space and time devoted to field crops have declined as river dwellers have focused on more lucrative enterprises, such as extraction of açaí fruit and palmito, the felling of timber, fishing, and raising water buffalo and cattle. In some instances, ribeirinhos have abandoned crop farming altogether; instead they buy basic staples with income derived from selling açaí fruit, shrimp, or livestock. Some farmers have been forced to give up growing crops because their neighbors' water buffalo invade their fields, devouring the succulent plants and trampling the others. Ironically, the tension here is not small versus big landowner. Water buffalo on large ranches keep to the interior of Marajó or graze in areas devoid of small farmers. It is small farmers who have recently adopted water buffalo who are causing problems with fellow smallholders in predominantly forested areas. Such is the case in the vicinity of Nascimento, a village at the mouth of a small river of the same name in northern Marajó. Often water buffalo graze on common lands in and around villages, making it difficult for residents to maintain home gardens let alone fields in the forest. Water buffalo eat the tender young fronds of recently planted açaí palm and literally mow through ba-

Floodplain forest recently cut and burned to plant crops. Watermelon and maize will be the first crops, to be followed by banana. Eventually the field will be turned into a grove of açaí palm. Sitio Caiçara, Rio Arapixi, municipality of Chaves, Marajó, August 15, 2000.

nana plantings. Those who abandon farming may adopt water buffalo themselves if they have sufficient resources, or try to make do with fishing and extraction of forest products.

MANIOC

Long a basic staple in the estuary, manioc is no longer grown on any significant scale on Marajó or its adjacent islands. In the first half of the twentieth century, for example, manioc was once cultivated in riparian forest snaking its way across savannas in the Anabiju watershed. Branches and small logs strewn in the slash-and-burn fields were gathered up and chopped for sale to steamships. Paddle steamers are now gone, and virtually all of the manioc flour eaten by residents on Marajó is produced on mainland farms. Forest has enveloped the long-abandoned manioc fields along the Anabiju and its tributary streams on the right bank. Nevertheless, pockets of manioc cultivation can still be found in the estuary. On Marajó, for example, river dwellers clear small patches of upland forest to plant manioc in the vicinity of Breves and along the Rio Camará. In the estuary, manioc is typically an intercrop.

Sweet manioc is boiled and eaten, like a potato. Small plots of sweet manioc, such as the Branca variety near Afuá or the Manteiga cultivar on Caviana Island, are sometimes grown in backyards or in fields. Because pigs are fond of the sweet type, locals surround the bushy plants near their homes with a wooden stockade. On Caviana, a grower has surrounded her manioc field with a sturdy fence fashioned from local bamboo (taboka) to keep out capybaras.

Most of the manioc grown in the estuary, as elsewhere in the Brazilian Amazon, is the bitter form, which must be converted to flour before eating. Bitter manioc tubers are carried in baskets from the slash-and-burn plot to the "flour house" (*casa da farinha*), where they are peeled, mostly by women, or left to soak for a few days in a flooded canoe or in a stream. The flour house is usually a few meters from the home. A couple of men or boys turn the large wheel that operates the grater, working up quite a sweat, especially if the oven is lit to toast the flour from a previous batch. After the tubers have softened in water or have been grated, they are put in a press, usually a sleevelike tipití or a boxlike device to which weight is added to squeeze out the water.

A family eating fish stew accompanied by manioc flour. The family makes a living from fishing and lives in a one-room house. Hammocks, used for sleeping, are hung up during the day. Manioc flour remains a basic staple on Marajó, although most of the flour is brought in from the mainland. Bairro do Choque, Cachoeira do Arari, Marajó, May 18, 2000.

The dough is removed and pressed through a sieve fashioned from arumã to remove larger fragments, which are then dried in the sun. The white pieces of manioc dough (*curueira*) are then boiled to make porridge or baked to make a sticky cake. The sieved dough is agitated on a large metal griddle over an oven for about an hour with a specialized paddle (*rodo*) until crunchy. In addition to making flour, some families make pancakes, known as beijú de mandioca, on the smooth griddle.

The yellow juice (*tucupí*) squeezed from the grated tubers is boiled to drive off the prussic acid and then added to a variety of dishes, especially those containing fish, shrimp, or poultry. One family along the Tauá-Pará River, which traverses part of the northern end of Colares Island, specializes in selling tucupí sauce to the nearby market in Vigia. Producers know that the more intense the color, the better the price tucupí will fetch. Accordingly, the family plants the Miriti variety of bitter manioc for such purposes because it yields a deep orange-yellow juice similar to the flesh of miriti (buriti) palm fruits. Tucupí vendors are invariably women who bring the product to market, especially on Saturdays, from their farms.

Tapioca is the starch that decants from the tucupí juice squeezed from grated manioc tubers and is used in a number of fish and shrimp dishes. A lucrative by-product from making flour, it is often sold in town by producers or handed over to vendors. Tapioca is especially popular at breakfast in the form of pancakes (*beijú de tapioca*) prepared on the spot at street stalls. Butter or margarine is spread on the warm pancakes, which may also be sprinkled with grated coconut. In Vigia, a breakfast gruel of tapioca, fresh maize, and condensed milk sprinkled with cinnamon is popular with shoppers and fishermen returning from a wave-tossed night on the freshwater sea.

All four products of manioc—flour, pancakes, tapioca, and tucupí sauce—can be stored for months, a major advantage in a hot, humid region where few rural folk have access to refrigerators. Manioc flour is eaten at virtually every meal, and manioc flour mixed with water, known as chibé, is a regional standby when there is no other food to be had. Chibé is either eaten cold or boiled first with salt. Butter may be added to boost the energy value of chibé, considered especially beneficial for anyone feeling weak. On Marajó, mothers feed their babies chibé when they think that they are underweight. Ironically, however, bloating can be a sign of protein malnutrition in babies. On Colares Island near Vigia, river dwellers prepare a manioc drink called maniocuera. An acquired taste, it is prepared with the Mandiocaba variety of bitter manioc; the tubers are boiled along with rice in tucupí sauce.

Farmers in the estuary cultivate a diverse array of manioc varieties for several reasons. The estuary is a patchwork quilt of habitats and microenvironments, and growers have learned to eke out a living in most of them by selecting plants and varieties that thrive under a variety of ecological conditions. Culinary tastes have been another fac-

Removing manioc dough from a tipití *press. This tipití is made with the fronds of the buriti palm.*
Nossa Senhora da Luz, Rio Tauaú near Breves, Marajó, August 11, 2000.

Manioc flour being scooped out of an oven with a specialized paddle (rodo) used to agitate the flour over the hot surface. This oven is designed to tip, thus facilitating flour removal. Nossa Senhora da Luz, Rio Tauaú near Breves, Marajó, August 11, 2000.

Street vendors selling juice
(tucupí), squeezed from
manioc dough, and tapioca.
Most of the vendors are
farmers who bring their
product to market year-round.
Vigia, November 14, 1998.

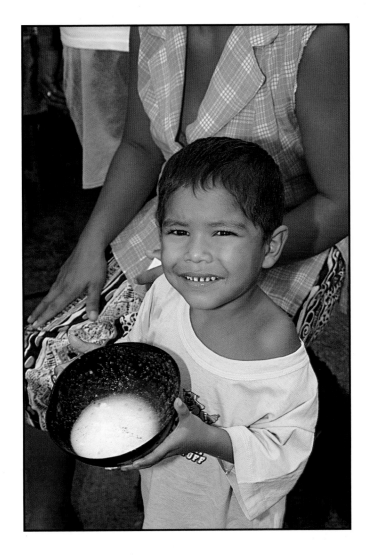

Tapioca, maize, and condensed
milk sprinkled with cinnamon
is a popular breakfast item in
street markets in the estuary.
The porridge is typically served
in a blackened calabash gourd.
Vigia, May 10, 1999.

tor motivating the selection of varieties. Locals appreciate nuances in taste, color, and texture and have retained the most desirable mutations. An added benefit of this diversity is that it helps to reduce disease and pest pressure, although farmers do not claim that is a factor in their decisions to intercrop varieties.

At Beiradão, a ferry crossing along the Camará, I visited a one-hectare manioc field planted with pineapple and coconut. The intraspecific diversity of manioc was quite high, even though the farmer was growing manioc for subsistence as well as for the market. In general, the greater the integration to markets, the fewer the crops and varieties grown. But on Marajó at least, this general rule does not always hold. The intercropped manioc field had four varieties of the bitter form (Pretinha, Paruí, Pacajá, Açaí) and one sweet variety (Manteiga). The Paruí variety is highly suited for agroforestry because it is tall and casts little shade; annual crops therefore thrive alongside it. The Açaí variety is so named for its purple skin, similar to that of the palm fruit. The name of the sweet manioc cultivar, Mantiega, means "butter," in reference to its rich, creamy texture. As in other parts of Amazonia, fewer varieties of sweet manioc are found, a reflection of its diminished importance as a food compared to the bitter form. Seis Meses (Six Months) appears to be one of the more common varieties of sweet manioc in the estuary, a logical choice for farmers who need to harvest the tubers before the annual flood.

Manioc cultivars are also diverse in nonflooded parts of the estuary. In the sandy interior of Colares Island near Vigia, for example, one field of bitter manioc had five varieties arranged in discrete patches. Treelike Pretinha Amarela and Pretinha Roxa soar to at least 2.8 meters, while the Sé variety, with its distinctive red leaf stems, and Mamaluca are not far behind at about 2.2 meters when fully grown. The Carimã variety is favored for making porridge for children. On another farm a few kilometers away, a bitter manioc field had four intercropped varieties: the narrow-leafed Pretinha Amarela; yellow tubered Gurijuba; Taresa, also with yellow tubers but with characteristic red leaf stems; and Mamaluca. Gurijuba, named after a catfish caught in coastal waters, produces an exceptionally fine flour called suruí. Gurijuba is likely a local selection or at least confined to the brackish coast of Pará.

Numerous other varieties of manioc, especially the bitter form, are cultivated in the estuary. The Bragança variety, named after an ancient town along the coast of Pará, and the Mamão cultivar, named for its broad, papaya-like leaves, are cultivated on Jurupari Island and its vicinity off northwestern Marajó. Both varieties are fairly widespread in the Brazilian Amazon, but with manioc in decline, locally selected varieties may become extinct even before they have been collected and placed in field gene banks for future breeding work. The Paruí variety, for example, appears to be confined to Marajó or at least is rarely encountered elsewhere. The same applies to several varieties of bitter manioc encountered on uplands near Breves: white-fleshed Garçinha, named after the snowy egret, which is common in the estuary; red-skinned Pepuí; and Curueira. On a floodplain island near Abaetetuba, a farmer cultivates two varieties of bitter manioc that appear to be confined to the mouth of the Tocantins: Pescada (named after a fish) and Tuíra. And at the village of Itupanema overlooking the confluence of the Tocantins and the southern arm of the Amazon, villagers cultivate Pucajá de Marajó, another bitter manioc variety apparently confined to the estuary.

RICE

The conventional view is that Asian rice (*Oryza sativa*) was introduced to the Amazon estuary from the Carolinas in 1772. But it seems likely that a rice domesticated in the Niger Valley of West Africa, *Oryza glaberrima*, was cultivated in the Amazon estuary a century or two earlier. Thanks to the careful historical sleuthing of Judith Carney, a geographer at the University of California, Los Angeles, it appears that African rice, with its distinctive red husk and grain, was brought to the New World in the sixteenth or seventeenth century in Portuguese slave ships. Rice is listed on cargo ships leaving Cape Verde for Brazil as early as 1530, and seed rice was being taken to Brazil in the mid-sixteenth century. Asian rice became widespread in West Africa only in the nineteenth century.

Paul Le Cointe, a French agronomist who spent most of his professional life in the Brazilian Amazon in the late nineteenth and early twentieth century, noted that a small-grained red rice was once cultivated in the Amazon estuary. Locals called it *abati* or *auati*, in contrast to *arroz*, the name for Asian rice. Le Cointe considered it indigenous. Although several species of wild rice thrive in freshwater marshes along the Amazon, none of them have red husks. African rice may have reached the estuary via traders from the Guianas or Maranhão, or slaves may have brought it with them from West Africa.

Red rice was soon stamped out after white rice was introduced from the Carolinas. The Portuguese crown wanted to generate a lucrative trade in Asian rice from Brazil. African rice tends to break easily when stone milled, in contrast to traditional threshing techniques in West Africa that avoid damaging the grain. Coastal areas of Maranhão, the state bordering Pará to the east, were the main rice-producing area of Brazil during the colonial period. When white Carolina rice was introduced, local farmers were reluctant to adopt it. The crown had to impose severe penalties on recalcitrant farmers: one year in jail and a fine, the latter to be split between the person denouncing the lawbreaker and a fund for public works. If slaves or Indians were caught growing red rice, they were jailed for two years. By 1800 African rice was essentially gone from the Amazon estuary and other parts of Brazil.

Annual production of Asian rice in Pará, mostly in the estuary, climbed from 13,747 kilograms in 1773 to about 2,000 metric tons in the first half of the nineteenth century. Still, the area devoted to the crop was small, and that some rice was exported in the late colonial period to Portugal is more a reflection of the Amazon's tiny urban and rural population at the time. By the close of the ninteenth century, Pará was no longer self-sufficient in rice and had to import the cereal from Maranhão.

Although the Amazon estuary has never been a major rice-producing area, several early travelers remarked on the high quality of the grain. In 1783 the Brazilian explorer and ethnographer Alexandre Rodrigues Ferreira reported that rice from the flood-plains of Marajó was esteemed for its especially large grains. In the mid-nineteenth century, the English naturalist Alfred Russel Wallace reported that rice was a small-holder crop and that farmers sold the harvest directly to mills. Rice mills were powered by steam engines or water wheels. For the latter, streams were dammed in a manner similar to those serving sugarcane mills. The rice was dehusked by grinding it between two flat millstones, followed by passage through boards armed with stiff wires to remove any remaining husks. In this process, some of the rice was broken, which fell through a sieve, while the whole grains were conveyed to a blower before final polishing with sheepskin. Wallace described Pará rice as "remarkably fine," at times equal to that from Carolina. But growers had a propensity to harvest some of the grain while still green because of insufficient labor at the peak of the harvest, thereby lowering the quality.

Rice lingered as a minor crop in the estuary until 1917, when farmers in the Breves area began to take it on as a cash crop. Rice yields on the rich alluvial soils of the estuary are in the 3,000-kilogram-per-hectare range even without fertilization, about three times those achieved on uplands. By the mid-1970s, however, the rice boom in the estuary was over, a victim of the asphalting of the Belém-Brasília highway, which greatly reduced transportation costs to central and southern Brazil. Rice from Goiás and Tocantins (which was carved out of Goiás state) is grown on a large scale with machinery and, because it is relatively cheap, now accounts for most of the cereal consumed in both urban and rural areas at the mouth of the Amazon. Manioc is still the basic staple in the estuary, but as income levels rise, the proportion of rice in the diet increases.

Today rice fields are a rare sight in the estuary. And rice is often planted as a transition crop before establishing an açaí grove. In 1999, for example, a farmer along the Xingu River on a floodplain island near Abaetetuba cleared two hectares of riverine forest and one hectare of adjacent upland woods to plant the Marajó variety of rice. The rice was hand sown among four varieties of banana (Prata, Missouri, Branca, and Perua). After the rice harvest, the farmer planned to plant açaí, which would eventually shade out the bananas. The rice was planted without any credit for the Abaetetuba market. Along the

Rio dos Macacos near Breves, a few farmers still cultivate rice but only for local consumption and to feed chickens and ducks. Planting seed corn is hung from rafters to keep it dry and out of harm's way. In the Brazilian Amazon, a snout beetle and a moth larva tunnel into stored rice, especially if it is damp, and farmers have learned that suspending seed rice from ceilings reduces such damage. Apparently, no Breves-based buyers are interested in rice anymore; the dryers once used to prepare the product for market have long since rusted or have been dismantled. The only other rice I saw in the estuary was a single field on the floodplain of the Pacajá River on Caviana.

The Marajó rice variety planted in cleared floodplain forest on an island in the southern estuary. Rio Xingu near the mouth of the Tocantins, municipality of Abaetetuba, December 11, 1999.

Maxixe squash, introduced to Brazil from Africa during the colonial period, is popular in stews. Ilha dos Porcos, municipality of Afuá, Marajó, August 17, 1998.

SQUASHES

As in the middle Amazon floodplain near Santarém, squash is a seasonal crop in the Amazon estuary. Grown on alluvial soils during the low water period for domestic consumption and market, squashes come in an intriguing variety of shapes and colors. No botanical research has been conducted on squashes grown along the Amazon, but two species of *Cucurbita* appear to be involved, known locally as jerimum and in English variously as the turban, winter, or gourd squash. Squash is typically cultivated as an intercrop, alongside maize or bananas.

Increased market integration has boosted the number of varieties of squash grown in the estuary. With the paving of the Belém-Brasília highway in 1974, twenty-ton trucks loaded with vegetables from southern Brazil now reach Belém in a few days. Most of the vegetables are taken to a large, government-operated wholesale facility (CEASA) on the outskirts of Belém. Vendors purchase their vegetables and fruits from CEASA and then resell them in street markets in Belém and other cities in the estuary. Some locals save seeds from these temperate and subtropical squashes, collectively called abóbra, and add them to the mix of varieties they already cultivate. The same process is under way with new varieties of capsicum pepper. Not all squashes from the temperate parts of Brazil do well in the Amazon, however. Accustomed to long summer days that trigger flowering, some temperate varieties wait for long days that never come at the equator. Consequently, they grow for tens of meters, sprawling like weeds, but do not produce fruit. Farmers in the estuary pull such Jack and the Beanstalk varieties when it becomes obvious that they are not going to flower.

The prickly West Indian gherkin, a peculiar-looking squash of African origin brought to Brazil during the slave trade, is another popular subsistence and cash crop in the estuary. The Ping-Pong ball–sized squash, known locally as maxixe, is covered with soft spines and resembles a pale green version of tropical Asia's deep red rambutan fruit. The soft cucumber-like flesh is cooked in stews.

WATERMELON

Watermelon, another African introduction during the colonial period, is also cultivated at low water, especially on the floodplain islands in the northern part of the estuary. It is often the first crop to produce in a relay race of plants cultivated in clearings on the floodplain. By the time the floods arrive, the annuals have been harvested, while bananas and açaí will survive and keep the land productive for many years.

Several watermelon varieties are cultivated in the estuary, but the most common are the light green, oblong-shaped Paulista and the round, dark green and lime Japonesa, with distinctive mottled skin. Like squash, watermelon is grown for domestic consumption and for sale. Market considerations dictate the selection of watermelon varieties: Paulista and Japonesa are commercial cultivars from southern Brazil and have won converts in Amazonian cities. Watermelon is an example of how market integration can boost agrobiodiversity; without the lure of customers in urban centers, few growers in the estuary would bother to plant the crop.

Two commonly cultivated watermelon varieties in the Amazon estuary: Japonesa (left) and Paulista (right). Ilha dos Porcos, municipality of Afuá, August 17, 1998.

One cannot grasp the economic history of Latin America without considering sugarcane. No single crop has had such a profound impact on the landscapes, cultures, and ethnic makeup of tropical America and the Caribbean. This bamboolike perennial grass ruled as king of the export crops for almost four centuries and is still the mainstay of the economy in many areas. The same is true of the Amazon estuary, even though the region is often considered an economic and cultural backwater.

Alongside cacao, sugarcane was the most important crop in the Amazon estuary throughout the colonial period. The Dutch were the first to bring sugarcane to the Amazon, in the early seventeenth century, which they planted next to their wooden forts, such as along the lower Xingu. By 1616 the Dutch were exporting small amounts of sugar from the lower Amazon to their homeland. After the Dutch were expelled from the estuary in 1645, the Portuguese continued to plant sugarcane at the mouth of the Amazon. In the mid-seventeenth century, the astute Jesuit father João Felippe Betendorf noted that cacao, annatto, and sugarcane were the principal plantation crops in the vicinity of Belém.

To protect the interests of growers in the northeast of Brazil, royal authorities prohibited the Amazon from exporting significant quantities of sugar. Even so, more than one hundred sugarcane mills were established in the Amazon by the late seventeenth century. Landowners in the Amazon estuary were allowed to grow cane to produce sugar for local consumption and to make potent white rum, known initially in the Brazilian Amazon as "aguardente," from *água* (water) and *ardente* (burning). "Firewater" is now more commonly referred to as cachaça. By 1751 three quarters of the sugarcane mills operating in the estuary were dedicated exclusively to cachaça production. And some of these mills functioned continuously for hundreds of years. Engenho Murutucu, now in ruins and being engulfed by the sprawling suburbs of Belém, was established sometime in the late seventeeth century but was only abandoned in the mid-nineteenth century. How many businesses in Belém will still have their doors open two and a half centuries from now?

Most of the mills were built in the southern part of the estuary because it was closest to Belém, the main population center and node for most of the regional shipping. On southern Marajó, for example, the municipality of Muaná alone had twenty cachaça distilleries operating in 1862. And thirty-six sugarcane mills were producing cachaça in the vicinity of Igarapé-Miri and Abaetetuba, also in the southern estuary, in 1886. Most of the sugarcane was grown on fields cleared from floodplain forests. In the early twentieth century, between 5,000 and 10,000 hectares of forest had been cleared for sugarcane. For example, the thirty-eight mills operating in the vicinity of Igarapé-

Miri and Abaetetuba in 1920 were supplied by cane harvested from approximately 3,500 hectares.

Sugarcane mills in the Amazon estuary were annually producing between four hundred thousand and four million liters of cachaça between 1861 and 1920. The throat-searing liquor found a ready market locally and all the way up the Amazon into Peru. Cachaça has always been accessible to even the poorest citizens. In describing the hard life of rubber tappers along the Anajás River on Marajó in 1879, an American collector of insect and bird specimens, M. Mauris, captured cachaça's role as a cheap high:

> It is the privilege of the woodland, particularly of the Ingapos, where the India rubber collector is most frequently found, to be the native land of the intermittent fever. Here man literally buried in lakes of verdure, breathing only the pestilential exhalations of decomposing vegetation and stagnant water, must be said to perish slowly rather than live, his mode of living hastening nature's destructive work. The fish upon which he feeds, the cachaça (Brazilian whiskey) he must drink to check artificially the action of the deleterious elements absorbed by his constitution and to give his system a fleeting strength, do not constitute the healthiest régime.[2]

Cachaça distilling was such a profitable enterprise that the Carmelites, Jesuits, and Mercedarians got into the act, even though the potent beverage is infamous for lowering inhibitions. The priests may have been partial to a few drams, but most of the production was destined to keep workers happy and to generate income. They learned that periodic libations of aguardente kept the local population content and that sale of the liquor helped the balance sheet. Travelers along the Amazon in the seventeenth, eighteenth, and nineteenth centuries often remarked that as long as stocks of manioc flour, cachaça, and tobacco were plentiful, boat crews could be persuaded to work long and arduous hours. Such was the demand for cachaça that little was left over for export. Indeed, in the mid-nineteenth century, Pará was importing cachaça from other parts of Brazil. For upscale consumers, an anise-flavored cachaça was produced using anise seed imported from Portugal or Gibraltar.

Most of the early sugarcane mills in the estuary were operated by tidal power, although a few employed oxen to turn the rollers. Virtually all of the sugarcane was grown on floodplains, because yields are higher than on uplands, so harnessing tidal power was a logical choice to squeeze the stalks. Locks were constructed on narrow streams and were closed at high tide. At low tide, water was slowly released to turn a wheel. The locks were made from wood or local sandstone exposed at eroding shorelines in the southern estuary.

On a visit to the ruins of one such lock in the headwaters of the Tauá-Pará River on Colares Island, several residents of nearby Vigia said they doubted that the masonry

walls constricting a stretch of the tidal stream were assembled for a water wheel. Rather local lore has it that the former owner of the mill, the baron of Guajará, had the lock built to impound water in case he had to travel at low tide. At such times, the locks would supposedly be opened so that the baron and his entourage could shoot down the dry creekbed in a canoe and make it to the river. Anyone who has been stuck in a mosquito-ridden mangrove swamp for six hours waiting for the tide to turn can understand how such explanations might arise.

By the late 1800s steam powered most of the sugarcane mills, and the locks and water wheels were abandoned. Only a few durable stumps in the mud or crumbling walls remain of the tidal mills. Steam offered the advantage of working at any time of day or night. The boilers were heated by burning bagasse, the squeezed stalks of cane, and fuelwood.

Sugarcane mills flourished in the estuary for close to three centuries. Cachaça was sold in large, dark-colored glass bottles called frasceiras. Plastic containers largely replaced the fifty-liter frasceiras by the mid-twentieth century, but I noticed a few still in use at the São João mill along the Furo do Seco River near Igarapé-Miri in 1999. The

A sugarcane mill in the Amazon estuary circa 1785. It is an undershot, tidal-powered mill with three upright cylinders for grinding the cane. The three-cylinder mill apparently originated in Brazil in the early seventeenth century. From A. R. Ferreira, Viagem Filosófica pelas Capitanias do Grão Pará, Rio Negro, Mato Grosso, e Cuiabá, 1783–1792, vol. 1: Iconografia (Rio de Janeiro: Conselho Federal de Cultura, 1971), pl. 46.

thick glass bottles were wrapped in fronds of ubím, held in place by a lattice of arumã leaf stems, for protection. Locals gather the slender fronds of ubím, a short under-story palm, in upland forests.

The decline of the sugarcane industry in the estuary has been precipitous. In 1960 some sixty cachaça distilleries were operating in the vicinity of Abaetetuba alone, but only sixteen were left in 1987, dropping to six by 1993. As late as the mid-1970s thirty-two sugarcane mills were producing cachaça in the vicinity of Igarapé-Miri, but by 1999 only one was left. The last mill producing sugar in the estuary, the steam-powered Engenho Palheta on an island at the mouth of the Atuá in southern Marajó, closed its doors in 1968 after operating for almost seventy years. By 1999 only two mills were still operating in the Amazon estuary, both producing cachaça.[3]

A brief description of the remaining two mills provides a glimpse of a way of life in its twilight years. Engenho Caprixo has operated along Furo Grande on a floodplain island of the lower Tocantins near Abaetetuba for more than fifty years. The bagasse-fueled boiler, obtained from Abaetetuba when the city switched to diesel generators, operates the steel rollers. After pressing the cane, the juice ferments for one or two days in concrete-lined brick vats. The fermented juice, called sugarcane wine (vinho de cana), is then pumped into a copper still and heated gently for several hours. The resulting steam is led through a coil immersed in cool water and the cachaça drips into a large wooden barrel (alambique) for storage. The five-meter-high barrel is about four meters wide at the base and tapers gently toward the top. The mill owner grows cane on his land and contracts out to about fifteen farmers to supply him with additional raw material. Engenho São João along Furo do Seco near Igarapé-Miri operates along similar lines and houses about half a dozen workers and their families adjacent to the mill.

The banks of estuarine rivers and creeks near those towns are littered with the hulks of huge boilers, typically made in the United States or England and dating to the nineteenth century, as well as rust-crusted cogs and rollers. Wooden rollers used in the colonial period have long since rotted away. A poem published in Muaná's now-defunct weekly newspaper in 1928 captures the spirit of a creaky wooden sugarcane mill that once operated near Marajó's southern coast:

> In the lethargic pace of the rustic ranch
> Under the hot light of the sun and the moon's cool glow
> Existing as if to atone for a painful wrongdoing
> The wooden mill groans and weeps
> Roars and grates as the graters rasp

Gnashing, grating, and crushing the cane
It seems that it has a soul, to guess and uncover
The ruin, the pain, the bad, that it may cause

Moved by sluggish and solemn oxen
Moans, as if expressing painful sorrow
Of misfortunes to come
All known by heart

Oh! From its sad sighs! Oh! Remorseful grinder
Alcohol! To forget the torments of life
And dig, God knows! A greater anguish.[4]

Most of the open boats (*batelão*) once used for hauling cane to the mill have been pressed into service to carry açaí heart-of-palm or have been converted for general cargo or passenger use. Planted açaí groves or forests have taken over where sugarcane once rustled in the summer trade winds or bowed in winter thunderstorms.

A few isolated sugarcane fields still cling to the banks of estuarine creeks near Abaetetuba and Igarapé-Miri, but most of the cane is now grown in small clumps alongside other crops in fields or in home gardens. In home gardens, a wooden fence usually surrounds clumps of sugarcane to keep out pigs. Children are especially fond of chewing on fresh cut cane; old-timers generally do not have enough teeth left to enjoy the snack.

Backyard sugarcane is the final resting place for traditional varieties once cultivated on a larger scale. On Fazenda Cajueiro, for example, some cowboys keep plots of the Taboka variety, a sugarcane cultivar not used in commercial operations, around their homes. Other traditional varieties of sugarcane, such as Cayena and Roxa, are also now confined largely to home gardens. In remote areas of the estuary, a few other traditional varieties are still grown in fields, such as Foguete along the Pacajá River on Caviana.

Growers in the vicinity of Abaetetuba used to plant the Cayena variety because it is easy to grind. More recently, other, higher-yielding varieties have been introduced, including Jota Branca (White J), Jota Marajó, Jota Azuluda (Blue J), Jota Preta (Black J), and Bambu. The latter hails from Pernambuco, a major sugar-producing state in the northeast, and has a very thick stem. These introduced varieties have been selected for industrial-scale operations using modern equipment. The yield is lower in the Amazon, where antiquated rollers are used. A politician in Abaetetuba who was lamenting the decline of the sugarcane industry in the area remarked on the inefficiency of the old mills; so much sugar is left in the cane stems after crushing that pigs devour the bagasse when given a chance.

Backyard sugarcane grown exclusively for domestic consumption. Home gardens have become repositories for genetic diversity in sugarcane now that one or two varieties dominate production on commercial estates. Fazenda Cajueiro, Igarapé Fundo, municipality of Chaves, Marajó, August 16, 2000.

Some growers near towns such as Breves send cut cane to market, where street vendors and stores pass the stalks through hand-operated rollers to extract the green juice. *Caldo de cana* or *garapa*, as the syrup is called, is cheaper than soda and considered a treat by young and old alike. It is also thought to calm the digestive tract.

Several factors account for the demise of sugarcane mills at the mouth of the estuary. The paving of the Belém-Brasília highway in 1974 led to the influx of cheaper cachaça from southern Brazil. Paulista brands such as Tatuzinho from Rio Claro and 51 from Pirassununga, as well as Duelo from Pinheiro Preto in Santa Catarina, now dominate cachaça sales in the Brazilian Amazon. Duelo is a current hit in the estuary because a half-liter plastic bottle costs only U.S. 75 cents. The 51 brand is available in one-liter glass bottles or pop-top cans; aggressive marketing tactics include deluging the mouth of the Amazon with baseball caps and T-shirts emblazoned with the slogan "51, a good idea." Sugarcane growers and processors in Brazil operate on a vast scale using efficient equipment, in contrast to the antiquated facilities of mills in the Amazon. Brazil's ever more stringent labor laws resulting from the country's return to democratic rule in the late 1980s are another factor in the decision of many mill owners to shutter their operations. Many of the mills operated an almost feudal system whereby instead of salaries and health benefits, workers were given food, lodging, and the occasional spending money to attend religious festivities.

If sugarcane mills are to survive in the estuary, they will need to market their cachaça as a premium product. With Brazil's favorite cachaça-based drink—*caipirinha*—a hit in trendy bars in New York, scope exists for marketing estate-bottled cachaça from the Amazon. For example, a white rum called Amazon Velvet or Pink Dolphin, named after the river dolphin that allegedly transforms into a handsome man to seduce women, might catch on with consumers in North America, Europe, and even São Paulo and Rio de Janeiro. A seal proclaiming that the cachaça was produced from organic cane, grown without any fertilizers or pesticides, and processed without artificial ingredients would enhance the cachet of limited edition cachaças from the Amazon.

Unfortunately, cachaça produced in the estuary has always been sold in large, brandless bottles. An expression has even arisen to describe this generic product: "bald cachaça" (*cachaça carreca*). Local taverns simply serve it to customers in doses, from recycled bottles. And the current practice of marketing cachaça from Abaetetuba and Igarapé-Miri in plastic containers does little to enhance the rum's flavor.

As in the case of some other alcoholic beverages, such as whiskey and wine, the wood used in storing the cachaça imparts subtle flavors. In the case of Engenho Caprixo near Abaetetuba, upland timber trees—piquiá, acapu, and itaúba—were used to make the large barrel for holding the spirits until sold. And here, surely, lies the secret for resurrecting Amazonian cachaça. With so many timber species to choose from, an almost infinite palette of unique flavors is possible. Just as the endless variety of single malt whiskeys have emerged from relative obscurity in the Scottish Highlands to be served in bars and restaurants all over the world, so too could Amazonian cachaça conquer coveted shelf space on the shelves of supermarkets and upscale bars. In Santa Catarina and São Paulo, for example, small distilleries have managed to stay in business by pitching their product as special and worth five to ten times the price of mass-produced cachaça.

Although Amazonian cachaça may be on its way out, the sugarcane industry has left an indelible cultural imprint. During the colonial period, some forty thousand African slaves were brought to Belém, mostly to work on sugarcane plantations and cacao orchards. Neither is a significant crop in the estuary today, but the slaves' descendants have made a noticeable impact on the ethnic makeup of the region. When Africans were brought to the mouth of the Amazon the indigenous population had largely crashed and few Europeans had settled there, so their impact was much greater than if they had been brought to the Amazon at the beginning of the sixteenth century before introduced diseases and slave raids decimated indigenous groups. Escaped African slaves established several settlements, called quilombos, in the Brazilian Amazon, including Quilombo Curiaú, perched on an upland bluff overlooking an estuarine floodplain some fourteen kilometers east of Macapá. Curiaú is a flourishing community that derives a livelihood from raising crops and cattle and from fishing. In 1999 the state government of Pará belatedly accorded quilombos legal rights to their land claims, similar to indigenous groups. For the most part, though, Africans have not lived apart from the rest of society. With a policy that encouraged miscegenation and the abolition of slavery in 1888, Africans soon made an impact on the ethnic appearance of the regional population.

Africans have also influenced the regional music scene. The carimbó dance, which originated along the estuarine coast of Pará between Belém and Marapanim, traces its origins to slave dances on sugarcane estates during the colonial period. In the vicinity of Vigia, river dwellers call the dance *zimba*, clearly an African word, and all carimbó songs feature the hypnotic rhythm of bongo drums. An elderly woman of mixed ethnic background who lives at the edge of a mangrove near Vigia recounted to me how much she used to enjoy letting her hair down dancing zimba during May Day celebrations.

HOME GARDENS

A few crops cultivated in fields, such as sugarcane, are also occasionally planted in home gardens, but they differ in several important aspects. Few if any ornamental or medicinal plants are found in fields, but they are common around the home. The calabash tree, grown for its oval to round gourds that can attain the size of basketballs, is one of the most common trees in home gardens in the estuary.

The insides of the ubiquitous calabash gourds are scraped out and dried to hold drinking water or are cut in half to make bowls for holding food or to bail canoes. While home gardens often contain small clumps of subsistence crops, such as co-coyam, sweet manioc, and sweet potato, fruit trees usually dominate. Fruit trees in home gardens come from all over the tropics, many of which were introduced during the colonial period. Coconut, for example, is common in home gardens in the estuary; although it dispersed naturally to the Pacific shores of Central America shortly before the arrival of Europeans, the ubiquitous palm was brought to Brazil during the colonial period and several varieties have been adapted for inland locations.

Asian fruit trees are particularly common in the estuary and include banana, jack-fruit, jambolan, lime, mango, Malay apple, and Java apple. Several varieties of each fruit tree are often maintained for distinct culinary purposes. The Pucuçu variety of

Java apple, known locally as jambo rosa, hails from tropical Asia and is occasionally found in home gardens in the Amazon estuary. Combu Island near Belém, May 10, 1999.

banana, for example, is especially good for making porridge according to cowboy families along the Tartaruga canal on Marajó. Other varieties of banana grown in home gardens in the estuary are Amapá (named after an Amazonian state), diminutive Baixota (Stunted One), Branca (White), Prata (Plate), and Sapo (Frog). Both Branca and Prata are common in other parts of the Brazilian Amazon and are equally adapted to upland and floodplain sites. Both Malay apple and Java apple cast deep shade, which is enjoyed by all family members while conversing, cutting hair, or performing other tasks. Malay apple, called jambo in Brazil, is common in street markets, but the smaller, walnut-sized fruits of Java apple are consumed locally and do not make their way to towns or cities.

Tropical American fruit trees—abiu, açaí, avocado (on well-drained sites), Barbados cherry, cashew, genipap, guava, ingá costela, papaya, peach palm, soursop, and yellow mombim—are commonly planted around homes. Some are indigenous to Amazonia, such as açaí, genipap, papaya, peach palm, and soursop, whereas others have been introduced, such as avocado and Barbados cherry. In savanna areas, cowboys and their families plant home gardens along the banks of artificial ponds, typically dug next to the house, where plants do well because they are not submersed as long during the rainy season.

Farmers are always interested in experimenting with new crops, and home gardens are the usual venue for testing exotics or domesticating useful forest trees. In two home gardens near Breves, for example, family members had planted umarí, a giant tree of upland forests that produces a rich, oily fruit. In one home garden, the umarí seedling was in a plant box containing mostly herbs on a walkway in front of the house. The stilted house is on a floodplain, an unsuitable environment for umarí. The river dweller explained that he intends to plant the seedling in a garden plot on a patch of upland about a kilometer from his home. Umarí is also planted in a home garden on an upland site along the only road leading north from Breves. In both cases, families had saved seed from umarí gathered in upland forest for planting. River dwellers along the Ucayali, some two thousand kilometers upstream from the mouth of the Amazon, also plant umarí and seedlings of other forest trees in their upland agroforestry fields. And Umarizal, a district in Belém, is named after the tree. At one time, that area, now entirely built over and sandwiched between the docks and the airport, was rich in umarí trees, many of which were likely planted by indigenous people.

In another upland home garden near Breves, a farmer has planted piquiá, a forest giant that bears an edible fruit. The seeds were obtained from nearby forest. The outer skin of piquiá fruit is first removed and the fruits boiled. People usually use a spoon to remove the oily but savory flesh so as to avoid ingesting any of the spines surrounding the seed. Piquiá fruits in the latter part of the rainy season, and the fruits are held in such esteem that they commonly find their way to urban markets.

(TOP) *A street vendor holding strong-smelling umarí fruits. The teenage boy on the bicycle is buying both net bags of the oily fruit, which is eaten fresh as a snack. Vigia, May 19, 1999.*

Piquiá fruit with the skin partially removed in a street market. The fruits are boiled with salt to render the flesh soft before eating. Portel, May 14, 2000.

Several wild trees encountered in home gardens are either spared when the land is cleared for settlement or are allowed to grow if they arise spontaneously. Examples include matutí, which is left to provide shade, and parápará, the gummy fruits of which are fed to pigs and chickens.

In a part of the world where rural folk may only go shopping once a month or even less frequently, home gardens also serve as convenient and affordable sources of folk remedies, spices, and vegetables. In some cases, women generate income by selling herbs and vegetables grown on raised beds or in baskets and pots on verandas. Home gardens, then, serve a wide array of utilitarian and aesthetic functions.

Home gardens in the estuary range from a relatively sparse collection of fruit and medicinal trees around cowboy huts to rich assemblages of flowers, fruit trees, vegetables, and medicinal herbs surrounding the homes of river dwellers. The composition of

(OPPOSITE PAGE)
An assortment of vegetables including spring onions, capsicum peppers, and string beans grown on a house dock in containers using mulched seeds of açaí palm. Some of the produce is sold in the nearby town of Breves. São Pedro, Rio Pararijós, Marajó, August 10, 2000.

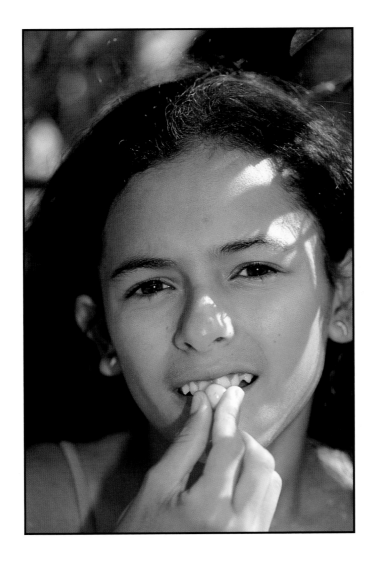

Murici is cultivated in home gardens for its abundant but small fruit. The tree also occurs spontaneously in open areas, such as early second growth and savannas. Near Vigia, November 15, 1998.

backyard plants varies, therefore, according to lifestyle and whether the occupants live on uplands or floodplain. Home gardens in the estuary embrace hundreds of annuals and perennials, and only a few of the fruit-bearing shrubs and trees are discussed here.

MURICI

Well adapted to sandy or degraded soils, murici is cultivated in home gardens in the estuary and throughout Pará for its blueberry-sized yellow fruits. The small tree also grows spontaneously in open environments, such as second growth and savannas. Known as nance in English and Spanish, murici grows from Mexico to northern South America. Although more common in the Bragantina Zone east of Belém, murici is occasionally cultivated in home gardens on upland portions of estuarine islands, such as near Breves on Marajó. Fruits of wild murici are also gathered on the savannas of Marajó, such as in the vicinity of Cachoeira do Arari and along the Rio Tauá near Muaná. Murici fruits are picked in the latter part of the dry season and eaten fresh or sold in towns to make a rather cheesy-tasting ice cream.

GUAVA

Like murici, guava is both cultivated and semiwild in open habitats. The weedy forms are dispersed by birds, such as tanagers and parakeets, and produce fruit up to the size of a billiard ball. In some cases, such as on Caviana Island, spontaneous guava forms veritable orchards, favorite haunts of pigs in their perennial quest for food. Children also enjoy gathering and eating the vitamin C–rich fruits, attracted by the haunting flavor that is both sweet and savory.

If there is one tropical American fruit that is the equivalent to the apple of temperate climes, it is guava. The flesh varies in color from pale yellow to orange. People take care to spit out the hard, BB-sized seeds lest they break their teeth.

Easily grown, guava produces year-round, and during abundant harvests, locals sell the fruits in town. At Santa Cruz do Arari on Marajó, for example, boys hawk the fruits in plastic net bags suspended from shoulder poles. Each bag fetches U.S. 75 cents and contains about a dozen fruits. In Abaetetuba, street vendors sell guava fruits in baskets made from the leaf stems of sororoca, a banana-like fleshy plant of dimly lit floodplain forests. Some mothers and grandmothers prepare a dessert from guava fruits called goiabada, a thick paste spread on crackers or eaten with cheese.

PEACH TOMATO

Peach tomato, known locally as cubiu, is a distant relative of the tomato and similar to a small persimmon. The fruit color of cubiu varies from yellow to ocher, even on the same bush. Domesticated in Amazonia thousands of years ago, the peach tomato

*Picking fruits of guava
growing spontaneously
on savanna. Fazenda São
Luis, Caviana Island,
May 22, 2001.*

hangs on in home gardens in both upland and floodplain sites. The billiard ball–sized fruits are eaten raw with a pinch of salt or cooked. The iron and niacin-rich fruits are also chopped to make a sauce to flavor fish dishes.

The agricultural origins of the peach tomato may not be entirely culinary. The obscure plant allegedly possesses supernatural powers. A street vendor in Portel explained that the astringent juice is also used as a body wash, especially in folklore cures that call for bathing to dispel evil influences. Interestingly, the only time I have encountered cubiu in markets was in Portel in May 1999, and the handful of the finely pubescent fruits were carried by a man selling folk remedies and hardware items rather than fruits and vegetables.

Cubiu cultivated in a home garden flooded daily at high tide during the rainy season. Lower Maracá, Amapá, May 4, 1996.

Cacao pods gathered in a cultural forest for the sweet white pulp surrounding the beans. The teenager is sporting a Bob Dylan T-shirt purchased in Belém. Combu Island near Belém, November 20, 1998.

CACAO

Native to western Amazonia, cacao was planted extensively at the mouth of the Amazon starting in the mid-eighteenth century. A mini cacao planting boom in the Amazon during the 1970s and early 1980s—in response to record high cocoa prices on world markets—bypassed the estuary. Instead, the Brazilian government provided incentives for small farmers to plant cacao on patches of relatively fertile soil cleared in forest along stretches of certain pioneer highways, such as the Transamazon Highway near Altamira.

Cocoa prices have since plummeted, but because cacao is only one of many economic plants in cultural forests in the estuary, river dwellers are getting by. Cacao is still harvested for markets, but it has lost ground to more lucrative enterprises, such as the gathering of açaí fruit and heart-of-palm. The sight of cacao beans drying on arumã mats after fermenting in baskets or wooden vats for a few days is increasingly rare. Rather pods from backyard cacao trees are more typically gathered and split open to access the sticky white pulp, which is sucked off the beans with relish, especially by kids.

Cupuaçu, a relative of the better-known cacao, is native to the upland forests of Amazonia east of the Xingu River. Cupuaçu also produces pods that encase seeds surrounded by creamy white pulp, except that beans have not yet been employed to produce chocolate, or cupulate, on a commercial scale. Women break open the brown pods and snip off the pulp with scissors. Sugar and water are added to make a refreshing drink. Long gathered in the wild and in backyards for its fruits, cupuaçu has emerged in the last two decades as a valuable cash crop in agroforestry systems for upland farmers with good road links to urban centers. Cupuaçu fruits in the rainy season, and unless roads are well maintained, the fruits can rot before reaching market. Commercial growers dispatch the fruits to processing centers where the pulp is removed and quickly frozen. Urban consumers purchase the frozen pulp to make juice, ice cream, and desserts.

Cupuaçu fruit in a street market. Cupuaçu is one of the most procured fruits in the Brazilian Amazon, and strong market demand has spurred growers to cultivate this relative of cacao in agroforestry fields as well as in home gardens. Portel, May 14, 2000.

Although most commonly found on upland sites, cupuaçu thrives in dooryard gardens in floodplain areas of the estuary, such as along the Camará River and in the vicinity of Afuá on Marajó. Cupuaçu is also occasionally cultivated alongside other crops in fields cleared in both upland and floodplain areas of Marajó. Spurred by a growing market for cupuaçu pulp, a pharmacy owner in Afuá started planting forty thousand cupuaçu seedlings in 1996 in partially cleared floodplain forest along the Curupaxizinho, about seven kilometers inland from the town. The seedlings were planted without credit over a two-year period on his three-thousand-hectare property at a cost of U.S. $200,000. Only the underbrush was cleared; the main trees were left intact. In a few years, the trees will start producing and the owner hopes to locate financing to set up a plant to process and freeze the pulp. Credit is difficult to come by for small-scale agricultural enterprises, so his gamble may not pay off. With only 6,000 inhabitants, Afuá is too small to absorb production from so many cupuaçu trees. Macapá, with 200,000 inhabitants, is only five hours away by boat, but the main money to be made with cupuaçu is frozen pulp during the off-season.

CHAPTER 7

Chainsaw Orgy

For Amazonia as a whole, the logging industry is second only to minerals in economic importance. The value and volume of timber extracted from the Amazon has soared during the last few decades. In 1974, for example, only 225 sawmills were registered in the entire Brazilian Amazon, and only three plywood factories were in operation. As of 1991, just over 1,000 sawmills were operating in Amazon estuary alone, 6 of which were large plywood plants.

In spite of the impressive number of sawmills at the mouth of the Amazon, the main logging action has leapfrogged the estuary to pioneer highways tearing across the forest canopy and to tributary rivers such as the Mojú, Anapú, and Pacajá. The Pacajá and its many affluents, once a remote wilderness, are now dotted with logging camps, most of which close at the height of the rainy season. Nevertheless, sawmills are still ubiquitous in the estuary, especially the southern part, and they have stayed in business by obtaining logs locally as well as from upland forests hundreds of kilometers away. Logs stacked on barges or lashed together in rafts are common sights in the estuary. Sawmills at the mouth of the Amazon range in size from industrial-scale facilities geared principally to the export market, particularly near Belém and Breves, to small, backyard affairs catering to local needs.

It would seem that by now the estuary would have been logged out. After all, the mouth of the Amazon is the region's gateway to international and domestic shipping. And a relatively short boat trip takes one to Belém, from which all-weather highways provide access to both foreign and domestic markets. The common perception that timber resources in the estuary have been exhausted is due to publicity regarding the excessive logging of virola, much in demand as a veneer for plywood since Georgia Pacific established the first plywood factory in the region at Portel in 1956. This floodplain species, also known locally as ucuúba, has been intensively logged for several decades, and only relatively small trees remain. Indeed, the plywood factory in Portel closed in the mid-1990s. But the concern over depleted stocks of virola obscures the fact that a suite of other floodplain trees, such as assacu, pracuúba, and pau mulato, are now receiving a good deal of attention from loggers in the estuary. And while it is true that much of the timber logged in the Amazon today is coming from upland forests outside of the estuary, both floodplain and upland areas of Marajó are still providing valuable timber.

A dugout fashioned from angelim on a ranch in northern Marajó. This canoe, large enough for at least thirty people, was made along the upper Mojú; large timber trees are now rare at the mouth of the Amazon. Fazenda Santa Maria, Rio Maruim, May 17, 2000.

Lumberjacks in the chow hut of a logging camp. Numerous such camps are strung out along the Pacajá and Anapú Rivers, formerly backwater areas at the periphery of the Amazon estuary. Rio Jacaré-Puruzinho, affluent of the lower Pacajá, May 15, 2000.

Assacu log being cut into planks. Serraria São Luis, Rio Capitarieuara near São Miguel de Pracuúba, Marajó, May 21, 1999.

Timber is thus big business in the estuary, surpassing even cattle ranching in economic importance. Precise figures for any economic enterprise in the Amazon are difficult to obtain because business owners typically underreport income to avoid taxes or regulations governing "sustainable management" of resources. The logging industry has an additional problem: it is a lightning rod for many environmental concerns. In response to worries about deforestation, the natural resource protection agency— IBAMA—has established "game rules" by which sawmills are supposed to operate. One of IBAMA's exigencies is that all sawmills must establish reserves where forests are managed sustainably for timber. The size of the management area depends on the volume of sawn timber; Brazil long ago prohibited the export of logs in order to generate local jobs. Sawmills must therefore either buy or lease land for forest management, and the smaller the volume of wood sawn, the lower the cost of meeting environmental requirements.

INVESTING IN TIMBER TREES

The timber industry in the Amazon is correctly characterized as predatory. Although laws have been enacted to promote forest management and replanting with timber species, they are largely ineffectual; enforcement is weak or nonexistent. As is often the case, private initiative rather than government bureaucracy can be more effective in achieving desired goals. Such is the case in the estuary where smallholders are investing in timber trees.

One might expect large landholders with secure title to their land to be spearheading the planting of timber trees. But in the estuary, as in many other parts of the Brazilian Amazon, small-scale farmers, many without land title, are at the forefront with respect to planting timber. Only a small fraction of rural inhabitants have undisputed title to their land anyway, and in the estuary smallholders occupy land that is not much in demand by speculators, so their ownership is rarely challenged. Further, smallholders are planting or allowing the spontaneous regeneration of a mix of quick-growing softwoods for the plywood industry, such as kapok (sumaúma), as well as hardwoods that take decades to reach market size. And timber planting in diverse agroforestry plots among smallholders will likely prove more successful than large monocrop plantations that are more susceptible to disease and pest pressure.

In Amapá, for example, one river dweller has an agroforestry plot of açaí and cupuaçu on the floodplain of the lower Maracá with several spontaneous timber trees, including andiroba, macacaúba, pau mulato, and kapok. In Jurupari village near Afuá, a spontaneous pau mulato is being spared in a home garden with a future eye on revenue. And near São Pedro village along the Pararijós near Breves on Marajó, some virola seedlings have sprouted in a fruit-dominated agroforestry field. The field's owner spec-

ulates that birds dispersed the virola seeds; several species of toucans, guans, and trogons have been recorded elsewhere feeding on virola fruits and spreading the seeds. The parents are protecting the young virola plants so that their children will benefit when the trees reach marketable size in about twenty years.

LUMBER AS A LOCAL RESOURCE

Much of the debate about the timber industry focuses on globalization issues, linking the rapacious appetite for wood in industrial countries with rampant deforestation in Amazonia. But such links are tenuous at best. Ranchers and small-scale farmers, rather than loggers, are primarily responsible for pushing back the forest in the Amazon, especially in frontier zones. In contrast to temperate areas, loggers in the Amazon and most tropical regions do not clear-cut. Species diversity is so high in tropical forests that the desirable species are scattered and must be removed selectively. And most of the timber in the Amazon is destined for domestic markets, both local and national.

Farmer with a kapok log, known locally as sumaúma, tethered to the bank of his property. A buyer will pay the farmer on the spot and tow the massive log away at high tide for resale to a plywood factory. Because kapok is in demand for plywood manufacture, river dwellers are protecting spontaneous seedlings in their fields and home gardens. Igarapé Grande near Breves, Marajó, August 10, 2000.

The point is that locals have a stake in the survival of forests because they provide wood for a wide variety of uses. Indeed, some river dwellers have become quite adept at cutting forest trees into planks using their own power saws. If forests disappear or are severely depleted, locals will be forced to purchase supplies from sawmills. Should their income levels rise sufficiently for them to be able to do this, biodiversity will be lost, but at least locals would have household essentials. But depletion of natural resources in the estuary is more likely to further impoverish locals. For this reason, it is useful to pinpoint how people use such resources, even if one cannot place a meaningful dollar value on them.

Maçaranduba being cut into planks using a hand-held power saw. Maçaranduba grows in upland forests, and this river dweller harvests trees from both floodplain and upland areas for domestic use and sale to neighbors. Near São Pedro, Rio Pararijós, Marajó, August 10, 2000.

Carpenter refurbishing a boat for a client in his backyard. The repair job is taking quite a while because the client, a neighbor in the small village, only occasionally has enough cash to buy supplies and pay for labor. São Pedro, Rio Pararijós near Breves, Marajó, August 10, 2000.

BOATBUILDING AND REPAIR

In a region dominated by water rather than freeways, hundreds of thousands of boats need to be constantly repaired and eventually replaced. And most of them are made of wood, often involving half a dozen or so timber species. Boatbuilding and repair facilities (*estaleiros*) range from large dry docks dedicated to the servicing of oceangoing vessels in Belém to small, backyard operations scattered along the numerous creeks that lace the estuary's islands. Some river dwellers make their own boats for hauling goods and family members to market, obtaining the necessary wood from the forest or buying the lumber as financial resources permit. River dwellers are typically strapped for cash for much of the time, so a homemade six-meter boat may take months to complete.

Both upland and floodplain timber is used in the construction and repair of boats in the estuary. Itaúba, an upland tree, is the preferred wood for the hull planks because it is rot-resistant and easily worked. The keel and bumper strip (*friso*) are often fashioned from gray-barked pracuúba, a floodplain tree anchored by massive buttress roots. At a boatbuilding facility in Breves, a large cattle boat under construction employed four timber species from upland forests: itaúba (keel), piquiá (spars), pau d'arco (floors), and acapu (cabin walls). And at a backyard facility in the village of São Pedro along the Pararijós near Breves, five different woods were being used to repair a small boat: andiboroba (ceiling), acapu (plank flooring and cabin walls), cumaru (runners),

Boat under construction in a river dweller's backyard. The hull planks were sawn from itaúba, an upland tree, whereas the keel is of pracuúba, a denizen of floodplains. Ilha dos Porcos near Afuá, August 17, 1998.

maçaranduba (posts), and piquiá (roof). Andiroba grows on both uplands and flood-plains; all the other species are from upland forest. As upland forests are increasingly logged out in the estuary and surrounding areas, costs for boatbuilders are sure to rise.

FUEL FOR HOME AND FACTORY

Most river dwellers cook their meals with wood. And in urban areas, the poorer res-idents—typically, most of the inhabitants—rely on charcoal to boil rice and beans and fry meat or fish. A few river dwellers own gas stoves that run on bottled propane, but they are typically used sparingly, such as to bake cakes or to cook when it has been raining for days and stores of dry wood have run out. In areas where floodplain forests dominate, pau mulato, pacapéua, and pitaíca are preferred for cooking because they burn slowly yet radiate intense heat.

Pracuúba timber is used in boat construction, among other uses. It grows in floodplain forests of the Amazon estuary, and a town on Marajó is named in honor of the tree: São Miguel de Pracuúba. Rio Coqueiro near Afuá, Pará, August 17, 1998.

River dwellers generally cook their meals and boil water for coffee using wood fuel. Rio Tauá-Pará, Colares Island near Vigia, November 15, 1998.

Three other activities in the estuary demand constant supplies of firewood: brick-making factories, heart-of-palm plants, and manioc ovens. Brick makers (olarias) are particularly common in the southern estuary because urban centers, including Belém, are concentrated there. The fine, light gray clay found along certain tidal creeks in the vicinity of Muaná on southern Marajó also accounts for the concentration of brick makers in the southern estuary; the clay is even taken to brick factories near Abaetetuba. Burgeoning cities and a relatively stable economy have triggered a building boom; bricks are even trucked in from the northeast of Brazil to satisfy demand in Belém. Brick makers need copious supplies of wood to fire the bricks, including trunks of açaí palm discarded by palmito gatherers, taperebá, and mututí. Owners of brick ovens are not fussy about the kind of wood they use and will turn to fruit trees such as mango or yellow mombim if available.

Palmito plants also use whatever wood is available to fire the boilers. In this regard, the timber boom has helped, because palmito plants typically scrounge scrap wood from sawmills, which are pleased to get rid of the debris. Steam-powered sawmills generate more scrap than they can use, in part because their machinery is antiquated and inefficient.

River dwellers who process manioc into flour are more discriminating in choosing wood to fire their ovens. Temperatures have to be more precisely controlled to prevent scorching the flour. For this reason, farmers prefer slow-burning hardwoods, such as paracaxi, for their manioc ovens. And wood from numerous upland and floodplain trees is harvested to equip the flour hut. For example, the manually operated wheel that is often used to grate the tubers is fashioned from a variety of woods, including acapu (from upland forest), anani (floodplains), andiroba (floodplains and uplands), and jutaí (floodplains). Because of its durability, acapu is also favored for making the stand for the grater and the container for tubers. The shaft of the pole used to stir the flour over the hot oven is made from envira, while the rectangular end piece is carved from assacu, a giant tree of floodplain forests.

ENVIRONMENTAL IMPACTS

Little is known about the ecological impacts of selective logging in floodplain forests. In upland areas of the Amazon with a pronounced dry season, such as southern Pará, logging can render forest more susceptible to fires. Normally, fires from slash-and-burn fields singe only the edge of the forest because of its relatively moist microclimate. The thinning of woods, however, allows desiccating winds to penetrate and debris left on the ground as well as trampled saplings provide fuel. In exceptionally dry years, such as in 1992, both natural and human-set fires can set patches of upland forest ablaze even without recent logging.

In floodplain forests of the estuary, rainfall amounts are higher than in southern Pará and the ground remains moist, so fires are not an issue. Rather, the removal of several dozen species of floodplain trees is likely removing food for some seed dispersal agents and pollinators. The natural history of most timber trees is poorly understood, so the impact of their being torn from the forest fabric remains largely unknown. Several lightwoods, such as aninga, buriti, and ventosa, are cut to float (emboiar) the high value timber species, which would otherwise sink on their way to the sawmill. People and some game animals, such as deer and peccary, seek the fruits of buriti, so the destruction of the noble palm by logging crews is detrimental to river dwellers. Aninga is plentiful and not eaten by locals; however, turtles eat its fruits. But, more aninga is chopped down to improve navigation than to float logs.

A fifty-six-year-old lumberjack in Portel explained how modern logging practices in upland areas are much more thorough than in the past. Raimundo, who still works at a logging camp but is now confined to domestic chores because of his failing eye-

Acapu planks cut with a hand-held power saw for use in the construction of a manioc grater. São Pedro, Rio Pararijós near Breves, Marajó, August 10, 2000.

sight and "tired" body, recalls that when he was in his teens and early twenties he used to fell trees with an ax along the Pacajá and its affluents. The larger trees were spared, because they were too much work to bring down and because they were too heavy to push to the water's edge. Massive trees, perhaps the superior genotypes, were thus left to produce seed to repopulate the area. Today gasoline-powered handsaws bring down forest giants in minutes.

Crews of about eight, known locally as calangos (lizards), used to heave the logs to the riverbank. Oxen were not used because no natural grasslands are found along the Pacajá, and no one raised cattle along the river decades ago. The "lizards" could only push logs for about a kilometer, so rivers were logged within a relatively narrow strip along their banks. Today skidders and tractors probe dozens of kilometers inland. Logs are stacked in cleared areas called patios and then taken by ancient trucks long retired from highway life for up to fifty kilometers along rutted and twisting trails to the river's edge. With markets growing for timber within the region as well as nationally and abroad, more sawmills and logging operations are willing to invest in heavy equipment to move larger volumes of timber out of forests.

CHAPTER 8

Fishing and Plants in the River-Sea

In stark contrast to the industrial fishing fleets that operate out of the main estuarine ports of Belém and Macapá, fishing for subsistence and small-scale commerce depends heavily on the plants gathered from wetlands. Destruction of wetland habitats eliminates plants needed by fishermen to fashion their gear and bait. It also undercuts the productivity of fisheries, for many species feed and shelter in floodplain forests, floating meadows, and mangroves. If the pace of deforestation quickens, catches obtained by the industrial fishing fleets would also likely suffer, because some species of shrimp and fish captured offshore depend on food resources and nutrients flushing through the estuary.

For many, fishing is a part-time profession. Fishermen based in urban centers engage in other remunerative activities, especially when catches are meager. In Vigia, for example, a fisherman who normally operates from his small boat on day trips is an accomplished carpenter and takes on construction work when the opportunity arises. Another fisherman in Vigia rents out his boat to clients wishing to transport goods to settlements on nearby islands. Town-based fishing boats may stay out for as long as three weeks and typically carry crews of three or four men. Gill nets buoyed from pieces of Styrofoam drape estuarine waters for several kilometers. The gill nets are so large that they pull the boats with them as the tide goes out or comes in. Longlines for catching dourada catfish are also let out in deep water and typically contain several hundred hooks.

In rural areas, fishing trips are generally shorter and provide supplemental income and subsistence to people who are also engaged in farming and extraction of timber and nontimber forest products. River dwellers use gill nets and longlines, but they are much shorter than those used in commercial fishing. They also employ fish traps of various designs and piscicides to "suffocate" fish so that they can be easily scooped out of the water.

Traditionally, fishing has been the domain of men for a number of cultural reasons, including supernatural beliefs. For example, pregnant or menstruating women are thought to be responsible for *panema*, a virulent form of bad luck that requires treatment by a healer (*pajé, curador*). However, in the last decade or so, women and girls have taken up fishing with hand lines or poles from docks in front of their homes or from canoes. In Cachoeira do Arari, some women spend a day or two fishing with gill nets on the flooded savannas. A fisherman explained to me that some women have to do this to "defend themselves" (*se defender*) when their mates have abandoned them or have taken a temporary job far from home. Women's involvement in fishing is primarily for domestic consumption, however, and men and boys still catch most of the fish for home and markets.

Nature's Tackle Shop

Wetland forests are a veritable warehouse of fishing supplies. Floodplain trees are used to prepare a wide variety of fishing gear, from roll-up fences for damming creeks to traps for capturing fish and shrimp. In addition, the fruits of a number of estuarine trees and bushes are gathered for bait.

FOREST FRUITS AS BAIT

Many fish important in commerce and for local consumption in the Amazon subsist partly or entirely on fruits. Although tambaqui, the most esteemed fruit-eating fish in the Amazon, is rare in the Amazon estuary, others that are highly regarded are caught at the mouth of the great river. According to fishermen at Santa Cruz do Arari and along the Cajueiro River on Marajó, for example, several widely appreciated fish feed on the bright orange-red fruits of jacitara palm, including aracu cavalo (the horse aracu), the jandiá catfish, and a small catfish called the "the Priest's dog" (cachorro do Padre).[1] The bright fruit of the climbing jacitara palm resembles that of holly trees at Christmas in temperate climes. Rattanlike jacitara fruits during the high water season and into the early part of the dry season and is relatively common in the wetter parts of Marajó Island, such as along the banks of the middle Arari and Cajueiro Rivers. On Caviana Island, jacitara fruit is also gathered to feed pigs.

Several forest fruits are gathered for pole and longline fishing. Near Vigia, heavily armored bacu pedra is hooked using the fruits of tapereba or murumuru palm. The one-meter-long catfish is also taken on longlines using the gummy fruits of aninga. Plump bacu pedra ("rock" bacu) may look unappetizing to Europeans and North Americans, but locals savor its flesh, rendered especially tantalizing because of its diet of wild fruits. Tapereba is widespread in the estuary and the lowland tropics of Latin America where it goes by various names, including yellow mombim. Spiny murumuru palm is relatively common in the understory of floodplain forests, whereas aninga, an aquatic aroid, typically grows in clumps along riverbanks and mudflats. The latter's distinctive arrow-shaped leaves, which point upward, add character to the landscape. In

The fruits of jacitara palm ripen during the wet months and into the early part of the dry season.
Several species of fish consumed on Marajó Island eat the fruits when they fall into the water. Rio
Cajueiro, municipality of Chaves, Marajó, August 15, 2000.

the vicinity of Cachoeira do Arari, pole fishermen use the fruits of the uriri tree to catch aracu and cachorro do Padre. Those fish are also hooked with bait balls consisting of manioc flour mixed with the orange flesh of tucumã fruits.

Many other fish fruits abound in the flooded forests of the Amazon estuary, and some are eaten by other animals, including game and humans. According to fishermen on Lake Arari, in Cachoeira do Arari, and along the Cajueiro River, aracu cavalo and two small catfish—the brown and black mottled Priest's dog and silvery mandí—eat the sweet, sticky fruits of parápará. Rural folk on Marajó also occasionally snack on the tan-gray, cranberry-sized fruits of parápará from January to May; this water-loving tree, whose scientific name is *Cordia tetrandra*, goes by different names along the Amazon. In the vicinity of Santarém, for example, it is known as uruá, and locals gather the fruits at high water for fish bait, to feed chickens, and as a snack. In the Vigia area, the same tree is called chapeu de sol ("sun hat"); there it is a favorite among woodcutters because it makes an especially fine charcoal. The growing market for charcoal in urban areas, such as Vigia, with ten thousand residents, is probably accelerating the removal of this fish food.

Fisherman entering a fish trap through a hinged door. This trap is made from taboka, a native bamboo. Opposite Vigia, November 14, 1998.

POLES

Fishing poles are about 1.5 meters long and are used primarily to catch small fish. Fruit, moistened manioc flour rolled into balls (*pirão*), meat, or fish are used as bait. In the vicinity of Cachoeira do Arari, poles are fashioned mostly from aturiá or the leaf spine (*tala*) of jupatí palm. In the northern estuary where jupatí is absent, such as Ilha dos Porcos, jacamin is preferred for fishing poles and is also an excellent source of firewood.

During the rainy season, broad, shallow lakes cover much of the savannas. The largest lake on the island, Arari, stretches for dozens of kilometers at high water. Such lakes become partially clogged by immense floating islands of vegetation, posing a major obstacle to navigation. Locals hack channels through these floating meadows, but the channels often close up after storms shift the buoyant islands, or water buffalo clog up the sinuous paths when they bulldoze aside plants as they feed. In such cases, paddling is arduous or impossible, and propellers quickly become entangled. The only way to make progress in such situations is to push the canoe along with a long pole. On Lake Arari, the preferred wood for punting is arara-canga, a sturdy wood from floodplain forests, particularly around Ponta das Pedras. Another suitable wood for this purpose is quaruba, also from wetland forests in the estuary. Taboka is also employed for poling boats near Cachoeira do Arari, but the native bamboo tends to split and is therefore less durable than hardwoods.

TRAPS

The fish traps employed in the Amazon estuary are of the same design used by indigenous groups thousands of years ago. A three-meter-high fence is erected perpendicular to the shore to channel fish into a bulbous holding area at the deep end of the fence. From above, the terminal portion of the trap resembles a keyhole. Fish traps vary in length, depending on how quickly the river bottom drops off and how much boat traffic is in the area. When the bank is steep and many motorized boats ply the area, the fence may extend for little more than three meters from the shore. Only on shallow mudflats shunned by motorboats do the fences stretch for some twenty meters or more.

Depending on the location of the trap, fish can be left high and dry at low tide, so they are removed promptly before tenacious black vultures and other scavengers arrive. In the case of traps built along the shore, such as by mangroves, some water remains in the trap at low tide; to facilitate capturing the fish, a wooden slatted platform is built at the bottom of the "shaft" where the prey accumulates. Fishermen paddle up to the enclosed part of the trap and enter by opening a small rectangular door. Once through

Taboka arching over fishing boats tied up to the entrance of a stream. Taboka is common in many parts of the estuary and is used extensively in the construction of fish traps, elevated walkways, and platforms around floodplain homes. Taboka is a disturbance indicator, one of the many economic species that form the cultural forests of the estuary. Confluence of Mandioca stream with the Cajueiro, municipality of Chaves, Marajó, August 16, 2000.

the narrow opening and with a secure footing on the wooden platform, the fisherman scoops out the fish with a hand-held net, known locally as puçá, which resembles those used to play lacrosse. The rim of the net is fashioned from the slender and pliable trunks of the jiriparana tree; the net is made of multifilament nylon.

Taboka bamboo is favored for building traps. The woody grass often grows in clumps along rivers on Marajó and tidal creeks in the estuary, and its arching stems adorned with feathery leaves impart an ethereal beauty to the estuary's numerous sloughs and bayous. The stem is split lengthwise with a machete into four strips to make the fish corrals. In the southern part of the estuary the trap is called a *curral*, whereas in the northern estuary it is called *cacuri*. When new, fish traps made from taboka are yellow, but they tan as they age and become coated with sediment. In areas where taboka is hard to find, the slender trunks of paxiúba palm are used instead to make the fish corral, as along Rio Coqueiro near Afuá. Along the eastern shore of Marajó, which faces the open sea, traps are made with sturdy seine nets strung between fence posts because they are less susceptible to wave damage. These traps can be assembled quicker, but the owner must be vigilant lest someone "borrow" the netting, as one fisherman remarked with a grin.

In addition to fish, other useful prey fall victim to the traps. Near Vigia, for example, the occasional siri crab is stranded in fish corrals during the low water season when the water is more brackish. Red-legged siri crabs are a delicacy and are taken home to cook. On Ilha dos Porcos in northwestern Marajó, much-prized tracajá turtles are occasionally diverted along the fence of fish traps and are a welcome surprise to the fisherman when he comes to retrieve the catch.

Fish traps require continuous maintenance, mainly because floating logs smash into them from time to time. Sections of old gill nets are sometimes used to repair holes, but after four or five years, the entire structure is abandoned. The banks of many a tidal river are studded with a line of small stumps perpendicular to the shore, vestiges of the fence posts from old fish corrals.

A mobile version of the taboka fish trap avoids the problem of damage from boats and storms because it is only erected for a few hours. Along the Maruim River in northwestern Marajó, fishermen unfurl a taboka fence at the mouth of streams at high

River dweller splitting taboka to make a fish trap. The strips will be lashed together with synthetic cord. Near Vigia, November 14, 1998.

tide. At low tide they return to remove fish trapped in the shallow water using a short seine with a stake at each end. A fisherman grabs each end of the seine and pulls the fish to shore. The taboka fence is stitched together with supple vine (cipó morcego), pulled from trees in floodplain forest.

The origin of the third type of trap, called *matapí*, is also likely indigenous. Matapís are used mainly for capturing freshwater shrimp, sometimes referred to as *camarão da região* to distinguish them from marine species caught by commercial trawlers. At Guajará on Ilha do Colares, however, larger versions of matapí made of taboka are used. Matapís can be found as far upstream as the Santarém area, close to the limit of tidal influence along the Amazon. Matapís for capturing shrimp are about one meter long and twenty centimeters in diameter. Matapís are typically cylindrical, but an interesting variant that is tapered toward the end is used in the vicinity of Colares Island in the southern estuary.

Shrimp traps stacked on the front porch of a river dweller's home. These traps are made from the midribs of jupatí palm fronds. Furo Flechal near São Miguel de Pracuúba, Marajó, May 20, 1999.

Whether tapered or cylindrical, matapís have coned entrances protruding inward at both ends that trap the shrimp inside. A hinged door in the middle is opened to shake the shrimp into a basket. The crushed nuts of babaçu palm are the most commonly used bait, wrapped in a little ball using a piece of plastic to prevent it from dissipating or being eaten. Babaçu seed cake is sold in general stores throughout the estuary and comes from Maranhão where the nuts are pressed for their oil, which is used in cooking. Babaçu is an upland palm and does not occur in the Amazon estuary. Rice bran, which smells offensive to the human nose when wet, is apparently highly attractive to shrimp and is used to bait shrimp traps along the southern margins of Marajó Island, particularly in the vicinity of Muaná and São Sebastião da Boa Vista.

Various plants are used to fashion matapís. The stems of arumã, a denizen of the shady interior of floodplain forest, are favored. In the southern estuary, fishermen use mostly the midribs of jupatí palm to make their traps. Jupatí is restricted to the south-

Jupatí palm with its generous, copper-tinged fronds along a riverbank on southern Marajó Island. The midribs of jupatí are employed to make shrimp traps. The distinctive fan-shaped leaves of young buriti palms can be seen on the left. Açaí palms are scattered in the foreground and background. Rio Anabiju near Muaná, May 19, 1999.

ern estuary, where its soaring fronds—the longest of any palm in the region—help to distinguish it from the other streamside palms at the mouth of the Amazon. Near Afuá, the midribs of moisture-loving urucrui palm, the floodplain equivalent of the closely related upland babaçu, are occasionally employed to make the traps. And in the vicinity of Vigia, the midribs of inajá palm are used to make shrimp traps.

Curiously, travelers in the eighteenth and nineteenth centuries do not mention matapís, probably because indigenous groups were largely wiped out from the estuary and lower Amazon soon after contact. The traps may have been reintroduced to the estuary in modified form from adjacent Maranhão state in the northeast of Brazil. Or they may have come back along the coast of Amapá from the Guianas. A nineteenth-century account of matapí-like traps along the Essequibo in Guyana suggests an indigenous origin for this technology:

> The Indian employs likewise different shaped baskets, which are made of thin twigs, or of a reed rather flat and held asunder by hoops; some are cylindrical, others conical, with an opening at both ends; and small sharpened sticks are placed, funnel-shaped, in such a manner that they point inward, to allow the fish to get in but not out again.[2]

Freshwater shrimp are caught in matapís year-round, but catches are especially abundant from May through September. Muaná, for example, held its first Festival de Camarão in late May 1999, following the example of Afuá, which started its annual shrimp festival in July 1997. Politicians and local businesses, especially tavern owners, are keen to promote the festivals because they attract customers. Occasionally, large freshwater prawns, known as *pitús* or *lagostinhos* (small lobsters), find their way into a matapí, welcome visitors as the fifteen-centimeter-long prawns fetch premium prices in the market. And in October and November, the height of the dry season, siri crabs come inshore and are also captured in matapí traps baited with crushed babaçu nuts, as I witnessed at Mosqueiro in October 1992.

Most rural households in the estuary put out several shrimp traps close to shore, safely tethered to a pole. Near Afuá, matapí traps are attached to poles with sections of the little bat vine (cipó morceginho). Canoes stacked high with five to ten matapís are a common sight along sloughs. Young boys and girls as well as adults take on the chore of baiting the traps and lowering them into the water. In areas with a strong current, the shrimp traps are weighted inside with a chunk of beach rock.[3] If placed in the water in late afternoon, the traps are left overnight, or they are checked in the afternoon if they were baited in the morning.

Submerged cages (*viveiros*) are used to stockpile live shrimp until there is enough to warrant a trip to market or until a traveling merchant comes by in his boat. Shrimp

Dried freshwater shrimp for sale in a boat serving as an itinerant store. Pickled fish, bread, and water buffalo milk are also in stock. The teenager on top of the boat is managing the store for his parents. Vila Antônio Lemos, Rio Tajapurú, August 11, 2000.

cages are made with the midribs of the urucuri or paxiúba palm. The cage may be rectangular or an oversize version of a matapí trap, measuring about 1.5 meters long by a meter or so deep. Sections of buoyant aninga are strapped to the side of the viveiro so that it floats just below the surface. Large, cylindrical cages are also used to take fresh shrimp to market. Aninga leaves are sometimes placed on top of baskets containing fresh shrimp to shade them in street markets.

Freshwater shrimp are also caught with small beach seines. A net is strung between two short posts and dragged through shallow water on foot, usually on the incoming tide. Boys or young men are usually employed in this task, and they often live in villages or small towns. Alternatively, boys entice shrimp close to shore with manioc flour then toss a castnet over them.

A roll-up fishing fence (pari) made with arrowcane. The fence is erected across the mouth of a creek at high tide to prevent fish from escaping. At low tide, fish are concentrated in the narrow channel of the stream. Fishermen put pounded and mashed timbó vine, which contains a compound that stuns the fish, into the water upstream. The fish then can be easily scooped out of the water with a basket. Ilha dos Porcos near Afuá, August 17, 1998.

Many of the shrimp caught in the estuary are boiled in salted water and then sundried, an ancient preservation practice. Few rural families have refrigerators, and although freezers and refrigerators are increasingly common in urban areas, several dishes still call for dried shrimp. Consequently, a brisk trade in dried shrimp continues in town and village as well as on boats that serve as traveling stores.

A regional dish that calls for dried shrimp—*tacacá*—is a broth of shrimp in warm manioc sauce resting on a gummy bed of tapioca. The thick soup also contains the leaves and stems of an herbaceous weed called jambu, which produces a tingling sensation on the lips, similar to Novocain. Because of its popularity in tacacá and some other regional dishes, jambu is cultivated in backyards. Tacacá is typically eaten standing up or perched on a narrow bench at street stalls in the late afternoon or early evening. A single bowl of tacacá suffices for dinner. Weight-conscious clients often ask tacacá vendors to hold the tapioca. Interestingly, fast-food restaurants in the larger towns have not driven tacacá vendors out of business; on the contrary, teenagers and young adults are among the more avid customers. And in towns such as Breves, teenagers rendezvous at tacacá stands to check out the action and flirt. Dried shrimp also find their way into dumplings (*costel*) and fried pastries (*pastel*) hawked by itinerant vendors or sold from street stalls and counters of bars and restaurants.

BASKETS FOR FISH AND SHRIMP

Baskets are fashioned from a variety of palms and other plants of floodplain forest to scoop out trapped fish or carry them to market. In the vicinity of Chaves in northern Marajó, for example, fishermen fashion open-weave baskets of jacitara palm to remove fish that have been driven against a seine net along narrow streams. At Abaetetuba, stevedores employ open-weave buriti baskets some 1.5 meters in diameter and 30 centimeters tall to carry fish from dockside to the market stalls.

PISCICIDES

Piscicidal plants are used in conjunction with portable fishing fences throughout the estuary. Known locally as pari, the roll-up fences are about 2.5 meters high and are placed across narrow creeks at high tide. As the tide withdraws, the fish are trapped in shallow water behind the fence. About twenty meters upstream, a piscicidal plant (*timbó*) is beaten with a wooden club and the mashed stem is then squeezed into the water so that the sap is carried downstream to stun the fish. Within minutes the active ingredient takes effect and the stupefied fish flop around near the surface and are easily scooped up into a basket. The fence is then rolled up, slung over the shoulders, and carried to the canoe. A number of plants are used to paralyze the "breathing" mechanism of fish in the Amazon. A river dweller on Ilha dos Porcos purchased his thick timbó vine from a supplier who apparently obtained it from upland forests near Gurupá. Fishermen in the Breves area of Marajó scour patches of upland forest near their homes for timbó vine.

The roll-up fishing fence is of indigenous design and is fashioned from a variety of plants, depending on local availability. These mobile fishing fences have likely been used in the estuary for millennia and were recorded by at least one explorer at the mouth of the Amazon in the mid-nineteenth century. In the southern estuary near Igarapé Miri, pari is made from the midribs of jupatí palm; elsewhere, the split trunks of young paxiúba palm are lashed together with vine or synthetic cord. Pari is also made from frecha (arrow), a native cane of the floodplain. Frecha is found sporadically along the Amazon from its mouth along the northern channel well into Peru. On Ilha dos Porcos off northwestern Marajó, locals plant frecha to make the pari fence trap. The fence is made by splitting frecha lengthwise and binding the pieces together near the top and bottom with twine.

FLOATS FOR FISHING NETS

Commercial fishers now use plastic bottles or Styrofoam to suspend gill nets and seines. Subsistence fishermen still resort largely to ubiquitous aninga to buoy their nets, a practice noticed as far upstream as Itacoatiara in Amazonas state. Fleshy aninga trunks are sliced into foot-long sections and notched to attach the net. A major advantage of aninga is that it is biodegradable. Already some beaches in the estuary are littered with plastic bottles and pieces of Styrofoam. For the most part, fishermen are not responsible for such flotsam; rather they obtain floats from such trash. Ironically, beaches touted as "ecological," such as Paraíso near Mosqueiro, are some of the most polluted.

DUGOUT CANOES AND PADDLES

A wide array of both upland and floodplain trees are used to fashion dugout canoes. These include acapu, angelim, itaúba, louro vermelho, and piquiá, the latter also a source of edible fruit. Several floodplain trees are felled to make dugouts, including black mangrove, known locally as ciriúba. Ciriúba does not have the distinctive stilt roots of the red mangrove and sits farther back from the shoreline, but the tall, broad trunks are straight and ideal for dugouts. Pracuúba and maúba are other trees of estuarine forests used to fashion dugout canoes for fishing and transportation. Paddles are fashioned from a variety of upland and floodplain trees. The wall-like buttress roots of the mututí, a common tree along the banks of tidal sloughs, are easily cut into sections and make ideal paddles. Jutaí do igapó, pitaíca, and urucurana are other wetland trees favored for making paddles on Marajó.

Canoes, whether dugout or consisting of planks, and small boats are sometimes treated with a red preservative obtained by boiling the bark of red mangrove. The resulting red liquid is painted on the wood, like a stain, to retard rotting. Sails are also treated in the same manner, although this practice is now less common as canvas sails have been largely replaced with synthetic materials.

IMPORTANCE OF MANGROVE FOR SHIPWORM AND CRABS

Red and black mangrove found at the mouth of the Amazon also occurs in other tropical waters, so some might argue that their conservation and management are not important. One could argue that even if they were to be completely eradicated in the Amazonian estuary, mangroves will survive elsewhere. But this reasoning fails to take into account that some animals that depend on mangroves in the Amazon estuary may not occur elsewhere, and the environmental services provided by mangroves in the mouth of the great river are irreplaceable. In addition to providing an important habitat for fish at high tide, mangroves are also home to crabs and shipworm, which are important locally for income and subsistence.

SHIPWORM'S ROLE IN SEX, SUSTENANCE, AND CURING

For millennia, several species of shipworm have been the bane of sailing vessels in the tropics, subtropics, and warm temperate regions. Shipworms can grow to a meter in length, and although they look like worms, they are actually bivalves (clams) with highly modified shells near their mouths that serve as rasping devices. These calcified blades enable shipworm to gnaw through submersed wood. The resulting tunnels, the diameter of a pencil, eventually cause planks to fail. On his fourth voyage to the Americas in 1502, Columbus had to abandon two of his four ships in Jamaica because shipworms had rendered them unsafe.

Shipworms enter wood virtually undetected in their microscopic larval stage. Once inside, they consume wood with the aid of bacteria that excrete enzymes capable of breaking down cellulose; the bacteria also fix nitrogen, thereby enriching the shipworms' diet with protein. The secretive habits of shipworms make them the equivalent of aquatic termites; they can seriously compromise wooden structures before they are discovered. Armand de Quatrefages de Bréau, an eighteenth-century French naturalist, aptly described shipworms as "obscure miners." Various means have been devised to combat them. More than two thousand years ago, the Greeks resorted to plating ship hulls with lead to discourage the pests.

With the advent of steel ships and concrete pylons, shipworms fell off the radar of public attention in many parts of the world. The spellchecker of my word processing program flags shipworm and wants me to change it to shopworn. Yet shipworms remain a nuisance in many parts of the world, including the United States. After shipworms were inadvertently introduced to San Francisco Bay in 1913, they caused hundreds of millions of dollars of damage to wharves and piers. In the early 1990s the New York City government spent more than $100 million trying to protect wooden pier pylons by wrapping them with plastic, or in a few cases replacing them with recycled plastic. The berth of Cunard's *Queen Elizabeth II* and structures at John F. Kennedy International Airport were threatened. In the preindustrial era, ships and wharves were frequently attacked by shipworms in the New York area. Then with mounting industrial pollution along the Hudson River, shipworms and many other forms of aquatic life disappeared. Protected by a chemical soup of oil and chemical effluent, the wooden pilings were safe until the passage of the Federal Clean Water Act in 1972. Eleven years later, shipworms reappeared in the inner harbor of New York, an unexpected problem resulting from the successful and much-needed campaign to clean up the waters of the Hudson. The bountiful supply of shipworms in the Amazon estuary is thus an indication that industrial pollution is not yet a large-scale problem at the mouth of the river.

In the Amazon estuary, river dwellers have to contend with shipworms, but they do not pose a serious problem. Shipworms are killed by taking boats and canoes out of the water and setting fires under the hull every six months or so. The fire must be sufficiently hot to cook the shipworms without setting the craft on fire. Quick-burning fronds of buriti or coconut palm are ideal for this purpose. Alternatively, a sack soaked in kerosene is tied to the end of a pole and after igniting passed along the underside of the hull. Shipworm damage can also be reduced by using itaúba wood for the hull and keel and by regularly painting the underside of the boat. Pilings for jetties are less susceptible to shipworm attack if they are made from "bitter" wood, such as andiroba or faveira.

Rather than pose a significant hazard, the slimy, chalky-colored worms are a resource. Known locally as turu, the worms are considered a delicacy, especially in the southern part of the estuary, as is the case among Australian aborigines and locals in coastal Thailand and Fiji. Furthermore, shipworms at the mouth of the Amazon are reputed to have medicinal powers and to enhance sexual performance. The aphrodisiac properties of turu may be attributed to its head, which bears some resemblance to the tip of an uncircumcised human penis. The body of the worm, however, is always limp. In the Brazilian Amazon, the consumption of turtles, especially the giant river turtle, is also thought to increase one's libido.

Shipworm is usually an acquired taste for outsiders but is akin to oysters in texture. The worm is first pulled between the thumb and forefinger to squeeze out the contents

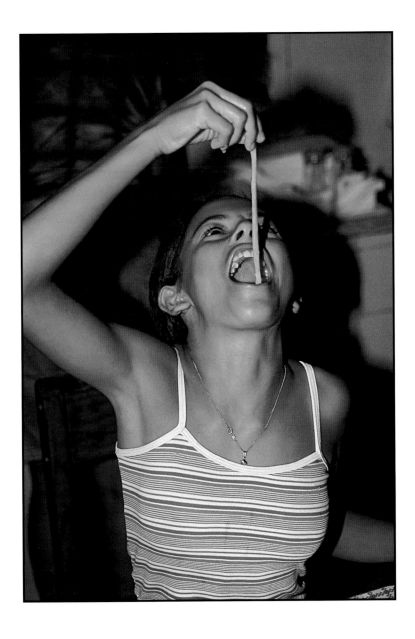

Raw shipworm for dinner in a fisherman's home in the estuary. Vigia, May 8, 1999.

of the intestines. A toothpick or some other sharp implement is sometimes used to slice open and empty the worm's gut. After the murky brown, digested wood is expelled, the gustatory delight is dropped whole into the mouth. Some youngsters slurp turu into their mouths, like spaghetti.

Some prefer to eat shipworms after they have marinated for a few hours in their own juices with salt, freshly squeezed lime, and garlic if available. Garlic is not grown in the Amazon and must be purchased in stores or street markets, which accounts for why it is sometimes left out of the marinating sauce. After soaking for a few hours, the lime juice bleaches the worms; individuals who cannot tolerate fresh shipworms appreciate the more sanitized flavor of marinated turu. Near Muaná in southern Marajó, I met a middle-aged couple canoeing their way to some red mangroves to extract shipworms. The wife explained that they normally boil shipworms in a stew flavored with salt, lime juice, tomatoes, and *cheiro verde* ("green smell"). Cheiro verde is a mixture of herbs and spices containing the tops of spring onions (*cebolinha*), parsley (*salsa*), and coriander leaves (*coentro*). These Old World plants are often sold in bundles or in plastic bags alongside fish stalls, and both rural and urban folk often keep a stock of them in raised herb gardens near their kitchens. It is not known whether indigenous peoples in the estuary ate shipworms; if they did, they would have used different spice plants to mask or enhance the flavor of the slippery bivalves.

River dwellers also gather shipworms to treat bronchitis. The sick drink the milky juice (*caldo*) that the worms exude after they die to alleviate coughs, particularly those caused by tuberculosis. Infants are force fed shipworm juice when in pulmonary dis-

Shipworms being shaken out of a section of red mangrove. Ilha Araqueçaua near Vigia, May 9, 1999.

tress. Manuel, a middle-aged curer in Vigia, pointed out to me that although he was not partial to turu, he drinks shipworm juice when he suffers from asthma. Manuel is a chain-smoker, so he has to resort frequently to chalk-colored turu juice.

Vigia is the only market in the Amazon estuary where shipworms are seen with any regularity. In other urban centers, turu is obtained by placing an order (*encomenda*) with people who know how to extract the worms. The practice of obtaining goods from forest, field, and waters outside of formal markets is quite common in the Amazon, which is one reason that market surveys do not capture the real contribution of extractive activities. Nevertheless, the consumption of shipworms seems to be largely confined to rural folk and town dwellers with limited income. Most middle- and upper-class families in the larger cities such as Belém and Macapá are unfamiliar with turu. One family in Belém even suggested that turu consumption is an indication that rural people have overexploited more desirable game and fish and are desperate. This perception reflects a widespread prejudice among the well-to-do against eating such unsavory-looking creatures.

Shipworms inhabit fallen trunks and branches of several trees, but for people living in the southern part of the estuary only those living in red mangrove are worth eating (*presta para comer*). Turu extracted from black mangrove, for example, allegedly tastes bitter. Shipworm is a more regular fixture in the diet in the southern part of the estuary, because the water there is more saline, especially in the dry season, and red mangroves are relatively common. In the northern part of the estuary where most of the Amazon flows out into the ocean, red mangrove is rare, so river dwellers occasionally resort to obtaining shipworm from submerged trunks and branches of rubber trees, the fruit-bearing yellow mombim, and certain timber trees such as ananí and pracuúba.

Shipworms are uncovered by chopping open fallen trunks and branches of red mangrove, aptly named because of the rich burgundy wood. The dead wood is either split or, if too large, cut into sections so that the worms can be shaken or pulled out. The secretive worms are fragile and die even before extraction; vibrations caused by chopping wood are apparently enough to do them in. The resounding thud of the ax attracts black vultures, which assemble and patiently wait their turn to mop up any leftovers. The heavy, wheezing sound of wingbeats and the argumentative hissing of black vultures accompany shipworm extractors as they work.

Shipworm gatherers (*tiradores de turu*) work singly or in small teams. Men usually do this work, unless the worms are being gathered for domestic consumption, in which case women and children may also be involved. If turu are destined for sale, they must be obtained around dawn so that they reach the town market by midmorning; otherwise they spoil. To save time, some turu gatherers scout suitable sites the previous afternoon. Tide permitting, shipworm extractors are typically at work just before dawn with the aid of small, cone-shaped kerosene lamps.

Turu is gathered at low tide, when the fallen branches and trunks of red mangrove are exposed on muddy shores of islands and sloughs. As in so many activities in the estuary, the waxing and waning of tides determines the rhythm of daily activities. High tide at dawn poses a problem for turu gatherers who plan to sell their product in the market; in such cases they must delay extracting the worms, a disadvantage because the catch will reach town in the afternoon when fewer customers are about and the higher temperatures promote spoilage. Most urban customers seeking produce, meat, and fish prefer to do their shopping in the early morning, because it is cooler and the ingredients are needed for lunch, the main meal of the day. Fortunately, high tide occurs about an hour later each day, so eventually favorable conditions return for commercial turu gatherers.

Turu extraction is a year-round activity, and a typical haul is twenty to thirty-five liters after a morning's work. Shipworm fetches between $0.60 and $1.80 per liter, depending on how much is available. Although shipworms do not fetch much money, turu extractors keep all the proceeds from sales, unlike most fishermen, who sell their catch to middlemen and therefore do not receive full market value for their labor. The only exception is when an occasional buyer arrives in Vigia from Belém and negotiates the purchase of shipworm to be sold in the state capital. In Vigia, customers interested in turu know where to look: against the outer wall of the meat market. In this manner, sellers keep their costs down by avoiding stall charges.

One sixty-six-year-old shipworm extractor who lives in Vigia told me that he prefers his outdoor profession to city life with its transient jobs. José, the father of thirteen children, noted that most of his sons and daughters live and work in Belém and are frequently laid off. However, one daughter works at a bank and was recently transferred to Rio, a source of some pride to José. Most commercial banks in Brazil have made money regardless of the state of the economy, so jobs in that sector tend to be more secure. José maintains a small house in Vigia, while his wife and children live in Belém, about a three-hour bus ride. When asked why the family spends so much time apart, José remarked it was a sacrifice they were willing to make so that the children would have a better education, access to superior medical care, and better job opportunities.

CRABFEST

Three main species of crab are captured in the Amazon estuary: sarara, siri, and carangueijo. Only the carangueijo, however, enters markets in significant numbers. The tiny sarara, which can be readily seen scurrying about mangroves, is scarcely bigger than the tip of a man's thumb and is gathered only when carangueijo are scarce. In the vicinity of Vigia, sarara are stewed with the coarse leaves of vinagreira da várzea, a wild

hibiscus with attractive purple flowers that grows on sandy beaches in the estuary. Because of their small size, boiled sarara are eaten shell and all.

Red-colored siri come near shore in brackish waters during the low water season. At such times, boys lower cylindrical traps baited with babaçu palm nuts into the water. The traps are similar in design to those used for catching shrimp but with larger openings at each end. Another method for catching siri from jetties and bridges over tidal sloughs involves a circular cloth or fishnet, about a meter in diameter, with a metal rim to maintain the trap's shape. The cloth or net is weighted immediately below the center with a rock or piece of metal so that it is cone shaped when suspended. The rim is attached to a central cord by four to five pieces of string to which some meat or gristle is tied to attract the crabs. When the device reaches the bottom, the bait rests in the middle of the cloth. Siri crabs crawl onto the cloth to feed on the bait and are captured when it is rapidly hoisted. Most of the siri are eaten locally, but some are sold in urban markets and along highways, strung together in groups of six to eight. Although siri enters mangroves, it appears to spend most of its adult life farther out to sea.

Shipworm extractors in a dugout canoe in the late afternoon. The young men have just returned from checking out a mangrove for sufficient quantities of dead wood to warrant returning at dawn to chop out the shipworms. One of the men is washing off mud accumulated during the scouting trip. Terra Amarela, Rio Tauá-Pará near Vigia, May 7, 1999.

Siri strung together for sale in an urban market. The crabs were captured in the vicinity of Vigia. Mosqueiro, August 2, 2000.

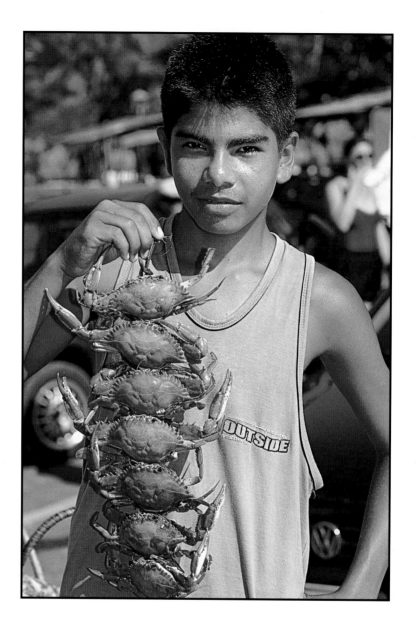

Purple-clawed carangueijo, on the other hand, lives in mangroves year-round. According to a fifty-year-old river dweller near Vigia, this crab, with its distinctive gray-turquoise shell and brushlike bristles on the back of its legs, chews fallen mangrove leaves, especially those of the black mangrove. The saucer-sized crabs excavate burrows about a meter deep in mangrove woods where they "hide" until low tide. As many as four occupied burrows have been recorded per square meter, an indication of how abundant the resource can be as long as the crabs are not overexploited. As the waters recede, exposing the muddy floor of the mangrove, the crabs are captured at their holes by one of three methods: grabbing them by hand; scooping them out with a metal hook; or snagging them in a lasso (*laço*).

Carangueijo crab and vendor in a fish market. This species of crab depends on mangrove for food and shelter. Continued destruction of this habitat will undercut a widely consumed food resource. Vigia, November 14, 1998.

When a fisherman near Vigia told me that he captures crabs with a lasso, I assumed that the gringo was in line again for a good ribbing. Trying to conceal a smile, I asked Raimundo exactly how he rounded up crabs using a rope. The technique is ingenuous and effective: a lasso snare. Whenever someone walks in a mangrove at low tide, the crabs immediately scurry for their holes in the mud. A noose is then placed around the burrow's entrance attached to a stake. When the crab deems that the coast is clear, the hapless creature reemerges and becomes entangled. The more the crab struggles, the tighter the noose becomes. An hour or so later, the crabber returns to remove the quarry. One hundred or more lasso stakes may be set out, each with a small brightly colored flag to identify its owner.

The other two methods for catching carangueijo, by hand and crook, are also employed at low tide. The crook consists of a short wooden pole with a U-shaped metal hook at the end. The hook is not barbed, and the object is to hoist out the crab uninjured. Crabs that are accidentally hurt are kept for home consumption as buyers in town purchase only healthy crabs. Experienced crabbers plunge their arms down the burrows and grab the crabs from behind, thereby avoiding their claws. This method reduces the chances of damaging the crabs but increases the risk of incurring a painful nip. Not all crab burrows are straight, forcing the crabber to use his hands or move on to another hole. According to local lore, the crab mother (*mãe do carangueijo*) hangs out in mangroves and keeps an eye on people who come to harvest the crabs. If a crab collector is greedy, the spirit guardian disorients the guilty soul so that he becomes lost.

Although carangueijo hunting is a year-round activity, unusually large numbers are caught during the rainy season, when river levels are high. From December to March, exceptionally high tides occur once a month (*lance do inverno*), a signal for sexual reproduction. Although it may appear that the high tides are flushing crabs from mangroves onto higher ground, they are simply seeking mates and seem quite oblivious to people. Crabs can even be seen wandering on roads and backyards and are easy to catch. The peculiar forays of carangueijo at such times have been incorporated into a regional carimbó song. Pinduca, a popular country singer, has a two-verse song titled "Siri and Carangueijo":

> I hear a knock on that door
> Oh my son, go see who it is.
>
> It's siri and carangueijo as well, Dad,
> Coming on their tiptoes.

Not all locals subscribe to the idea that carangueijo is courting when on prolonged sorties from its normal habitat in the mangroves. A teacher in Vigia attributed the carangueijo's disoriented behavior to the cooler and fresher waters at the height of the rainy season (*água de sauatá*).

Carangueijo sells briskly in urban markets in the southern part of the estuary, especially Belém, the largest city in the region. The crabs are taken to market in wooden crates or metal boxes and then transferred to baskets or tied together for sale. In some of the towns, crabs in the market are kept in tiled holding tanks. Carangueijo crabs are often displayed in markets tied together with string; piled into one-meter-high, close-weaved baskets or in smaller, open-weave baskets. When stringing crabs, they are stacked on top of each other, some six to a side, so that they can be sold in bunches of a dozen. Held together tightly by twine, the crabs are easily displayed by holding them up to passing motorists or pedestrians. Baskets for selling crabs are fashioned from the fronds of inajá, a native palm of uplands, or introduced coconut and have their tops tied together to prevent the crabs from escaping. Known locally as *pêra*, or by the older name *cofo*, the shopping bag–sized baskets have no holes, but the weave design is porous enough to prevent the crabs from suffocating. Smaller, open-weave baskets are usually fashioned from arumã twine and hold about a dozen crabs.

In "people's" eating establishments in the poorer parts of Belém near the waterfront, such as the Condor district, boiled crabs are cracked open with clubs on wooden tables to the accompaniment of blaring dance music. But in more refined restaurants and the homes of the well-to-do, boiled carangueijo is prepared in a number of dishes. One of the most popular is *casquinho de carangueijo*, cooked crabmeat mixed with spices and fried manioc flour (*farofa*) and served in a shell. Most chefs recycle the same shell many times for this purpose. Crab in its shell is typically served as a first course; as a main course, the same ingredients are served in a large bowl. As society becomes increasingly urbanized, fewer people are aware of the connection between this highly esteemed delicacy and the fate of mangroves, belief in the mother of crabs, the amorous wanderings of the crabs, or the skill and ingenuity of the crab hunters who spend hours up to their knees in mud.

CHAPTER 9

The Hunt between Land and Water

In a world dominated by water, game might seem a sideshow when so many people have access to fish, shrimp, crabs, and shipworms, as well as domestic livestock. Yet wild animals are a significant source of meat for rural folk, especially when one considers that most of the cattle and water buffalo roaming the seasonally flooded plains of Marajó and Mexiana end up on lunch and dinner plates in urban centers. River dwellers eat beef infrequently if at all. During the rainy season, when fish are harder to find and families draw down their backyard stocks of ducks, chickens, turkeys, goats, and pigs, game is particularly welcome.

Each game animal has a unique flavor and texture, and in some industrial countries customers are willing to pay a premium for such delicacies. The taste of the forest and the field helps some urban dwellers in Europe and North America to feel connected once again to the countryside they have long since left. Chewy partridge on the verge of spoiling elicits grunts of pleasure from gentlemen in posh London clubs, even though the more succulent chicken on the menu is considerably cheaper. In the estuary, game is not suffused with such romantic connotations; although locals appreciate game's fruity nuances, they view it as a matter of subsistence. A shotgun hanging from the wall is therefore a common sight in houses in the estuary and throughout Amazonia.

Most of the game in the estuary is consumed in the interior rather than in towns and cities. Unlike Iquitos in the Peruvian Amazon, which has a thriving game market, in Brazil the commercialization of wildlife is prohibited. Even so, game is brought to town clandestinely, especially high-value items such as certain turtles. Because game does not turn up in market surveys or in government production figures, it is often deemed unimportant by development authorities. This erroneous perception has important implications for conservation. Game depends on the integrity of its habitat for survival, a fact well recognized by organized hunting clubs and associations in developed countries. Because sport hunting is not a significant business activity in the estuary, the safeguarding of habitats for game is not usually considered in development plans.

Dozens of mammals, birds, and reptiles are hunted for food in the estuary, and they span habitats that range from marshes and upland forests to tidal woods and mangroves. Furthermore, some animals, such as the muçuã turtle, spend the wet part of the year in the forest and the dry season in grasslands. A mosaic of habitats therefore warrants conservation, and, most important, the interconnections between the diverse environments need to be better understood to promote sound management. Of the numerous animals captured for the table, only a few are discussed here, and their dependence on a variety of habitats is highlighted.

A Furry Repast

DEER

Two species of deer inhabit the estuary, and they occupy entirely different niches. The red brocket deer seeks shelter and food in floodplain and upland forests, whereas the white-tailed deer is confined to savannas that border forest.

The diminutive red brocket deer, known by various names but most commonly referred to as veado, is solitary and secretive. Found throughout the Amazon basin, it is shot at night when it comes to feed on fallen fruit, such as that of the açaí, buriti, and paxiúba palms. Indeed, the diet of red brocket deer is mostly fruit, hence the importance of maintaining forest for the creature's survival. The red brocket deer has evolved tiny antlers so that they do not become entangled in the rank jungle. Seamstresses use the stubby antlers for awls.

The red brocket deer is far more common in the estuary than its larger cousin, the white-tailed deer. And because its flesh is held in such esteem, it is not surprising that it surfaces in local lore. André, a thirty-year-old river dweller on Ilha dos Porcos, one of an archipelago of alluvial islands off northwestern Marajó, recounted a story he was told when he was younger:

> Some twenty years ago, João Nena was killing a lot of red brocket deer. He went out to hunt just about every night, even though he did not need to. One evening, he was paddling up Tesouro stream on Ilha dos Porcos with a companion; they were periodically scanning the banks of the stream with a flashlight [*lanternando*], trying to pick up the red reflecting eyes of a deer or perhaps a paca. Suddenly the crunch of leaves; it was a heavy animal. João turned on the flashlight and discerned a deer, but it was in thick vegetation. So instead of shooting, he and his companion continued paddling upstream, following the rustling sound of the moving deer. When they turned on the flashlight again, an old lady came into view rather than the deer they were expecting. The flashlight was quickly turned off. Then the footsteps in the dark forest started up again. Instead of heading home, the hunters pressed forward. After a while, João again clicked on the flashlight. This time a large upright hand appeared, signaling for them to halt. João

shot at the hand and immediately reeled back and fell down in the canoe. João became crazy [endoidou] and his companion had to tie him up to prevent injury. After he was taken home, João was brought to a nearby healer who declared that the Mother of the Forest had punished [malinado] João because he was persecuting game. The healer instructed João to cut back on hunting.

On Marajó, the white-tailed deer browses on savannas along the right bank of the middle and upper Anabiju, a transition zone between savanna and forest. It is absent on open savannas in central and eastern Marajó, as well as the thick forests that cloak the western portion of the island. The white-tailed deer ranges from eastern North America sporadically into South America. Marajó appears to be the southernmost extension of its range, the only place where it occurs south of the equator. At some point in the past, a founding population swam across the treacherous currents in the northern estuary from Amapá, where vast savannas abound, to northern Marajó and its adjacent islands.

Unlike the red brocket deer, the white-tailed deer displays impressive antlers because it roams in the open. The local name for the deer on Marajó is apropos: galheiro, the branched one. The multipronged antlers, which cowboys and ranchers sometimes hang on the walls of their houses, come into play during the mating season and when under attack. Other than people, jaguar and puma are the only significant predators of both deer.

Although white-tailed deer are avidly hunted in North America, venison from this species is not particularly popular among cowboys and river dwellers on Marajó. Meat from bucks is avoided altogether because its odor is reportedly too strong (catinga muito); instead it is fed to dogs. Doe meat is considered milder and therefore fit for human consumption. Ranchers on the middle and upper Anabiju report that helicopters filled with hunters from Belém occasionally sweep across their properties. After picking off their targets from the air, the hunters do not even bother to land and remove the carcasses. Needless to say, ranchers are not happy about such incursions, but there is little they can do to stop it. The hunters are evidently successful businesspeople—helicopters cost $1,000 an hour to rent in Belém—and well connected politically.

PECCARY

Two species of peccary live in the forests of Amazonia, the collared and the white-lipped, and both inhabit Marajó. White-lippeds, known locally as queixada, roam widely in herds that sometimes exceed one hundred animals and are avidly hunted by cowboys and river dwellers alike. Because they travel in such large groups, white-lippeds attract a lot of attention. When they are rumored to be in the vicinity, neighbors in-form each other and set off for the forest in great excitement and anticipation. With well-trained dogs, a hunter can force some of the peccaries to turn and fight; they can then be dispatched at short range with a shotgun. A full-grown peccary attains forty kilograms or more, about as much as the scrawny backyard pigs. White-lippeds are more common in headwaters, such as the upper Anabiju and Anajás Rivers, where fewer people live and hunting pressure is consequently lighter.

As in the case of the brocket deer, white-lippeds eat mostly fruit. According to a cowboy along the upper Anajás, white-lipped peccaries are especially fond of the oily nuts of murumuru, a spine-studded palm of floodplain forests. They also feast on the fallen fruits of buriti and paxiúba palms. During the high water season, white-lippeds presumably migrate to higher ground in southwestern Marajó.

The smaller collared peccary (caitetu), weighing up to twenty-five kilograms, has a much smaller home range than the white-lipped. Like its cousin, however, collared peccaries are fond of fruit, so river dwellers reportedly collect the fruits of buçú palm and pile them in the forest to attract them within shooting range. Without forest for cover and food, then, white-lipped and collared peccaries would disappear from Marajó Island.

CAPYBARA

Capybara, a rottweiler-sized rodent with webbed feet and a stumpy tail, thrives in the savannas and floodplain forests in the estuary, where it grazes on aquatic plants. For at least a century, ranches have profited from the sale of capybara meat and hides. According to the record book of the now-extinct Ferreira Teixeira Company, which was headquartered at the Espiritu Santo ranch along Anabiju on Marajó, cowboys were bringing in about one hundred fifty capybara skins each month in the late 1920s. The ledger has a regular section titled "Capybara Movement" (*Movimento de capivara*). Cowboys were paid a bonus depending on how many skins they brought to headquarters. Some of the meat was eaten, but much of it was probably discarded and consumed by vultures. At that time, Espiritu Santo encompassed sixty-five thousand hectares, but the ranch has since been divided into separate properties.

The practice of selling capybara meat on ranches continues, although technically it is illegal. Ranchers involved in the trade avoid confrontation with the law by selling to middlemen who have set up a scheme (*esquema*) for getting the meat to urban markets. Abaetetuba, known as a smugglers' haven for contraband whiskey, perfume, and cigarettes, is reputed to be one of the main markets for capybara meat.

Capybaras are social animals, living in groups of a dozen or so individuals, and give themselves away by leaving large, deep tracks in the mud and by flattening the vegetation in rest spots. The telltale piles of droppings, similar to those of rabbits, only

larger, also tell the hunter how long ago capybaras passed through the area. Capybaras are wary and fleet, so well-trained dogs are a great help on the hunt. A cowboy or river dweller enters a stream in a canoe and releases his dogs so that they can run along the banks. Once the dogs detect the scent of capybaras, they attempt to round them up and chase them toward the stream. If fresh tracks are spotted along the bank, the hunter may get out of the canoe and join the dogs for a while by walking inland. The hunter makes periodic calls to let the dogs know where he is. As the capybaras jump into the stream they are shot, harpooned, or attacked with a machete. Instead of trying to cross the stream, a capybara may remain submerged for several minutes under a bank or fallen tree. The hunter probes such spots with his paddle to flush out his quarry. Before the hunter is able to catch up with the action, his dogs sometimes yelp in pain; either a capybara has sunk its chisel-like front teeth into its pursuers or electric eels have discharged powerful shocks, none too happy about all the commotion around their resting spot. A cowboy on Caviana Island lamented that he lost his best hunting dog to an adult capybara when it bit the dog's neck, severing the jugular vein.

Fisherman with a butchered capybara in his canoe. The man was fishing with companions when his dog came upon the scent of the capybara and chased it into the stream, where it was killed. Igarapé Mandioca, affluent of the Cajueiro, municipality of Chaves, Marajó, August 17, 2000.

215

To prevent dogs from being lazy, they are not fed before the hunt. Sometimes the dogs appear tired—understandably so when they are famished—and want to get back into the canoe. But if they have not found any capybara, boarding is denied. If the hunt is successful, the quarry's stomach may be wrapped over the head of a novice hunting dog for a few seconds to provoke hatred for capybara and make it more eager on the next outing.

Poachers sometimes penetrate ranches in search of capybara. One of the owners of Fazenda Monte Alegre, in the headwaters of the Anabiju, expressed dismay but also admiration for the stealth of poachers after capybaras. The intruders, who often work in small teams, erect lean-to shelters in the middle of higher, wooded parts of savannas, taking care not to create an obvious path into the forest island. They then capture a baby capybara and tie it to a tree so that its desperate cries attract others. The hunters wait overhead on a branch, then jump down and club the adult capybaras that have come to investigate. Thus, by not using guns, the poachers escape detection. Further, the capybara meat is salted and covered with a thick pile of grass and small branches so that vultures do not circle above and give away the hunters' position.

At least one rancher on Marajó raises capybaras. Quickly tamed, they are unpredictable only when females are in heat. One captive female on the ranch wanders off during the day and returns at night to be fed. On one of her sorties, she became preg-

An agouti searching for food. Agoutis are important dispersal agents for several forest trees, including the Brazil nut. Near Macapá, Amapá, May 2, 1996.

nant by a wild capybara and subsequently gave birth to six young, which are being raised in a pen. Along the middle Amazon near Santarém, a small farmer is also raising the animals but lives in fear that he will be discovered by the federal wildlife protection service and fined. It is ironic that people can clear forest to raise Old World cattle but are punished for attempting to raise capybaras that require no land clearing.

Capybaras forage on savannas near streams and seek shelter as well as food in floodplain forest. During the dry season, suitable forage becomes increasingly scarce on the grasslands, so the versatile animals feed on forest fruits, such as caxinguba, a wild fig. According to locals living in the vicinity of Cachoeira do Arari, capybaras are fond of the succulent fruits when they fall to the ground during the dry months. Capybaras are also partial to the marble-sized yellow fruits of aturiá, a small floodplain tree with contorted branches, which drops its fruit from the end of the wet season in May until well into the drier months.

AGOUTI AND PACA

Rodents come in all shapes and sizes in the Amazon, and people in the estuary eat them large and small. Diurnal agoutis (cutia) are about the size of a rabbit and are often shot in the late afternoon as they feed on fallen fruit in floodplain forests before retiring. Agoutis feed on the fruits and nuts of several floodplain forest trees, including the spiny murumuru palm. Agoutis bury nuts for later consumption but forget the whereabouts of some of their stash; they thus serve as dispersal agents for several forest trees. Because they forage in second-growth as well as mature forest, agoutis also thrive in upland areas and tolerate habitat disturbance. Agoutis are prepared for the table by singeing off the fur, removing the internal organs, and then rubbing the carcass down with fresh lime. The meat is then cut into pieces and boiled in a stew.

The mother of the forest (mãe da mata) sometimes adopts the guise of an agouti to warn people when they have been hunting too much. Tuffi, a fifty-year-old river dweller who has lived much of his life on Ilha dos Porcos but who has also worked in several places as a carpenter, recounted a bizarre experience he had trying to kill an agouti one afternoon in 1987. He was paddling up the Lobato River, which traverses part of Ilha dos Porcos, when he came upon an agouti eating the oily nuts of andiroba. It was about three o'clock on a bright afternoon, and the agouti was in plain view as Tuffi released a volley from his 20-gauge, single-barrel shotgun. Although he fired from only four meters away, the agouti kept chewing the andiroba nut as if nothing had happened. Tuffi tried to reload, but the cartridge shell was stuck. After locating a stick, he was able to force the cartridge out and quickly loaded and fired again. This time the agouti dropped the nut. But instead of collapsing, it simply ambled away into nearby ground cover. Tuffi put another cartridge in his gun and fired a third time from only one meter. The agouti walked toward him, then reared up and clasped its front paws, as if in prayer. It then ran to the stream, where Tuffi was able to drown it. Although he was finally able to kill the agouti, he deemed it supernatural and vowed not to hunt so much anymore. "The forest boss is in charge" (*Chefe da mata toma conta*), he explained.

As agoutis head for hollow logs as the sun goes down, their place is taken by bull-dog-sized pacas, which are also avid fruit eaters. Hunters shoot pacas from canoes as they feed along stream banks. Unlike agoutis, however, pacas do not do well when their forest habitat is perturbed, because forest fruits constitute a major part of their diet. Paca meat is more succulent than that of agouti and is esteemed enough to reach urban markets. Certain vendors keep dressed paca carcasses in coolers, because it is illegal to sell game meat in the Brazilian Amazon. Authorities can evidently be persuaded to ignore such infractions, however. It is relatively easy to find out which vendor carries game in any given market in the estuary. Henry Walter Bates, a venerable English naturalist who spent eleven years in the Amazon in the mid-nineteenth century, described paca meat thus:

> The meat of the Paca, in colour, grain, and flavour, resembles young pork; it is much drier, however, and less palatable than pork. The skin is thick, and boils down to a jelly, when it makes a capital soup with rice.[1]

SPINY RAT

Spiny rats, know locally as soiyá, are a delicacy in rural parts of the estuary but would not be considered edible by most North Americans, Europeans, or residents of the larger towns in the Amazon. Prejudice in polite society against rats stems from their association with trash and sewers. Rats adapted to living in cities and in rural homes are invariably black or Norwegian rats, both originally confined to the Old World but now well established on every continent. Black rats are common in many rural and urban homes in the estuary, but no one eats them.

The flesh of spiny rats, however, is appreciated in rural areas. These forest rats grow plump on fruits, which gives the rats a savory flavor. Spiny rats reach twenty centimeters from the tip of the nose to the base of the tail and are so named because longer hairs, which are tipped black or gray, protrude from their fur. After skinning, the carcass is parted and fried. On Ilha dos Porcos near Afuá, I joined a family for a dinner of crispy soiyá, manioc flour, and açaí juice. The rat's meat tastes like something between the dark meat of chicken and pork: strong but not overpowering. Rural folk eat spiny rats because they taste good, not because there is nothing better to eat, as one urban-bound scientist in Belém suggested to me.

Spiny rats are nocturnal, but they are hunted during the day and at night. During

*A spiny rat alongside the dog that killed it in nearby floodplain forest. The family will soon be dining on
the tasty rodent. Ilha dos Porcos near Afuá, August 18, 1998.*

the day, the animals rest inside hollow logs or among tangled roots of streamside trees. At night, when the rats emerge to feed on fruit, they are chased to their diurnal resting places by dogs. The excited barking of dogs reverberating through the forest guides the hunter to the rat's lair. The hunter quickly prepares a prod, known as *basculho,* with the frond of a buçú or açaí palm. The end of the frond is bent down to form a stopper so that the rat is forced to flee in the opposite direction. The rat usually has at least one escape hatch, and the dogs wait in anticipation at the potential exit. If only one dog is present, the rat has a better than 50-50 chance of escaping. When the rat attempts to bolt, the dog snaps it up. The dogs are trained not to eat the rats, which they could do in a matter of seconds. Instead, the hunter tears off the fatty tail, which is quite plump at the base, and gives it to the eager dog for its reward.

Maria, the mother of five children on Ilha dos Porcos, who are all fond of soiyá, recounted an attempt she made to raise the rat in captivity. She kept a female spiny rat in the bottom of a fifty-five-gallon oil drum and fed it açaí fruits. Eventually, the rat gave birth to young, which also ate the palm fruits. One night a black rat either climbed or fell into the steel barrel and the spiny rat killed it. Unfortunately, the baby rats were also killed in the melee, and so ended that attempt at domestication. It seems likely, however, that other river dwellers living on Marajó or adjacent islands are raising the rats in their homes or backyards.

GIANT ANTEATER

The giant anteater, with its distinctive long tail draped with coarse hair—hence its Brazilian name, tamanduá bandeira (flag anteater)—inhabits the grasslands of Marajó and is killed opportunistically for its meat. How the giant anteater reached Marajó is a mystery as it shuns forest. Perhaps it arrived when the climate was drier and savannas extended to the banks of the Amazon. A likely dispersal route would be from Amapá; today savanna can be encountered a few kilometers inland from the estuary. Curiously, though, giant anteaters are absent from Caviana Island, which is nearer to Amapá, possibly because the savannas are not big enough to sustain the creature.

Cowboys on horseback most commonly encounter giant anteaters while they are checking on cattle. The anteaters are either shot or lassoed and clubbed. A cowboy along the Mandubé River in northern Marajó once killed a giant anteater because it was bear-hugging his dog. Giant anteaters have no teeth, but they are equipped with formidable front claws for tearing open termite mounds. Even after the giant anteater stopped breathing, it would not release the dog. The owner had to cut off the front paws of the dead anteater to extricate his struggling canine companion, which was fortunate to survive.

Only one species of armadillo seems to have become established on the islands that dot the estuary: the nine-banded armadillo. Considered roadkill in Florida and a nuisance to gardeners trying to protect their plants, the nine-banded armadillo (tatu) is widespread in Amazonia, where it is considered fair game. Cowboys on Caviana Island hunt the nocturnal creature with the help of their dogs, which chase their quarry down a hole and bark until their master arrives. The hunter may then partially dig out the burrow with a machete before probing the hole with a steel-tipped pole, called an *estoque*. The specialized pole has a wooden shaft a little over a meter long with a metal

THE HUNT BETWEEN
LAND AND WATER

A young nine-banded armadillo captured when its mother was killed in the forest. Caviana Island, May 21, 2000.

Black-bellied tree duck stew served over rice. This family makes its living by buying locally caught fish and taking them on ice for resale in Belém. Cachoeira do Arari, Marajó, May 18, 1999.

prong attached to one end. The notched prong is about half a meter long and is thrust through the bony plating of the armadillo. Thus skewered, the armadillo is pulled to the surface and dispatched. Fatty armadillo is cooked in stews or roasted.

One cowboy family on Caviana is raising a couple of young nine-banded armadillos in their home. The inquisitive creatures are kept in a wooden box, which is opened at night so that they can have free range of the kitchen. Dogs are not allowed in the house, so they are safe for now. Once they reach adult size, however, the "pets" will probably end up in the cooking pot.

A Feathered Feast

Many birds are shot opportunistically on Marajó and some adjacent islands, but only one is bagged in any numbers: the black-bellied tree duck. Known locally as marreca, the easily tamed duck nests in tree holes but forages in marshes and flooded savannas. In the dry season, the ducks are confined to permanent swamps studded with buriti palms. These bogs, known on Marajó as *mondongos*, occur in the transition zone between forest and savanna, especially in the northern part of the island. When the rains begin in January, the multicolored ducks migrate to vast, temporarily submerged campos to feed on the abundant aquatic plants. Loose formations of up to a few hundred ducks can be seen at such times, with smaller groups splitting off from the main formation from time to time. The ducks fly even on moonless nights, and their high-pitched, wheezy whistles can be heard overhead in towns and villages as well in open country. In the last century, flocks of black-bellied tree ducks were so thick they darkened the sky. Today hunting pressure has reduced the number and size of flocks, but enough of the fast-flying ducks survive to make organized hunts worthwhile.

Men dedicated to hunting black-bellied tree ducks are known as *marrequeiros*. During the rainy season, marrequeiros fan out across the flooded savannas to shoot the ducks from canoes or while stalking in knee-deep water. Sometimes hunters use cattle as cover to approach flocks as they feed. After a successful hunt, marrequeiros send their sons to town, such as in Cachoeira do Arari, to sell the ducks, which are slightly smaller than mallards, suspended from wooden poles laid across the shoulders. The ducks fetch about U.S. $1.25 each, cheaper than chicken. Customers eagerly snap up the ducks for boiling in savory stews.

Locals on Caviana Island and along the Mandubé River in northern Marajó also capture black-bellied tree ducks at night with cast nets normally used for fishing. During a heavy downpour, two people working as a team approach the ducks, which are huddled together for warmth. The sound of the rain masks the footsteps of the approaching hunters. When only a few meters away, the lead person turns on the flashlight. Momentarily startled, the ducks fly up but soon descend and waddle in unison toward the light. When deemed close enough, the person with the flashlight turns it off and drops down while his companion hurls the net.

On Caviana Island, southern lapwings, known locally as téu-téu, are caught in a similar manner, except that they are clubbed rather than caught in a net. The diurnal birds huddle together for warmth on rainy nights, making it easier to knock several of them down. Not much larger than a seagull, the long-legged birds disperse during the day and are too wary and small to waste a shot on.

The list of birds shot opportunistically would make any avid bird-watcher cringe. Some are relatively common, such as the great egret and the neotropic cormorant, while others, such as the buff-necked ibis, are relatively rare. Known on Marajó as curi-caca, the buff-necked ibis is vulnerable because it is relatively large and its loud cackle gives its position away. It also likes to roost in isolated trees near houses, where it can be easily spotted. At Fazenda Diamantina along the shores of Lake Arari, for example, groups of about half a dozen buff-necked ibises like to spend the night perched on the fronds of a royal palm planted decades ago near the main ranch house.

Another strikingly handsome bird of estuarine wetlands, the rufescent tiger heron, is also shot whenever encountered within range. Young ones, left defenseless when their mothers are killed, are sometimes taken home, where they are tethered and fattened until ready for the pot. Children have learned to give tiger herons wide berth, for their long, pointed bills can inflict severe injury, especially to the eyes.

The stately maguari stork, known locally as cauaúa, arguably the largest bird on Marajó, also succumbs to the occasional shotgun. Unlike buff-necked ibis, however, maguari are much harder to approach because their long necks and legs enable them to see far afield. The wary bird soars to great heights when traveling, well beyond the range of any shotgun or rifle. On one ranch in northern Marajó, a cowboy family keeps an adult maguari stork in a small enclosure containing a clump of sugarcane. Rather than display an aggressive nature like the rufescent tiger heron, the captive maguari is tame and accepts fish and table scraps from the family. When asked why the handsome bird was being held in captivity, the mother replied matter-of-factly that it was just a pet. Yet a faint smile hinted at the stork's real destiny. The only other bird that rivals the maguari in size is the ungainly looking jabiru stork, known in the estuary as tuiuiú. With its thick, leathery neck, reminiscent of a vulture's, and large fat bill, the jabiru stork may not be particularly attractive, but its meat is certainly appreciated.

Small wooden traps (*irapucas*) that collapse when the quarry trips a string are used to catch ground doves and pigeons that feed on fruits and seeds in savannas. Ubiqui-tous pale-vented pigeons, known locally as galego, are tempted into the traps with rice. The birds do not have much flesh, so they are typically boiled, rather than roasted, and served with manioc flour.

A Reptilian Banquet

Unlike in temperate regions, reptiles have long served as important food items for peoples inhabiting coastal regions and inland waterways in the tropics and subtropics. And the Amazon, straddling the equator, is no exception. Presumably, year-round warm temperatures have fostered not only the evolution of numerous species, but have allowed relatively large populations to thrive. Several species of caimans, aquatic lizards, turtles, and tortoises provide welcome variety to the diet in the Amazon estuary.

It is worth mentioning that not all reptiles are persecuted. Young boas sometimes take up residence in the rafters of rural homes, where they are welcome because they prey on rats. Locals assert that boas are particularly successful hunters because they "hypnotize" (*mundiar*) their prey. A cowboy family on Fazenda Coração de Jesus near Santa Cruz do Arari claims that their sleep was no longer disturbed within just a few days of a jiboiá setting up shop in the roof of their wooden home. As boas approach maturity, they apparently move back into the wild, just as well considering they can reach a length of four meters.

LIZARDS

At least three large lizards are eaten in the estuary, and all of them are associated with water. Two, the caiman lizard and the jacururú, are confined to floodplain forests, where they hunt in the water or chase their prey along the exposed banks of rivers and streams. The caiman lizard and jacuraru are in the same family (Teiidae) and resemble monitor lizards of the Old World. The iguana is in a different family and eats leaves; it inhabits forests on floodplains and uplands. Iguanas are excellent swimmers and avoid predators by dropping off branches into the water below. By the time a predator reaches the ripples signaling where the iguana landed with a loud crash, it is nowhere to be seen. All three species can be found in the same patch of flooded forest.

The caiman lizard, known locally as jacuruxi, is so named because of its thick, corrugated skin. In the 1960s and 1970s it was hunted heavily for its skin, but now it is captured opportunistically for its meat. Almost the length of an otter when fully grown, the caiman lizard is relatively easy to capture because it often remains motionless when approached, evidently thinking that it has not been noticed. A noose can then be slipped over its broad, triangular-shaped head as it lies on a branch, usually over water. For such purposes, men, or more usually boys, attach a noose of jungle vine to a makeshift pole fashioned from a buçú or açaí frond. At times youngsters can get close enough to grab the placid lizard by hand or mortally wound it with the swipe of a machete or paddle. After removing about half of the tail and the innards, the plump lizard is skinned and cooked in a stew (*guisada*).

A caiman lizard captured in floodplain forest with a noose tied to the end of pole. The semiaquatic lizard will be cooked in a stew. Near Breves, Marajó, August 11, 2000.

The eggs of the caiman lizard are even more sought after than the flesh. The leathery-skinned eggs are surprisingly large, almost as thick as a hen's egg. The caiman lizard is able to pass its ample eggs because they are elongated and have a supple shell. Three to six eggs are laid in arboreal termite nests during the dry season; only active termite nests are used for such purposes, presumably because the termite activity helps to incubate the intruder's eggs. People can tell which termite nests have been targeted by caiman lizards because the entrance hole is surrounded by scratch marks.

Smooth-skinned jacururú, a smaller and more slender cousin of the caiman lizard, also lays eggs in active termite nests. People climb up trees to remove the eggs, which are smaller than those of the caiman lizard. Cowboys on Caviana report that, unlike the caiman lizard, it also lays eggs at the base of rotten trees. Furthermore, it lays twice as many eggs as its distant cousin. Jacuráru is also captured in the water or along stream banks but is more skittish than the caiman lizard and a faster runner. Jacuráru is therefore more commonly shot rather than snagged with a noose. Dogs are also a great help in chasing and pinning down the agile lizard, which can reach one meter from its snout to the tip of its tail. All but the tip of the tail and feet go into the pot for dinner. Iguana eggs are among the favorite prey of sleek jacurarú.

Iguana, known in the Brazilian Amazon as camaleão, has tender, chickenlike flesh. Iguanas are typically snagged with a lasso tied to a long pole and may be kept for a few days at home with their legs tied together before being skinned and stewed. Iguana meat is considered light and therefore indicated when a person is not feeling well. In the food classification of rural folk, some meat, such as that of the peccary or pig, is considered *reimoso*, which means it is risky for someone who is sick or harboring a latent illness.

A jacurarú lizard captured by dogs in floodplain forest. The lizard will be served for dinner. Near Afuá, Marajó, September 9, 1997.

The oval, three-centimeter-long eggs of the iguana are also greatly appreciated. They are hard boiled and eaten with rice or manioc flour. During the dry season, female iguanas descend trees and seek out open, sandy soils to excavate a burrow where they lay about three dozen eggs. Suitably coarse soils for iguanas to nest are found along stretches of certain streams and in patches of the grasslands in eastern Marajó and the interior of other estuarine islands. Islands of sandy savannas are called *campinas* or *ilhas* and are ancient beaches laid down by rivers or during a marine incursion. On Colares Island near Vigia and along the Mandubé River in northern Marajó, locals set fire to grasslands to entice iguanas to lay their eggs. The singed landscape also makes it easier to spot iguana burrows. Indigenous groups likely set fires for the same reason in the distant past, thereby helping to maintain an open landscape.

Iguanas anxious to lay are also attracted to cemeteries. Locals prefer to bury the deceased in sandy soils because it is easier to dig and because coarse soils tend to be on higher ground. Manuel, a forty-five-year-old cowboy along the Mandubé River, suggested that pregnant iguanas are partial to cemeteries because they are kept relatively clear of weeds. Eggs laid in cemeteries are safe, at least from humans. Manuel explained that people resist the temptation to dig up the eggs out of "respect" for the departed.

CAIMANS

Three species of caimans are killed for food in the estuary: the fearsome black caiman, which can attain a length of five meters; the medium-sized spectacled caiman; and the relatively small smooth fronted caiman. Caiman populations, especially the black caiman, have universally declined because of overhunting. At one time black caimans were so numerous along the Amazon, including the estuary, that they threatened people. In describing life along the Amazon in 1691, Father Samuel Fritz, a Jesuit missionary, wrote:

> There are in this river lizards, otherwise called crocodiles, exceedingly numerous, and very large and horrible; they are so daring that frequently they attack and upset the canoes, carrying away and devouring the Indians. In the time of the high flood, when the huts are inundated, they cause horror with the noise that they make with their ceaseless grunting, and at times entering into the houses they seize the inhabitants.[2]

Black caimans were once so common that they could be easily harpooned from lakeshores during the dry season. The Swiss zoologist Emílio Goeldi reported that a rancher friend of his on Marajó had two thousand caimans killed on his ranch during the summer of 1897. And in a two-week period in 1915, cowboys killed some five hun-

Cowboys harpooning caimans on a ranch on Marajó in the early twentieth century. When caimans were more plentiful, ranch owners encouraged such hunts to reduce caiman predation on calves and to obtain the fat, which was rendered into lamp oil.

From Percy Lau, Tipos e Aspectos do Brasil *(Rio de Janeiro: Instituto Brasileiro de Geografia e Estatística, 1949), 3.*

dred caimans in a single lake on Marajó. Ranchers on Marajó and neighboring Mexiana Island organized black caiman hunts in the nineteenth and early twentieth century for two purposes: to reduce livestock losses and to obtain the fat around the intestines, which was rendered into oil for burning in lamps. Black caiman has never been considered good eating.

After 1940 black caiman populations came under additional attack from the leather trade. Around 1950 approximately five million black caiman skins were being exported annually from the Brazilian Amazon. By 1960 the annual offtake of black caiman for the international leather trade had plummeted to less than 700,000 skins and by the early 1980s had slipped further to less than 1,000 skins. Black caiman once outnumbered spectacled caiman, but now the latter is more common throughout the Amazon, including Marajó, and accounts for most of the caiman meat eaten on the island.

The skull of a black caiman killed on a ranch in the Amazon estuary. Fazenda Campo Limpo, head-waters of the Anajás, Marajó, April 23, 2000.

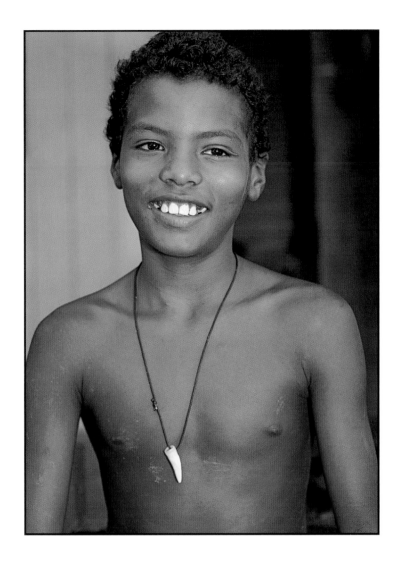

*A black caiman tooth on a
necklace. Some men and boys
on Marajó wear such necklaces
to ward off snakes. Rio
Cajueiro, municipality of
Chaves, Marajó,
August 15, 2000.*

The black caiman, known in the Brazilian Amazon as jacaré-açu (big caiman), re-sembles an alligator with its broad snout and is capable of inflicting a mortal wound on large mammals with a single bite. In 1999, for example, a cowboy on the Cajueiro ranch in northern Marajó was fishing on a murky lake when he nearly lost his life. He stepped out of his canoe for a moment and trod on a submerged black caiman; the lat-ter reared up and clamped on to his knee. After a brief struggle, the cowboy was able to free himself and was rescued by some companions who heard his calls for help. He was airlifted to Belém and doctors were able to stop the bleeding, but the wound left him crippled. And a decade ago along Jutaí Creek on Caviana Island, a cowboy was fishing with a companion using a short seine attached to two poles when they acciden-tally scooped up a black caiman. Before they could let go of the net, the ill-tempered creature lunged at one of the cowboys and almost severed his arm. The cowboy managed to escape and survived with the help of a traditional curer. In centuries past, rural people had to keep their eyes on children playing along the water's edge when black caimans were around. Now adult black caimans are rare, so such incidents are unusual.

Such is the prestige of the black caiman that men and boys on Marajó sometimes wear a caiman tooth suspended from a string necklace. The tapered tooth, about the size of a man's thumb, is worn to prevent snakebites. Pieces of black caiman hide are also kept to ward off evil. A cowboy in the northern part of Marajó burns black caiman leather so that the smoke wafts over his dogs and domestic livestock; the putrid smoke allegedly shields the animals from illness.

Black caimans are most often captured with a harpoon, but in 1998 one was hooked on a trotline baited with a possum along the middle Anabiju on Marajó. The cowboy who spotted the caiman lurking in the river had set out the trotline to eliminate any risk to his children. The cowboy was surprised by the stomach contents of the fully grown caiman: it contained the remains of several snakes and an empty tin of cooking oil.

The spectacled caiman, which can reach a length of nearly three meters, is preferred for roasting. The base of the tail is the filé, just as in the southeastern United States where gator tail is a regional delicacy. Known in the Brazilian Amazon as jacaré-tinga (white caiman, so named because it is much lighter than its larger cousin), the specta-cled caiman is sometimes smuggled into urban markets. Certain vendors are known to carry illicit game, usually kept in burlap sacks or Styrofoam containers below the counter. Salted and sun-dried caiman meat is sold openly in the Barcarena street market.

The spectacled caiman is captured with a harpoon or when it becomes entangled in a gill net set out to catch fish. While traveling along rivers and streams, locals always keep their eyes open for game, such as capybara or caiman. Spectacled caiman lying on the bank of a river can be an easy target because it will often allow a canoe to approach quite close before bolting for the water. Once harpooned, the first order of business is to pull a noose tightly around the caiman's jaws. The legs are then bound, and the ani-mal is kept alive until the day it is to be cooked, usually by roasting over an open fire. The white, crumbly flesh is something between haddock and turkey breast in taste and texture.

The hard, rough-shelled eggs of the spectacled caiman are also considered a deli-cacy. The caiman lays her oblong eggs, about thirty at a time, at the base of a buriti palm and then covers them with leaves. The telltale pile of debris alerts fishers, hunters, and cowboys that eggs are incubating in the warmth of the decaying vegetation. The nest is opened and the eggs removed and taken home. In the vicinity of Lake Arari on Marajó, the yolk is beaten with salt and sugar and then mixed with finely sieved manioc flour (*farinha coada*) before frying.

A harpooned spectacled caiman being subdued by tying its jaws shut. The harpoon point is embedded near the caiman's shoulders. Rio Cajueiro, municipality of Chaves, Marajó, August 17, 2000.

The eggs of the smaller smooth fronted caiman are also removed when encountered in floodplain forest. This species, known locally as jacaré-curuá, lays thirty to forty eggs in a pile of leaves, which are apparently left unguarded to incubate. The smooth fronted caiman is a denizen of forest streams and is not as plentiful as the spectacled caiman.

TURTLES AND TORTOISES

About half a dozen species of turtle and one land tortoise are eaten in the estuary, not counting occasional marine stragglers such as the green sea turtle. They range in size from the one-meter-long giant river turtle, known as tartaruga, now exceedingly rare due to overhunting, to salad plate–sized muçuã-lalá.

Muçuã turtles are caught on savannas in the estuary and often kept in backyard pens or in confined areas of the house for periodic consumption. Santa Cruz do Arari, Marajó, May 13, 1999.

Perema turtles are often fattened on kitchen scraps until they are cooked in stews. Rio Tamacuri near Breves, Marajó, August 9, 2000.

If there is one turtle that characterizes the estuary it is the muçuã, or scorpion mud turtle. In the Brazilian Amazon, this soup bowl–sized turtle is apparently found only in the estuary where seasonally flooded savannas abound. Diced meat of the scorpion mud turtle cooked with spices and served with manioc flour in its shell (*casquinho de muçuã*) is one of the delights of Paraense cuisine. Patrons at certain restaurants in Belém have to ask for the dish in a subdued voice; it is not featured on the menu because the restaurant owner could be fined.

Muçuã is another example of a game resource that depends on both forest and savanna. It lays its eggs in floodplain forest in August and spends the rest of the year on savannas, where most of them are caught. According to a river dweller along the Cajueiro in northern Marajó, the muçuã prefers to lay its ten or so eggs at the base of taboka. This native bamboo is surrounded at its base with short, twisting branches that have no leaves but are armed with fearsome spines. Muçuã have learned to take advantage of this protection for their eggs. People get around the thorns by burning them off; they can then excavate the eggs unscathed. Taboka thrives in disturbed sites, so burning increases its competitive advantage.

During the annual flood, horsemen spot muçuã as they swim through the grass, causing the stems to tremble. Just before dismounting, however, the hunter makes sure that he is not about to grab an electric eel or a venomous snake. In the dry season, locals torch the savannas to stampede muçuã; the fleeing turtles are then scooped up and taken home or sold to a trader. Curiously, the turtles refuse to eat even when kept in backyard pens or closets at home for a month or more. In the wild, locals claim that the muçuã eats leaves and silt (*limo*).

The twist-neck turtle, known on Marajó as muçuã-lalá, looks like a flattened version of the scorpion mud turtle. No larger than a salad plate, muçuã-lalá stays in floodplain forests and seeks out high ground in the wet season. At the camp of an açaí fruit gatherer on an indigenous mound along the lower Camutins, I encountered a circular pen containing two red-footed tortoises and a twist-neck turtle; these were being kept for a future dinner. The pen had a diameter of about a meter and was made by sticking one-meter-high slender poles, cut from the surrounding forest, into the ground.

The matamatá is a long-necked, flattened turtle about the size of a briefcase that lives in swamps dominated by aninga where it waits to ambush its prey. The pointy-nosed matamatá buries itself in leaves and mud when alarmed; locals locate the secretive animal by prodding the lakeshores with a pole. Matamatá is apparently a rural delicacy for it is not found in urban markets. Genteel suburbanites might be put off by matamatá's unwholesome appearance.

Perema turtles, another inhabitant of floodplain forests, are often encountered while weeding açaí stands. Agile swimmers, they are gathered up quickly before they reach water and are kept in corrals, sometimes containing several dozen individuals. When scared they burrow into the mud but come out to feed on manioc flour mixed with water, açaí juice, or milk. In the wild, they are reputed to eat fruit, particularly açaí and murumuru. Although most peremas are consumed by river dwellers, sufficient numbers of rural folk have migrated to cities to create urban markets for the turtle. The well-to-do in such cities as Belém and Macapá eat only the better-known giant river turtle or muçuã; indeed, demand for those turtles in cities has driven up the price beyond the reach of most urbanites. Peremas, because they are more plentiful and less prestigious, are more affordable to the mass of poorer people crowded into settlements in the outskirts of cities. Peremas are put into boiling water, dead or alive, until the shell (carapace) softens enough to pull it apart from the bony underplate (plastron). The meat is then simmered with salt and lime juice.

The giant river turtle, one of the world's largest freshwater turtles, is a prize because the flesh and eggs are considered an aphrodisiac and an adult can feed a family for several days. Heavily exploited in the colonial period for its eggs, which were rendered to provide lighting fuel and cooking oil, tartaruga, as the turtle is known in the Brazilian Amazon, is now essentially confined to the northern part of the estuary. A man-made canal in northern Marajó, Canal das Tartarugas, is named after the turtle.

Tartarugas seek out sandy nesting beaches in the dry season. One such beach, Praia do Maruim along the northeastern coast of Marajó, is checked periodically by locals during the low water season for the telltale tracks in the sand. Egg gatherers must work quickly, however, because biting midges, known as *maruim*, swarm on those who tarry. Aptly named punkies or no-see-ums in English, the tiny blood-sucking flies make one feel like a pincushion. The raw eggs are mixed with manioc flour that has soaked in water for a few minutes to soften it; salt is added to taste. The Ping-Pong ball–sized eggs, as many as one hundred to a nest, are also boiled and eaten with manioc flour.

When the first Europeans descended the Amazon in 1542, they encountered villages with as many as one thousand giant river turtles in pens. Although today a few ranches stock tartaruga in ponds, the turtle is so valuable that it is generally sold to urban markets. Manuel, a sixty-four-year-old river dweller along the Ganhoão River in northern Marajó, however, is raising a baby tartaruga for domestic consumption. Manuel has drilled a hole through the carapace and keeps the turtle tethered in his kitchen. Scarcely the size of a computer mouse, the turtle will take a decade or so to reach adult size. In the meantime the baby turtle feasts on shrimp and fish, wallows in a small cal-

Hunter armed with a specialized harpoon (tapuã) designed to capture tracajá turtles. Yellow arum fruits in the bottom of the canoe are broken up and tossed into the water to attract the turtles. Igarapé do Lago, affluent of the lower Maracá, Amapá, May 3, 1996.

A red-footed tortoise held captive for eventual eating. Dogs belonging to this cowboy family found it in nearby floodplain forest. Canal das Tartarugas, Marajó, May 17, 2001.

abash gourd filled with water, and could well outlive Manuel if he weans his tethered turtling on to fruit, the creature's normal diet.

The tracajá is known in English as the yellow spotted Amazon turtle but only retains the bright spots while a turtling. Hubcap-sized adults are uniform olive brown and during the flood season climb up on partially submerged logs and branches to sunbathe. Tracajá is also a fruit eater, so its flesh is particularly tasty. Tracajás are caught on trotlines baited with forest fruits, in fence-type fish traps, or jabbed with a specialized harpoon (*tapuã*). The short harpoon point is unbarbed and detachable. Once embedded in the turtle's shell, the locally made metal point unravels from the shaft, which is held firmly by the hunter. The quarry is then hauled in. If the point were fixed to the shaft, the turtle would be able to wiggle free. To entice the tracajá within striking range, the hunter breaks up the spongy, yellow fruits of aninga and drops the pieces into the water to serve as chum. The shells of tracajás are sometimes painted and hung on walls of the homes of rural folk for decoration, as on Fazenda Tres Marias along the upper Anabiju.

In a landscape where water reigns, it is not surprising that most of the turtles in the estuary are aquatic. But at least one species is terrestrial: the red-footed tortoise, known locally as jabutí. This fruit-eating tortoise is most commonly encountered during the rainy season when it congregates on higher ground. A grandmother along Canal das Tartarugas in northeastern Marajó explained that the family dogs discovered the red-footed tortoise that she has tethered under her house. The dogs were barking excitedly in the nearby riparian forest, so she resolved to investigate. Red-footed tortoises are sometimes sold in pet stores in North America, but when they encounter humans in the Amazon an entirely different fate awaits them.

CHAPTER 10

Misty Dawn

As the Amazon is increasingly integrated into domestic and international markets and the cities continue to grow, land use at the mouth of the great river will surely intensify. Although "globalization" can be a threat to the environment and the livelihoods of locals, in the case of the estuary it is improving standards of living and reducing pressure on forests, mangroves, and other habitats important for fisheries and other natural resources. The boom in açaí fruit is likely to strengthen, thereby providing further incentive for river dwellers to maintain or even expand their cultural forests. Economic activities that pose the greatest threat to forests are timber extraction, cattle ranching, and the arrival of the soybean front in the Amazon.

TIMBER: ANOTHER TRAGEDY OF THE COMMONS?

Boom-and-bust cycles have dominated much of the economic history of Amazonia since colonial times, and by the end of the twenty-first century, timber will likely count among them. The tempo of logging activities in the Amazon started rising sharply in the 1960s and shows no signs of stopping. How long it will last is anyone's guess, but it will likely further accelerate before slowing. A century and a half ago, Prince Adalbert of Prussia made a brief visit to the lower Amazon and declared that at Belém "there would be no want of timber for the next thousand years."[1] More likely, the boom will be over in a little more than a century.

But the eventual passing of the timber boom will not devastate the estuary, as only the most valuable trees are cherry picked, leaving much of the forest intact. By the twilight of the twenty-first century, planted trees will likely account for more than half the timber extracted from the Amazon, and growers in the estuary will be among those reaping the benefits from a growing global appetite for tropical hardwoods and veneers. By the middle of the century, it may make economic sense to manage Amazonian forests for timber production. At the moment, though, "sustainable" management of forests in Amazonia for lumber is a chimera.

CATTLE RANCHING INTENSIFICATION

Intensification of agricultural operations, including ranching, is generally considered beneficial to the environment because in theory it reduces pressure to clear more land. Some would argue that intensification, with justification in some cases, actually exacerbates environmental damage, by promoting the use of agricultural chemicals, such as insecticides. In the case of crop farming and ranching, however, moderate use of fertilizers and herbicides can boost productivity and therefore spare the forest, haven to so much of the region's biodiversity. Intensification in the case of ranching embraces a wide range of approaches, from weed management in pastures to application of fertilizers, pasture rotation, and genetic upgrading of the herd.

When discussing intensification of ranching in the Amazon, it is important to distinguish between upland and floodplain environments. Management issues are different in each case, ranging from soil type, the nature of the weed problem, and the choice of pasture grasses for replanting. On Marajó, the area of upland pasture is small compared to that on seasonally flooded savannas; most of the terra firme pasture, amounting for little more than three thousand hectares, is concentrated around Breves. Compared to upland ranches on the mainland, only modest efforts are under way to recuperate pastures near Breves, all of which are in various stages of degradation. Lacre is one of the most serious pasture weeds in the Breves area, as in many other upland areas of Amazonia. Although lacre is periodically slashed and burned, the aggressive weed quickly resprouts and gains a stronger foothold. If herbicide was applied to lacre immediately after it is cut and the pasture disked and fertilized with phosphorus every decade or so, quicuio would have an opportunity to outcompete the weeds. With no technical assistance available in the area and with limited resources to invest in upgrading operations, ranchers typically abandon pastures in a few years and clear more forest.

Fazenda Santa Teresa along Igarapé Grande near Breves is having so many weed problems that the herd has withered from 1,000 head to 300. In this case, vassoura de botão is the main problem in the one thousand hectares of pasture, planted to quicuio in stages over a thirty-year period. None of the pasture has ever been fertilized, and as nutrients have leached from the soil and been removed with cattle, weeds adapted to infertile soils have gained a comparative advantage. Vassoura de botão is deceptive. From a distance, pastures infested with the herbaceous weed look green and healthy in the rainy season. But on closer inspection, the damage becomes evident: the squat weed has smothered the quicuio. As an experiment, the rancher has disked fifteen hectares of degraded pasture and replanted with quicuio. Without applying fertilizer, however, botão de vassoura will soon reassert itself.

The pace of intensification on the seasonally flooded parts of Marajó and adjacent estuarine islands varies considerably from ranch to ranch. Most of the ranches on periodically wet savannas are essentially free-range operations with a low carrying capacity. Still, some ranches on low-lying campos are intensifying their operations by planting more nutritious pasture, suppressing weeds with large tractor-drawn mowers (*roçadeiras*), fencing pastures to avoid overgrazing, and upgrading the genetic makeup of their herds. On Fazenda Vitória near the mouth of the Anapú, for example, the 585 hectares of pasture in cleared floodplain forest are kept clean by periodic mowing with a tractor. Carrying capacity, at almost two head of cattle per hectare, is relatively high as a consequence. Along portions of a creek in the Santa Teresa ranch near Breves, the owner has planted canarana erecta lisa, a nutritious floodplain grass favored especially by water buffalo. This grass, native to the Amazon floodplain, does not occur naturally on the ranch but was planted on muddy banks of the stream to provide additional forage for one hundred forty water buffalo.

Ranchers on seasonally flooded campos are aware of signs of overgrazing, such as infestation of algodão bravo, which despite its name (wild cotton) is actually a member of the sweet potato family. One way to reduce the buildup of algodão bravo is to relieve grazing pressure by rotating pasture. Until relatively recently, fencing on Marajó was rare, except to delineate property boundaries. Now some ranchers are separating grazing areas with fencing to improve productivity and prevent overgrazing.

Although many ranchers would like to intensify their operations, credit is too expensive for them to do so. Also, cattle ranching still has an image problem, both socially and environmentally. The Brazilian government is unlikely to provide subsidized credit for any aspect of ranching in the near future, including upgrading pastures, because it might damage efforts to secure international funding for development and conservation efforts, particularly from Europe, the United States, and Japan. Yet such policies probably do more harm socially, because many smallholders also raise cattle and water buffalo, as well as environmentally, because they encourage extensification rather than intensification.

The need to intensify cattle production in the estuary and elsewhere in Amazonia is likely to increase as a result of a generally successful campaign to eradicate foot-and-mouth disease in parts of southern Brazil. Although a few outbreaks of the disease were reported in Rio Grande do Sul in 2000 and 2001, the cases were attributed to infected herds in neighboring Uruguay and Argentina and were quickly contained. Beef producers in zones declared free of foot-and-mouth disease will opt for more lucrative export markets, thereby creating a supply deficit for beef in the southern part of the country where people are concentrated and where incomes are highest. In 1999 exports of Brazilian beef jumped 86 percent and reached U.S. $1 billion in export earnings in 2001. Supermarket chains will therefore purchase more beef from the north, which is not free of the disease and therefore cannot tap the international market for chilled beef. Consequently, pressure on forests in Amazonia is likely to increase unless producers intensify their operations. Should foot-and-mouth disease be eliminated in Amazonia, then pressure on the remaining forests will further intensify.

Another justification for intensifying cattle operations in the Amazon is the havoc caused by mad cow disease on world beef markets. With several European nations, notably Britain, Germany, France, and Italy, registering occurrences of mad cow disease in their herds, which can prove fatal to humans if they eat meat contaminated by the pathogen, many countries have banned beef imports from Europe. Brains are not recycled into livestock feed in Brazil. In fact, Brazil has the world's largest cattle herd—about 165 million head—and it is entirely range fed. Exports of "green" beef from Brazil are thus likely to climb, propelling further deforestation in the Amazon unless operations are intensified.

In February 2001 Canada briefly imposed a ban on imports of Brazilian beef, allegedly as a precautionary measure citing North American Free Trade Agreement regulations. However, Brazilians suspected that the move had more to do with the success of their national aircraft company, Embraer, which is winning orders for its commuter jets in North America, in direct competition with Canada's Bombardier. Bombardier has accused the Brazilian government of subsidizing sales of Embraer aircraft. After the president of Brazil threatened an all-out trade war over the issue, the Canadian government lifted the ban on Brazilian beef within a few weeks.

Conservation Opportunities on Ranches

In debates about conservation and development in Amazonia, ranchers are typically cast as villains because of their propensity to clear extensive patches of forest. While it is true that cattle owners have destroyed enormous areas of floodplain forests along certain stretches of the Amazon, they are also key players in any bid to safeguard the remaining forests. A major advantage of ranches is that substantial blocks of forests can be better protected from loggers and illegal encroachment than most parks and reserves. Also, large blocks of forest can be maintained, critical for the integrity of ecosystems because pollinators, seed dispersal agents, and top predators have a better chance of survival in large patches of habitat.

As long as conservation does not threaten their economic interests, most ranchers would likely be open to discussing ways to promote habitat conservation. In the Amazon estuary, ranchers maintain forest on their property for a variety of reasons, including income from the sale of timber, as a source of construction material for corrals, and the high market value of açaí fruits. Some are planting açaí along streams, just as river dwellers do. And because timber is valuable, many ranchers are reluctant to eliminate their woodland to create pasture. Efforts by ranchers to diversify their operations can, in some cases, promote conservation.

Several ranchers have opted for ecotourism, similar to the dude ranches popular in various parts of the United States, particularly in the Rockies. A large ranch on Mexiana Island has invested in an extensive infrastructure for guests that includes individual cabins and a swimming pool. Guests are typically flown in on chartered planes, and activities include horseback riding, fishing, and bird-watching. Ecotourism on ranches is a seasonal affair because of the heavy rains during six months of the year. To keep costs down, tour operators might consider organizing jeep safaris to Marajó by boarding the regular ferry service from Belém to the mouth of the Camará River. At the height of the dry season, it is possible to reach many of the ranches on the savanna by land. Vehicles could thus bring in supplies, especially food and drinking water, and tourists could see several ranches and different environments.

While potential exists for developing ecotourism on ranches, the product should not be oversold. The market appears to be modest, at least at the moment, and the use of chartered planes to bring in tourists makes it quite expensive. The relatively high cost of air travel to Belém from North America, compared to airfares to Central America and Europe, acts as an additional damper on ecotourism in the estuary. Also, one of the most lucrative parts of the ecotourism business in the Brazilian Amazon— sportfishing—has limited appeal in the Amazon estuary where the main species sought by well-heeled foreign fishermen, the peacock bass (tucunaré), is rare or absent in most waters. Still, it should be possible to expand ecotourism modestly in the estuary based on ranches with relatively intact wildlife populations and containing a mix of savanna and forest. Cowboys and river dwellers who formerly hunted to supplement their diet, could be hired as nature guides and to help protect wildlife.

Another way to promote conservation in the estuary would be to arrange debt-for-nature swaps, especially popular with several governments in developing countries during the 1970s and 1980s. Some ranches on Marajó have no cattle because the owners are in arrears with a bank, usually the Banco da Amazônia (BASA), the regional development bank. As every year passes, the debt mushrooms as a result of accumulating interest and penalties. In many cases, the banks are unlikely to recover the amounts owed or even a fraction thereof. The cattle on ranches with debt problems have been sold in an attempt to pay off loans, or more likely removed to someone else's property so that the bank cannot seize them. Scope exists for conservation foundations to negotiate with banks and debtors so that liens are removed on properties and debts paid off with a discount. In theory, the banks would be happy because they would at least collect something, and in turn the ranch owners would agree to set aside conservation easements. Such deals could be arranged in domino fashion so that contiguous properties provide wildlife corridors.

Banks could play another role in promoting conservation by providing low-interest loans to livestock owners who want to intensify production on already cleared areas. While some might argue that would be unwise, because if successful, ranchers might attempt to expand production into areas by cutting forest or draining marshes, intensification usually increases options for conservation. Furthermore, if ranching operations on Marajó were intensified successfully, pressure would be taken off upland forests on the "mainland" where so many calves are taken to fatten on artificial pastures cleared from forest.

Tax incentives would be another means to encourage landowners to set aside areas for conservation purposes. The problem in the case of Brazil is that tax collection is still weak, a drawback fully recognized by government officials in Brasília who are trying to tighten procedures for reporting income and paying taxes. Many rural residents in the estuary do not report income or pay any taxes, and even wealthy landowners who are known to taxing authorities have devised innovative ways to shield income. Eventually, though, tax incentives could be put in place to encourage livestock owners to set aside conservation easements, as is the case in many industrial nations.

THE SOYBEAN FRONT

The soybean wave has finally swept into the Amazon, stirring concerns about environmental and social impacts. Spurred by growing international demand for soybeans, especially for the "natural" product, Brazil is making efforts to prevent the planting of transgenic soybean and is thus likely to reap its reward from the European market where consumers are particularly agitated over the potential health and environmental risks of planting genetically mutated crops.

The soybean front penetrated the Amazon in the 1990s along pioneer highways that link the Amazon to the industrial heartland of Brazil, especially the Belém-Brasília and the BR 364 from Porto Velho in Rondônia to Mato Grosso. Some voices in the Amazon have expressed alarm at this new development, suggesting that soybean cultivation will accelerate deforestation and displace the rural poor.

Soybean, however, is likely to enhance conservation efforts and improve livelihoods in the interior as well as in urban areas. Soybean is unlikely to accelerate deforestation; on the contrary, it may slow rates of forest destruction. At the moment at least, soybean is being planted mostly as a rotational crop in degraded pastures. It is planted with fertilizer after weed-infested pasture is torn up and burned. Pasture is replanted after the soybean harvest. Not only does soybean help to recoup the cost of upgrading pastures, it helps to fertilize the soil with nitrogen. Where soybean is being planted year after year, the fields occupy degraded pastures rather than cleared forest because fewer tree stumps remain to impede mechanization. Furthermore, the infrastructure for drying and transporting soybean creates jobs for people in urban areas.

Soybean is unlikely to be planted on Marajó, except perhaps on upland portions, in the near future, given the large areas of degraded pastures along upland highways on the mainland. The savannas of Marajó are flat and largely free of tree stumps, but soils are poor. Soybean would have to be planted during the dry season, and irrigation costs would be high. And fertilizer costs on Marajó would likely be too high considering the modest yields. Cattle have roamed the campos of Marajó for centuries, and water buffalo have thrived there for more than one hundred years; they are not likely to be displaced soon by soybean or any other field crop.

GLOBAL WARMING

Scenarios for the estuary could all be scrambled if global warming continues. Even a modest rise in sea levels from the melting of ice caps would permanently flood large tracts of savanna, mangrove, and forest at the mouth of the Amazon. Some are predicting that sea levels will rise by close to one meter in the twenty-first century if global warming continues. During the last million years, sea levels have fluctuated much more widely at the mouth of the Amazon, but now millions of people live there, and even a modest rise of half a meter would shift the mosaic of vegetation communities and force people to move and change their lifestyles. Eventually, a new equilibrium would be reached and people would once again adjust to a stabler environment, but considerable social and economic disruption could ensue over the next few decades.

While Brazilians are often berated in the press for not "doing something" about deforestation in the Amazon, they rightly ponder who occupies the moral high ground when consumers in the United States continue to purchase eight- and ten-cylinder sports utility vehicles with names resembling subdivisions. Residents at the mouth of the Amazon have long altered the landscapes without destroying their resiliency. If industrial nations, which pump most of the carbon dioxide into the atmosphere, curb their appetite for fossil fuels and promote more fair trade and donors and lending agencies appreciate the needs and aspirations of all stakeholders in the estuary, from river dwellers to loggers and ranchers, the future looks bright.

Common and Scientific Names of Plants

LOCAL	ENGLISH	SCIENTIFIC
Abiu	Abiu	*Pouteria caimito*
Açaí	Açaí palm	*Euterpe oleracea*
Acapu	Acapu	*Vouacapoua americana*
Acerola	Barbados cherry	*Malpighia glabra*
Algodão bravo	Algodão bravo	*Ipomaea fistulosa*
Ameixa	Jambolan	*Eugenia cumini*
Ananaí, ananás do miúdo	Ananaí	*Ananas ananassoides*
Ananás	Pineapple	*Ananas comosus*
Ananí	Ananí	*Symphonia globulifera*
Andiroba	Andiroba	*Carapa guianensis*
Andrequicé	Andrequicé	*Leersia hexandra*
Angelim	Angelim	*Hymenolobium* spp.
Angelim vermelho	Angelim vermelho	*Dinizia excelsa*
Aninga	Arum	*Montrichardia linifera*
Arara-canga	Arara-canga	?
Arroz bravo	Wild rice	*Oryza* spp.
Arumã	Arumã	*Ischnosiphon obliquus*
Arumã-rana	Arumã-rana	*Thalia geniculata*
Assacu	Assacu	*Hura crepitans*
Aturiá	Aturiá	*Macherium lunatum*
Babaçu	Babaçu palm	*Attalea speciosa*
Bacaba	Bacaba palm	*Oenocarpus distichus* and *O. bacaba*
Bacuri	Bacuri	*Rheedia benthamiana*
Bacuripari	Bacuripari	*Rheedia* cf. *macrophylla*
Baleira	Baleira	?
Brachiarão	Brachiarão	*Brachiaria brizantha*
Buçú	Buçú palm	*Manicaria saccifera*
Buriti, miriti	Buriti palm	*Mauritia flexousa*

LOCAL	ENGLISH	SCIENTIFIC
Cacau jacaré	Caiman cacao	*Theobroma mariae*
Caju	Cashew	*Anacardium occidentale*
Caju-açu, cajuí	Caju-açu	*Anacardium giganteum*
Cajuí do campo	Cajuí do campo	*Anacardium microcarpum*
Camutim	Camutim	*Mouriri grandiflora*
Canarana	Canarana	*Echinochloa polystachya*
Canarana erecta lisa	Canarana erecta lisa	*Echinochloa pyramidalis*
Capim arroz	Capim arroz	*Panicum zizanioides*
Caraipé	Caraipé	*Licania* sp.
Caraná	Caraná palm	*Mauritiella carana*
Caroba	Caroba	*Tecoma caraiba*
Caxinguba	Caxinguba	*Ficus anthelminthica*
Cedro	Cedar	*Cedrela odorata*
Ceru	Ceru	*Allantoma lineata*
Cipó morcego, morceginho	Bat vine	*Bignonia vespertilia*
Ciriúba	Black mangrove	*Avicennia germinans*
Coatá	Coatá	*Bromelia* cf. *karatas*
Côco	Coconut palm	*Cocos nucifera*
Coentro	Coriander	*Coriandrum sativum*
Colonião	Guinea grass	*Panicum maximum*
Conde	Custard apple	*Annona reticulata*
Cubiu	Cubiu, Tupiro	*Solanum sessiliflorum*
Cuia	Calabash gourd	*Crescentia cujete*
Cumaru	Cumaru	*Dipteryx odorata*
Embaúba	Cecropia	*Cecropia* spp.
Envira	Envira	Various genera and species
Faveira	Faveira	Species of *Parkia* and *Enterolobium*
Frecha, flecheira	Arrowcane	*Gynerium sagittatum*
Graviola	Soursop	*Annona muricata*
Guaraná	Guaraná	*Paullinia cupana*
Inajá	Inajá palm	*Attalea maripa*
Ingá costela	Ingá costela	*Inga capitata*
Itaúba	Itaúba	*Mezilaurus itauba*
Jacamin	Jacamin	*Aspidosperma inundatum*
Jacitara	Jacitara palm	*Desmoncus polyacanthos*

LOCAL	ENGLISH	SCIENTIFIC
Jambo	Malay apple	*Eugenia malaccensis*
Jambo rosa	Java apple	*Syzygium samarangense*
Jambu	Jambu	*Spilanthes oleracea*
Jiriparana	Jiriparana	?
Junco	Junco	*Heleocharis mutata*
Jupatí	Jupatí palm	*Raphia taedigera*
Jussara	Jussara palm	*Euterpe edulis*
Jutaí	Jutaí	*Hymenaea* spp.
Jutaí do igapó	Jutaí	*Hymenaea palustris*
Lacre	Lacre	*Vismia guianensis*
Louro vermelho	Louro vermelho	*Ocotea rubra*
Macacaúba	Macacaúba	*Platymiscium ulei*
Maçaranduba	Maçaranduba	*Manilkara huberi*
Mamoncillo, pitomba das Guianas	Mamoncillo	*Melicoccus bijugatus*
Mandioqueira	Mandioqueira	*Qualea* sp.
Mangaba	Mangaba	*Hancornia speciosa*
Mangue	Red mangrove	*Rhizophora mangle*
Marajá	Marajá palm	*Bactris brongniartii*
Maúba	Maúba	*Licaria mahuba*
Maxixe	West Indian gherkin	*Cucumis anguria*
Mucajá	Mucajá palm	*Acrocomia aculeata*
Murici	Nance	*Byrsonima crassifolia*
Murumuru	Murumuru palm	*Astrocaryum murumuru*
Mututí	Mututí	*Pterocarpus officinalis*
Pacapéua	Pacapéua	*Swartzia racemosa*
Paracaxi	Paracaxi	*Pentaclethra macroloba*
Parápará	Parápará	*Cordia tetrandra*
Patauá	Patauá palm	*Oenocarpus bataua*
Pau d'arco, ipê	Pau d'arco, ipê	*Tabebuia serratifolia*
Pau mulato	Pau mulato	*Calycophyllum spruceanum*
Paxiúba	Paxiúba palm	*Socratea exorrhiza*
Piquiá	Piquiá	*Caryocar villosum*
Pitaíca	Pitaíca	*Swartzia acuminata*
Pitomba	Pitomba	*Simarouba versicolor*
Pracuúba	Pracuúba	*Lecointea amazonica*
Pupunha	Peach palm	*Bactris gasipaes*

COMMON AND
SCIENTIFIC NAMES
OF PLANTS

LOCAL	ENGLISH	SCIENTIFIC
Quaruba	Quaruba	Various species and genera
Quicuio	Quicuio	*Brachiaria humidicola*
Salak	Salak palm	*Salacca edulis*
Salsa	Parsley	*Petroselinum sativum*
Seringa	Rubber	*Hevea brasiliensis*
Sororoca	Sororoca	*Ravenala guianensis*
Sumaúma	Kapok	*Ceiba pentandra*
Taboka	Taboka	*Guadua* sp.
Tamaquaré	Tamaquaré	*Caraipa densifolia*
Taperebá, cajá	Yellow mombim	*Spondias mombim*
Tarumã	Tarumã	*Vitex cymosa*
Tento	Tento	*Batesia floribunda*
Timbó	Timbó	*Derris* sp.
Tucumã	Tucumã palm	*Astrocaryum vulgare*
Ubim	Ubim palm	*Geonoma* sp.
Umarí	Umarí	*Poraqueiba paraensis*
Uriri	Uriri	?
Urucurana	Urucurana	*Hieronyma alchorneoides*
Urucuri	Urucuri palm	*Attalea phalerata*
Vassoura de botão	Vassoura de botão	*Borreria verticilata*
Ventosa	Ventosa	*Hernandia* spp.
Vinagreira da várzea	Vinagreira da várzea	*Hibiscus* sp.
Virola, ucuúba	Virola	*Virola surinamensis*

APPENDIX 2

Common and Scientific Names of Animals

LOCAL	ENGLISH	SCIENTIFIC
Fish		
Apaíari	Oscar	*Astronotus ocellatus*
Aracu cavalo	Aracu cavalo	*Leporinus* sp.
Bacu pedra	Bacu pedra	*Lithodoras dorsalis*
Cachorro do Padre, cachorrinho do Padre, anijá, anujá	Priest's dog, Priest's puppy	*Auchenipterichthys* sp.
Dourada	Dourada	*Brachyplatystoma flavicans*
Gurijuba	Gurijuba	*Arius parkeri*
Jandiá	Jandiá	*Leiarius marmoratus*
Mandí	Mandí	*Pimelodus* sp.
Pirarucu	Pirarucu	*Arapaima gigas*
Tambaqui	Tambaqui	*Colossoma macropomum*
Tamoatá	Tamoatá	*Hoplesternum littorale*
Traíra	Traíra	*Hoplias malabaricus*
Xareu	Jack	*Oligoplites* sp.
Crustaceans		
Carangueijo	Carangueijo	*Ucides cordatus*
Camarão da região	Shrimp	*Machrobrachium amazonicum*
Pitú, lagostinho	Pitú	*Machrobrachium carcinus*
Siri	Siri	*Callinectes bocourti*
Mollusks		
Turu	Shipworm	*Neoteredo reynei*
Reptiles		
Camaleão	Iguana	*Iguana iguana*
Jabutí	Red-footed tortoise	*Geochelone carbonaria*

LOCAL	ENGLISH	SCIENTIFIC
Jacaré-açu	Black caiman	*Melanosuchus niger*
Jacaré-curuá	Smooth-fronted caiman	*Paleosuchus trigonatus*
Jacaré-tinga	Spectacled caiman	*Caiman crocodilus*
Jacurarú	Jacurarú	*Tupinambis teguixin*
Jacuruxi	Caiman lizard	*Dracaena guianensis*
Jiboiá	Boa constrictor	*Boa constrictor*
Matamatá	Matamatá	*Chelus fimbriatus*
Muçuã	Scorpion mud turtle	*Kinosternon scorpioides*
Muçuã-lalá	Twist-neck turtle	*Platemys platycephala*
Perema	Perema	*Rhinoclemys punctularia*
Tartaruga	Giant river turtle	*Podocnemis expansa*
Tracajá	Yellow-spotted Amazon turtle	*Podocnemis unifilis*

Birds

Cauauá	Maguari stork	*Ciconia maguari*
Curicaca	Buff-necked ibis	*Theristicus caudatus*
Galego	Pale-vented pigeon	*Columba cayennenis*
Garça	Great egret	*Casmerodius albus*
Marreca	Black-bellied tree duck	*Dendrocygna autumnalis*
Mergulhão	Neotropic cormorant	*Phalacrocorax brasilianus*
Socó	Rufescent tiger heron	*Tigrisoma lineatum*
Téu-téu	Southern lapwing	*Vanellus chilensis*
Tuiuiú	Jabiru stork	*Jabiru mycteria*
Urubu	Black vulture	*Coragyps atratus*

Mammals

Caitetu	Collared peccary	*Tayassu tajacu*
Capivara	Capybara	*Hydrochaeris hydrochaeris*
Cutia	Agouti	*Dasyprocta* sp.
Galheiro	White-tailed deer	*Odocoileus virginianus*
Onça pintada	Jaguar	*Panthera onca*
Onça vermelha	Puma	*Felis concolor*
Paca	Paca	*Agouti paca*
Queixada	White-lipped peccary	*Tayassu pecari*
Soiyá	Spiny rat	*Proechimys steereii*
Tamanduá bandeira	Giant anteater	*Myrmecophaga tridactyla*
Tatu	Nine-banded armadillo	*Dasypus novemcinctus*
Veado	Red brocket deer	*Mazama americana*

Notes

CHAPTER 1

1. L. Agassiz, *A Journey in Brazil* (Boston: Houghton, Mifflin and Company, 1896), 139.

2. Quoted in J. Lorimer, *English and Irish Settlement on the River Amazon, 1550–1646* (London: Hakluyt Society, 1989), 137.

3. Ibid., 142.

4. A maré esta muito braba, tá cheio de pororoca
   Vai passando as ondas doidas, vai passando as gaivotas

   Vem cá prá ver as gaivotas pousar
   Depois que passa as pororocas do mar

   From CD: *Música e o Pará: Carimbó de Marapanim*

CHAPTER 2

1. *Discurso recitado pelo Exmo. Sr. Desembargador Manoel Paranhos da Silva Vellozo, Presidente da Provincia do Pará, na Abertura da Primeira Sessão da Quarta Legislatura da Assembléa Provincial no dia 15 de Agosto de 1844* (Belém: Typographia de Santos, 1844).

2. P. Marcoy, *A Journey across South America from the Pacific Ocean to the Atlantic Ocean* (London: Blackie and Son, 1873), 4:490.

3. Ibid., 480.

4. Pedro Vicente de Azevedo, *Relatorio apresentado ao Exm. Senr. Dr. Francisco Maria Corrêa de Sá e Benevides pelo Exm. Senr. Dr. Pedro Vicente de Azevedo por occasião de Passar-lhe Administração da Provincia do Pará no dia 17 de janeiro de 1875* (Belém, 1875).

CHAPTER 3

1. Quoted in J. Lorimer, *English and Irish Settlement on the River Amazon, 1550–1646* (London: Hakluyt Society, 1989), 273.

CHAPTER 4

1. N. I. Vavilov, *Five Continents* (Rome: International Plant Genetic Resources Institute, 1997), 142.

2. H. H. Smith, *Brazil, the Amazons and the Coast* (New York: Charles Scribner's Sons, 1879), 44.

3. Quoted in J. Lorimer, *English and Irish Settlement on the River Amazon, 1550–1646* (London: Hakluyt Society, 1989), 136.

Chapter 5

1. G. P. Marsh, 1882. *The Earth as Modified by Human Action* (New York: Charles Scribner's Sons, 1882), 343. The first edition of Marsh's book appeared in 1870. The history of civilization's often aggressive attitude toward forests is also explored in J. Perlin, *A Forest Journey: The Role of Wood in the Development of Civilization* (New York: W. W. Norton, 1989).

2. Pitomba (*Taliisia esculenta*). For a discussion of the origins and distribution of this species, see P. Cavalcante, *Frutas Comestíveis da Amazônia* (Belém: CEJUP, 1996).

3. T. Roosevelt, *Through the Brazilian Wilderness* (New York: Charles Scribner's Sons, 1926), 290–91.

Chapter 6

1. "Não existe cultura alguma e não ha outra indústria e occupação além do fabrico de borracha." Pedro Vicente de Azevedo, *Relatorio apresentado ao Exm. Senr. Dr. Francisco Maria Corrêa de Sá e Benevides pelo Exm. Senr. Dr. Pedro Vicente de Azevedo por occasião de Passar-lhe Administração da Provincia do Pará no dia 17 de janeiro de 1875* (Belém, 1875).

2. M. Mauris, "At the Mouth of the Amazons," *Harper's* 58 (1879): 365–79.

3. The sugarcane mill near Abaetetuba is Engenho Caprixo along Furo Grande on a floodplain island of the lower Tocantins (01° 46.74 S, 49° 01.59 W). The mill near Igarapé-Miri is Engenho São João, Furo do Seco, about five kilometers upstream from the town (1° 54.85 S, 49° 01.98 W).

4. Na remansosa paz da rustica fazenda
   Á luz quente ao sól e á fria luz do luar
   Vive, como a expiar uma culpa tremenda
   O engenho da madeira a gemear e a chorar
   Ruge e range rouquenha a rigia moenda
   E ringindo e rangendo a canna á triturar
   Parece que tem alma, adivinha e desvenda
   A ruina, a dor, o mal, que vae talvez causar

   Movida pelos bois tardos e somnolentos
   Geme, somo a exprimir em doridos lamentos
   Que as desgraças por vir
   Sabe todas de cór

   Ai! Dos seus tristes ais! Ai! Moenda arrependida
   Alcool! para esqueceros tormentos da vida
   E cavar, sabe Deus! Um tormento maior

   Costa e Silva, "O engenho," *Publicação Semanal
   do Município de Muaná* 7, no. 276 (1928): 1.

CHAPTER 8

1. Cachorro do padre is known as anujá along the Rio Cajueiro in the municipality of Chaves.

2. R. H. Schomburgk, *Fishes of British Guiana, Part I* (Edinburgh: W. H. Lizards, 1841).

3. Beach rock is sandstone impregnated with iron oxide, hence its dark red color. Water rich in iron compounds seeps into the porous sandstone and eventually dries out, leaving behind the iron, which then oxidizes. Alternating wet and dry periods occurred during the Pleistocene, but some of the beach rock could be older than one million years. Also known as duricrust, beach rock occurs in sizable blocks sporadically in upland parts of the Amazon estuary, often where waves are eroding the headland. Wave action breaks the boulders and wears them down to a size manageable for building or for use as shrimp trap weights.

CHAPTER 9

1. H. W. Bates, *The Naturalist on the River Amazons* (London: John Murray, 1863), 1:203.

2. G. Edmundson, *Journal of the Travels and Labours of Father Samuel Fritz in the River of the Amazons between 1686 and 1723*, 2d ser., no. 51 (London: Hakluyt Society, 1922), 146.

CHAPTER 10

1. P. Adalbert, *Travels of His Royal Highness Prince Adalbert of Prussia in the South of Europe and in Brazil, with a Voyage Up the Amazon and Xingu*, vol. 1 (London: David Bogue, 1849), 158.

Further Reading

CHAPTER I

ON THE MIXING OF SALT AND FRESHWATERS AND IMPACTS ON FISHERIES

Barthem, R. B. 1985. Ocorrência, distribuição e biologia dos peixes da Baia de Marajó, estuário Amazônico. *Boletim do Museu Paraense Emílio Goeldi, Série Zoologia* 2 (1): 49–69.

Barthem, R. B., and H. O. Schwassmann. 1994. Amazon River influences over the seasonal displacement of the salty wedges in the Tocantins estuary, Brazil, 1983–1985. *Boletim do Museu Paraense Emílio Goeldi, Série Zoologia* 10 (1): 119–13.

Egler, W. A., and H. O. Schwassmann. 1964. Limnological studies in the Amazon estuary. *Verhandlungen Internationale Verienigung Theoretische und Angewandte Limnolologie* 15: 1059–66.

Ryther, J. H., D. W. Menzel, and N. Corwin. 1967. Influence of the Amazon River outflow on the ecology of the western tropical Atlantic. I. Hydrography and nutrient chemistry. *Journal of Marine Research* 25 (1): 69–83.

ON THE POROROCA TIDAL BORE

Fritsch, P. 2000. On Brazil's pororoca, the ride is risky and totally gnarly: Surfers love the tidal wave that runs up the Amazon; rogue logs and icky fish. *Wall Street Journal*, 27 March, A1, A17.

Lynch, D. 1982. Tidal bores. *Scientific American* 247 (4): 146–56.

ON THE SPECIES COMPOSITION, DISTRIBUTION, AND THREATS TO MANGROVES

Almeida, S. S. 1996. Identificação, avaliação e impactos ambientais e uso da flora em Manguezais Paraenses. *Boletim do Museu Paraense Emílio Goeldi, Série Ciências da Terra* 8: 93–100.

Almeida, S. S. 1996. Estrutura e florística em áreas de Manguezais Paraenses: Evidências da influência do estuário Amazônico. *Boletim do Museu Paraense Emílio Goeldi, Série Ciências da Terra* 8: 93–100.

Bastos, M. N. C., and L. C. B. Lobato. 1996. Estudos fitossociológicos em áreas de bosque de mangue na Praia do Crispim e Ilha de Algodoal-Pará. *Boletim do Museu Paraense Emílio Goeldi, Série Ciência da Terra* 8: 157–67.

Gama, J. R. V., M. P. M. Bentes, and M. M. Tourinho. 1996. Composição e fitossociologia de um ecossistema de mangue no Nordeste Paraense. In *Anais do Workshop sobre as Potencialidades de uso do Ecossistema de Várzeas da Amazônia*, 1:114–20. Manaus: EMBRAPA.

ON THE DISCHARGE AND SEDIMENT LOAD OF THE AMAZON AT ITS MOUTH

Eisma, D., and H. W. Van der Marel. 1971. Marine muds along the Guyana coast and their origin from the Amazon basin. *Contributions to Mineralogy and Petrology* 31: 321–34.

Gibbs, R. J. 1967. The geochemistry of the Amazon River system: Part I. The factors that control the salinity and composition and concentration of the suspended solids. *Bulletin of the Geological Society of America* 78: 1203–32.

Gibbs, R. J. 1971. Amazon River: Environmental factors that control its dissolved and suspended load. *Science* 156: 1734–37.

Grabert, H. 1983. Der Amazonas-Geschichte eines Stromes zwischen Pazifik und Atlantik. *Natur und Museum* 113 (3): 6–70.

Meade, R. H. 1994. Suspended sediments of the modern Amazon and Orinoco rivers. *Quaternary International* 21: 29–39.

Meade, R. H., T. Dunne, J. E. Richey, U. M. Santos, and E. Salati. 1985. Storage and remobilization of suspended sediment in the lower Amazon River of Brazil. *Science* 228: 488–90.

Meade, R. H., C. F. Nordin, W. F. Curtis, F. M. C. Rodrigues, C. M. Vale, and J. M. Edmond. 1979. Transporte de sedimentos no rio Amazonas. *Acta Amazonica* 9 (3): 543–47.

Milliman, J. D., and R. H. Meade. 1983. World-wide delivery of river sediment to the oceans. *Journal of Geology* 91 (1): 1–21.

Prost, M. T. R., and B. V. Rabelo. 1996. Variabilidade fito-espacial de manguezais litorâneos e dinâmica costeira: Exemplos da Guiana Francesa, Amapá e Pará. *Boletim do Museu Paraense Emílio Goeldi, Série Ciência da Terra* 8: 101–21.

Sternberg, H. O'R. 1975. *The Amazon River of Brazil*. Wiesbaden: Franz Steiner.

On the geologic history of the Amazon

Ackerman, F. L. 1964. *Geologia e Fisiografia da Região Bragantina (Estado do Pará)*. Cadernos da Amazônia No. 2. Manaus: INPA.

Bigarella, J. J., and G. O. Andrade. 1965. Contribution to the study of the Brazilian Quaternary. *Geological Society of America, Special Paper* 84: 433–51.

Frailey, C. D., E. L. Lavina, A. Rancy, and J. P. Souza Filho. 1988. A proposed Pleistocene/Holocene lake in the Amazon Basin and its significance to Amazonian geology and biogeography. *Acta Amazonica* 18 (3–4): 119–43.

Francisco, B. H., P. Loewenstein, O. F. Silva, and G. G. Silva. 1971. Contribuição à geologia da fôlha de São Luís (SA-23), no Estado do Pará, III: Estratigrafia; IV: Recursos minerais. *Boletim do Museu Paraense Emílio Goeldi, Nova Série, Geologia* 17: 1–40.

Grabert, H. 1983. The Amazon shearing system. *Tectonophysics* 95: 329–36.

Haseman, J. D. 1912. Some factors of geographical distribution in South America. *Annals of the New York Academy of Sciences* 22: 9–112.

Hoorn, C. 1996. Miocene deposits in the Amazon. *Science* 273: 122.

Hoorn, C., J. Guerrero, G. A. Sarmiento, and M. A. Lorente. 1995. Andean tectonics as a cause for changing patterns in Miocene northern South America. *Geology* 23 (3): 237–40.

Huber, J. 1943. Contribuição à geografia física dos furos de Breves e da parte ocidental de Marajó. *Revista Brasileira de Geografia* 5 (3): 449–74.

Lundberg, J. G., L. G. Marshall, J. Guerrero, B. Horton, M. C. S. L. Malabarba, and F. Wesselingh. 1998. The stage for Neotropical fish diversification: A history of tropical South American rivers. In *Phylogeny and Classification of Neotropical Fishes*, edited by L. R. Malabarda, R. E. Reis, R. P. Vari, Z. M. S. Lucena, and C. A. S. Lucena, 13–48. Porto Alegre: EDIPUCRS.

Räsänen, M. E., A. M. Linna, J. C. R. Santos, and F. R. Negri. 1995. Late Miocene tidal deposits in the Amazonian foreland basin. *Science* 269: 386–90.

Reclus, E. 1900. *Estados Unidos do Brasil: Geographia, Ethnographia, Estatistica*. Rio de Janeiro: H. Garnier.

Sioli, H. 1966. General features of the delta of the Amazon. In *Proceedings of the Symposium on Humid Tropics Research: Scientific Problems of the Humid Tropical Zone Deltas and their Implications* (Dacca, 1964), 381–90. Paris: UNESCO.

Sioli, H. 1968. Hydrochemistry and geology in the Brazilian Amazon region. *Amazonia* 1 (3): 267–77.

ON THE ANTHROPOGENIC NATURE OF SAVANNAS

Wallace, A. R. 1853. *A Narrative of Travels on the Amazon and Rio Negro, with an Account of the Native Tribes, and Observations on the Climate, Geology, and Natural History of the Amazon Valley*. London: Reeve and Co.

ON THE IMPORTANCE OF MANGROVES FOR SHRIMP NURSERIES

Silva, L. M. A., and V. J. L. Nahum. 1997. Ocorrência e estrutura das populações de camarões (Crustacea, Decapoda), no estuário do Rio Caeté, Município de Bragança, Pará, Brasil. In *Resumos do Terceiro Workshop Internacional Dinâmica e Recomendações para Manejo em Áreas de Manguezais de Bragança, Pará, 11 a 12 de novembro de 1997*, 11–12. Belém: MADAM.

ON THREATS TO MANGROVES

West, R. C. 1956. Mangrove swamps of the Pacific Coast of Colombia. *Annals of the Association of American Geographers* 46: 98–121.

CHAPTER 2

ON BAMBOOS AS INDICATORS OF HABITAT DISTURBANCE

Judziewicz, E. J., L. G. Clark, X. Londoño, and M. J. Stern. 1999. *American Bamboos*. Washington, D.C.: Smithsonian Institution Press.

Soderstrom, T. R., and C. E. Calderón. 1979. A commentary on the bamboos (Poaceae: Bambusiodeae). *Biotropica* 11 (3): 161–72.

ON FERAL PINEAPPLE

Meggers, B. J., and C. Evans. 1957. *Archeological Investigations at the Mouth of the Amazon*. Smithsonian Institution, Bureau of American Ethnology, Bulletin 167. Washington, D.C.

ON INDIGENOUS SETTLEMENTS IN THE AMAZON ESTUARY

Braga, T. 1945. *Apostillas de História do Pará*. Belém: Imprensa Oficial do Estado.

Hartt, C. F. 1871. The ancient Indian pottery of Marajó, Brazil. *American Naturalist* 5 (8): 259–71.

Lorimer, J. 1989. *English and Irish Settlement on the River Amazon, 1550–1646*. London: Hakluyt Society.

Meggers, B. J., and C. Evans. 1957. *Archeological Investigations at the Mouth of the Amazon*. Smithsonian Institution, Bureau of American Ethnology, Bulletin 167. Washington, D.C.

Roosevelt, A. C. 1987. Chiefdoms in the Amazon and Orinoco. In *Chiefdoms in the Americas*, edited by R. D. Drennan and C. A. Uribe, 153–84. Lanham, Md.: University Press of America.

Roosevelt, A. C. 1991. *Moundbuilders of the Amazon: Geophysical Archaeology on Marajó Island, Brazil*. San Diego: Academic Press.

Schaan, D. P. 1997. *A Linguagem Iconográfica da Cerâmica Marajoara*. Porto Alegre: EDIPUCRS.

Schaan, D. P. 2000. Recent investigations on Marajoara culture, Marajó Island, Brazil. *Antiquity* 74: 469–70.

On steamship navigation in the Amazon

Lamare, J. R. 1867. *Relatorio apresentado á Assembéa Legislativa Provincial por S. Exc. O Sr. Vice-Almirante e Conselheiro de Guerra Joaquim Raymundo de Lamare, Presidente da Provincia, em 15 de agosto de 1867*. Belém: Typographia de Frederico Brossard.

Le Cointe, P. 1922. *L'Amazonie Brésilienne: Le Pays-ses Habitants, ses Resources, Notes et Statistiques jusqu'en 1920*. Paris: Augustin Challamel.

Melby, J. F. 1942. The rubber river: An account of the rise and collapse of the Amazon boom. *Hispanic American Historical Review* 22 (3): 452–69.

On the environmental consequences of steamship navigation

Marcoy, P. 1873. *A Journey across South America from the Pacific Ocean to the Atlantic Ocean*. Vol. 4. London: Blackie and Son.

CHAPTER 3

On the introduction and growth of cattle and water buffalo herds

Arima, E. Y., and C. Uhl. 1997. Ranching in the Brazilian Amazon in a national context: Economics, policy, and practice. *Society & Natural Resources* 10: 433–51.

Dias, M. N. 1970. *A Companhia Geral do Grão Pará e Maranhão (1755–1778)*. Coleção Amazônica, Série José Veríssimo. Belém: Universidade Federal do Pará.

Ferreira Penna, D. S. 1876. *A Ilha de Marajó*. Belém: Tip. do Diário do Grão-Pará.

Lange, A. 1914. *The Lower Amazon*. New York: Putnam's Sons.

Le Cointe, P. 1918. *A Industria Pastoril na Amazonia, Particularmente no Baixo-Amazonas*. Belém: Imprensa Official do Estado.

Le Cointe, P. 1922. *L'Amazonie Brésilienne: Le Pays-ses Habitants, ses Resources, Notes et Statistiques jusqu'en 1920*. Vol. 2. Paris: Augustin Challamel.

Lima, R. R. 1994. *Várzeas da Amazônia Brasileira: Principais Características e Possibilidades*. Belém: Faculdade de Ciências Agrárias do Pará.

Marajó, J. C. 1992. *As Regiões Amazônicas: Estudos Chorographicos dos Estados do Gram Pará e Amazônas*. Belém: Secretaria de Estado da Cultura.

Miranda, N. 1993. *Marajó: Desafio da Amazônia*. Belém: CEJUP.

Reis, A. C. F. 1957. *A Amazônia que os Portugueses Revelaram*. Rio de Janeiro: MEC.

Teixeira, J. F. 1953. *O Arquipélago de Marajó*. Rio de Janeiro: Instituto Brasileiro de Geografia e Estatística.

ON MORTALITY OF CATTLE DURING THE DRY SEASON

Ferreira, A. R. 1964. Notícia histórica da Ilha de Joanes ou Marajó. *Revista do Livro* 7: 145–64.

Lustosa, A. A. 1976. *No Estuário Amazônico "À Margem da Visita Pastoral."* Belém: Conselho Estadual de Cultura do Pará.

ON CATTLE AND WATER BUFFALO BREEDS

Maule, J. P. 1990. *The Cattle of the Tropics.* Edinburgh: Centre for Tropical Veterinary Medicine, University of Edinburgh.

Payne, W. J. A., and J. Hodges. 1997. *Tropical Cattle: Origins, Breeds and Breeding Policies.* Oxford: Blackwell Science.

Soares, L. C. 1949. Vaqueiros do Marajó. In *Tipos e aspectos do Brasil: Ilustrações do Percy Lau.* Rio de Janeiro: Instituto Brasileiro de Geografia e Estatística.

FURTHER READING

ON CATTLE RUSTLING

Acatauassú, D. 1998. *Marajó Minha Vida.* Belém: Cejup.

Ferreira Penna, D. S. 1876. *A Ilha de Marajó.* Belém: Tip. do Diário do Grão-Pará.

Gallo, G. 1977. *Marajó: A Ditadura da Água.* Cachoeira do Arari: Edições o Museu do Marajó.

Teixeira, J. F. 1953. *O Arquipélago de Marajó.* Rio de Janeiro: Instituto Brasileiro de Geografia e Estatística.

Viana, J. 1955. *A Fazenda Aparecida.* Belém: Gráfica Falangola Editôra.

ON SOURCES OF BEEF FOR THE BELÉM MARKET

Camargo, F. C. 1948. *Sugestões para o Soerguimento Econômico do Vale Amazônico.* Belém: Instituto Agronômico do Norte.

DDR/OEA. 1974. *Marajó: Um Estudo para Seu Desenvolvimento.* Washington, D.C.: Departamento de Desenvolvimento Regional, Estado do Pará/Organização dos Estados Americanos.

Lange, A. 1914. *The Lower Amazon.* New York: Putnam's Sons.

Lemos, A. J. 1907. *O Municipio de Belém: Relatorio apresentado ao Conselho Municipal de Belém, Capital do Estado do Pará.* Belém: Archivo da Intendencia Municipal.

Penteado, A. R. 1968. *Problemas de Colonização e do uso da Terra na Região Bragantina do Estado do Pará.* Lisbon: Centro de Estudos Vasco da Gama, Sociedade de Geografia de Lisboa.

Rahan, H. 1857. *Relatorio apresentado á Assemblea Legislativa Provincial do Pará no dia 15 de agosto de 1857 por Occasião da Abertura da Segunda Sessão da Decima Legislatra da mesma Assembéa, pelo Presidente Henrique de Beuarepaire Rahan.* Belém: Typographia de Santos.

ON THE AMOUNT OF CATTLE SLAUGHTERED FOR THE BELÉM MARKET

Araújo, H. C. 1922. *A Prophylaxia Rural no Estado do Pará.* Belém: Typographia da Livraria Gillet.

Azevedo, P. V. 1875. *Relatorio apresentado ao Exm. Senr. Dr. Francisco Maria Corrêa de Sá e Benevides pelo Exm. Senr. Dr. Pedro Vicente de Azevedo por occasião de Passar-lhe Administração da Provincia do Pará no dia 17 de janeiro de 1875.* Belém.

Lemos, A. J. 1907. *O Municipio de Belém: Relatorio apresentado ao Conselho Municipal de Belém, Capital do Estado do Pará.* Belém: Archivo da Intendencia Municipal.

Marajó, J. C. 1992. *As Regiões Amazônicas: Estudos Chorographicos dos Estados do Gram Pará e Amazônas.* Belém: Secretaria de Estado da Cultura.

On exports of Brazilian beef

Brazil: Harvesting farming's potential. *The Economist* 9 (September 2000): 36–37.

On schooling opportunities on ranches

Acatauassú, D. 1998. *Marajó Minha Vida.* Belém: cejup.

On the introduction and diseases of horses on Marajó

Ferreira Penna, D. S. 1876. *A Ilha de Marajó.* Tip. do Diário do Grão-Pará, Belém.

On the sale of horses from Marajó

Spix, J. B., and C. F. P. Martius. 1976. *Viagem pelo Brasil, 1817–1820.* Vol. 3. São Paulo: Edições Melhoramentos.

On the antiquity of pigs in the Amazon

Lorimer, J. 1989. *English and Irish Settlement on the River Amazon, 1550–1646.* London: Hakluyt Society.

On the diet and value of pigs

Anderson, A. B., and E. M. Ioris. 1992. Valuing the rain forest: Economic strategies by small-scale forest extractivists in the Amazon estuary. *Human Ecology* 20 (3): 337–69.

Anderson, A. B., A. Gely, J. Strudwick, G. L. Sobel, and M. G. C. Pinto. 1985. Um sistema agroflorestal na várzea do estuário Amazônico (Ilha das Onças, Município de Bacarena, Estado do Pará). *Acta Amazonica,* Supl. 15 (1–2): 195–224.

Carney, J., and M. Hiraoka. 1997. *Raphia taedigera* in the Amazon estuary. *Principes* 41 (3): 125–30.

On the introduction of sheep and goats

Smyth, W., and F. Lowe. 1836. *Narrative of a Journey from Lima to Pará, across the Andes and Down the Amazon.* London: John Murray.

CHAPTER 4

On transformation of the estuary into a cultural forest

Anderson, A. B., and E. M. Ioris. 1992. Valuing the rain forest: Economic strategies by small-scale forest extractivists in the Amazon estuary. *Human Ecology* 20 (3): 337–69.

Hiraoka, M. 1993. Mudanças nos padrões econômicos de uma população ribeirinha do estuário do Amazonas. In *Povos das Aguas: Realidade e Perspectivas na Amazônia,* edited by L. G. Furtado and W. Leitão, 133–57. Belém: Museu Paraense Emílio Goeldi.

Hiraoka, M. 1995. Land use change in the Amazon estuary. *Global Environmental Change* 5 (4): 323–36.

Hiraoka, M., and N. Hida. 1998. Human adaptation to the changing economy and ecology on the estuarine floodplain of the Amazon estuary. *Geographical Review of Japan* 71 (1): 45–58.

Huber, J. 1910. Mattas e madeiras amazônicas. *Boletim do Museu Goeldi de Historia Natural e Ethnographia* 6: 91–225.

Moran, E. F., E. Brondizio, and P. Mausel. 1994. Secondary succession. *National Geographic Research & Exploration* 10 (4): 458–76.

ON THE ANTIQUITY OF AÇAÍ IN THE LOCAL ECONOMY

Le Cointe, P. 1922. *L'Amazonie Brésilienne: Le Pays — ses Habitants, ses Resources, Notes et Statistiques jusqu'en 1920.* Vol. 1. Paris: Augustin Challamel.

Roosevelt, A. C. 1991. *Moundbuilders of the Amazon: Geophysical Archaeology on Marajó Island, Brazil.* San Diego: Academic Press.

ON PRODUCTION, CONSUMPTION, AND MANAGEMENT OF AÇAÍ

Anderson, A. B. 1990. Extraction and forest management by rural inhabitants in the Amazon estuary. In *Alternatives to Deforestation: Steps Toward Sustainable Use of the Amazon Rain Forest*, edited by Anthony B. Anderson, 65–85. New York: Columbia University Press.

Balick, M. J. 1984. Ethnobotany of palms in the Neotropics. *Advances in Economic Botany* 1: 9–23.

Brondizio, E. S., E. F. Moran, P. Mausel, and Y. Wu. 1994. Land use change in the Amazon estuary: Patterns of caboclo settlement and landscape management. *Human Ecology* 22 (3): 249–78.

Coradin, L., and E. Lleras. 1988. Overview of palm domestication in Latin America. *Advances in Economic Botany* 6: 175–89.

Gates, R. R. 1927. *A Botanist in the Amazon Valley: An Account of the Flora and Fauna in the Land of Floods.* London: H. F. & G. Witherby.

Jardim, M. A. G. 1996. Aspectos da produção extrativista do açaízeiro (*Euterpe oleracea* Mart.) no estuário Amazônico. *Boletim do Museu Paraense Emílio Goeldi, Série Botânica* 12 (1): 137–44.

Mesquita, S. A. J., and M. A. G. Jardim. 1996. Avaliação das populações nativas de açaízeiro (*Euterpe oleracea*) na comunidade do Rio Marajoí, Município de Gurupá (PA). *Boletim do Museu Paraense Emílio Goeldi, Série Botânica* 12 (2): 265–69.

Muñiz-Miret, N., R. Vamos, M. Hiraoka, F. Montagnini, and R. O. Mendelsohn. 1996. The economic value of managing açaí palm (*Euterpe oleracea* Mart.) in the floodplains of the Amazon estuary, Pará, Brazil. *Forest Ecology and Management* 87: 163–73.

Pollak, H., M. Mattos, and C. Uhl. 1995. A profile of palm heart extraction in the Amazon estuary. *Human Ecology* 23 (3): 357–85.

Sampaio, F. X. R. 1825. *Diário da Viagem que em Visita, e Correição, das Povações da Capitania de S. Joze do Rio Negro fez o Ouvidor, e Intendente Geral da Mesma, no Anno de 1774 e 1775.* Lisbon: Typographia da Academia.

Veríssimo, J. 1887. As populações indigenas e mestiças da Amazonia. *Revista Trimensal do Instituto Historico e Geographico Brazileiro* 50: 295–90.

ON DESTRUCTION OF AÇAÍ CAUSED BY THE HEART-OF-PALM INDUSTRY

Arima, Eugênio, N. Maciel, and C. Uhl. 1998. *Oportunidades para o Desenvolvimento do Estuário Amazônico.* Instituto do Homem e Meio Ambiente da Amazônia (IMAZON), Série Amazônia No. 15, Belém.

ON NONFOOD USES OF AÇAÍ

Anderson, A. B. 1988. Use and management of native forests dominated by açaí palm (*Euterpe oleracea* Mart.) in the Amazon Estuary. *Advances in Economic Botany* 6: 144–54.

Strudwick, J., and G. L. Sobel. 1988. Uses of *Euterpe oleracea* Mart. in the Amazon estuary, Brazil. *Advances in Economic Botany* 6: 225–53.

Van den Berg, M. E., and M. H. L. da Silva. 1986. Plantas medicinais do Amazonas. In *Anais do Primeiro Simpósio do Trópico Úmido, 12–17 November, Belém, Pará*, vol. 2, Flora e Floresta, 127–33. Brasília: EMBRAPA.

On the use of açaí seeds for mulch in Belém

Madaleno, I. 2000. Urban agriculture in Belém, Brazil. *Cities* 1 (1): 73–77.

On markets for açaí

Bezerra, J. A., and E. Souza. 2000. Açaí: Carga de energia. *Globo Rural*, Ano 16, No. 181.

On the fruiting behavior, nutritional value, and nonfood uses of buriti

Cavalcante, P. B., and D. Johnson. 1977. Edible palm fruits of the Brazilian Amazon. *Principes* 21 (3): 91–102.

Kahn, F. 1991. Palms as key swamp forest resources in Amazonia. *Forest Ecology and Management* 38: 133–42.

Le Cointe, P. 1922. *L'Amazonie Brésilienne: Le Pays-ses Habitants, ses Resources, Notes et Statistiques jusqu'en 1920*. Vol. 1. Paris: Augustin Challamel.

Milliken, W., R. P. Miller, S. R. Pollard, and E. V. Wandelli, 1992. *The Ethnobotany of the Waimiri Atroari Indians of Brazil*. Kew: Royal Botanic Gardens.

Plotkin, M. J., and M. J. Balick. 1984. Medicinal uses of South American palms. *Journal of Ethnopharmacology* 10: 157–79.

On supernatural protectors of buriti

Fock, N. 1963. *Waiwai: Religion and Society of an Amazonian Tribe*. Copenhagen: National Museum.

On the use of buçú fruits to attract collared peccary

Henderson, A., H. T. Beck, and A. Scariot. 1991. Flora de palmeiras da Ilha do Marajó, Pará, Brasil. *Boletim do Museu Paraense Emílio Goeldi, Série Botânica* 7 (2): 199–221.

On the nutritional value of buriti and tucumã

Aguiar, J. P. L., H. A. Marinho, Y. S. Rebêlo, and R. Shrimpton. 1980. Aspectos nutritivos de alguns frutos da Amazônia. *Acta Amazonica* 10 (4): 755–58.

Pechnik, E., I. V. Mattoso, J. M. Chaves, and P. Borges. 1947. Possibilidade de aplicação do buriti e tucumã na indústria alimentar. *Arquivos Brasileiros de Nutrição* 4 (1): 33–37.

Chapter 5

On domestication of indigenous "Cinderella" trees

Leakey, R. R. B. 1998. Agroforestry for biodiversity in farming systems. In *Biodiversity in Agroecosystems*, edited by W. W. Collins and C. O. Qualset, 127–45. New York: CRC.

ON THE DISTRIBUTION AND CHARACTERISTICS OF CERU NUT

Ducke, A. 1949. Árvores amazônicas e sua propagação: Adaptação de frutos ou sementes de árvores amazônicas a diversos meios de propagação em espécies de estreita afinidade botânica, porém em condições mesológicas diferentes. *Boletim do Museu Paraense Emílio Goeldi* 10: 81–92.

Prance, G. T., and S. A. Mori. 1979. *Lecythidaceae, Part 1: The Actinomorphic-flowered New World Lecythidaceae (Asteranthos, Gustavia, Grias, Allantoma, and Cariniana)*. Flora Neotropica Monograph 21. New York: New York Botanical Garden.

ON THE TAPPING OF MANGABA FOR LATEX

Polhaumus, L. G. 1962. *Rubber: Botany, Production, and Utilization*. London: Leonard Hill.

Wisniewski, A., and C. F. M. Melo. 1982. *Borrachas Naturais Brasileiras, III. Borracha de Mangabeira*. Belém: EMBRAPA.

CHAPTER 6

ON AGRICULTURAL INTENSIFICATION AND THE ROLE OF AGROFORESTRY

Brondizio, E. 1999. Agroforestry intensification in the Amazon estuary. In *Managing the Globalized Environment: Local Strategies to Secure Livelihoods*, edited by T. Granfelt, 88–113. London: Intermediate Technology Publications.

Laurance, W. F., M. A. Cochrane, S. Bergen, P. M. Fearnside, P. Delamônica, C. Barber, S. D'Angelo, T. Fernandes. 2000. The future of the Brazilian Amazon. *Science* 291: 438–39.

ON FLOODPLAIN FARMERS NOT BENEFITING FROM URBAN GROWTH IN THE AMAZON

Loureiro, V. R. 1985. *Os Parceiros do Mar: Natureza e Conflito Social na Pesca da Amazônia*. Belém: Museu Paraense Emílio Goeldi.

Sternberg, H. O'R. 1998. *A Água e o Homem na Várzea do Careiro*. Belém: Museu Paraense Emílio Goeldi.

ON THE DIVERSITY OF MANIOC CULTIVARS

Smith, N. J. H. 1999. *The Amazon River Forest: A Natural History of Plants, Animals, and People*. New York: Oxford University Press.

ON GOIÁS AS A MAJOR RICE-PRODUCING AREA OF BRAZIL

Katzman, M. T. 1975. Regional development policy in Brazil: The role of growth poles and development highways in Goiás. *Economic Development and Cultural Change* 24: 75–107.

ON THE INTRODUCTION, YIELDS, AND PRODUCTION OF ASIAN RICE IN THE AMAZON ESTUARY

Le Cointe, P. 1922. *L'Amazonie Brésilienne: Le Pays-ses Habitants, ses Resources, Notes et Statistiques jusqu'en 1920*. Vol. 1:297, vol. 2:173. Paris: Augustin Challamel.

Lima, R. R. 1956. A agricultura nas várzeas do estuário do Amazonas. *Boletim Técnico do Instituto Agronômico do Norte* 33: 1–164.

On the introduction of African rice to Brazil and the Amazon

Carney, J. A. 2001. *Black Rice: The African Origins of Rice Cultivation in the Americas.* Cambridge, Mass.: Harvard University Press.

Carney, J. A. 1998. The role of African rice and slaves in the history of rice cultivation in the Americas. *Human Ecology* 26: 525–45.

Le Cointe, P. 1922. *L'Amazonie Brésilienne: Le Pays-ses Habitants, ses Resources, Notes et Statistiques jusqu'en 1920.* Vol. 2:173. Paris: Augustin Challamel.

On punishment for cultivating red (African) rice

Dias, M. N. 1970. *A Companhia Geral do Grão Pará e Maranhão (1755–1778).* Coleção Amazônica, Série José Veríssimo. Belém: Universidade Federal do Pará. P. 435.

On the high quality of rice from Marajó

Ferreira, A. R. 1964. Notícia histórica da Ilha de Joanes ou Marajó. *Revista do Livro* 7: 145–64.

On rice exports from the Brazilian Amazon during the colonial period

MacLachlan, C. M. 1974. African slave trade and economic development in Amazônia. In *Slavery and Race Relations in Latin America*, edited by R. B. Toplin, 112–45. Westport, Conn.: Greenwood Press.

On pests of stored rice in the Amazon

Sefer, E. 1959. Pragas que ocorrem no Estado do Pará atacando produtos armazenados. *Boletim da Inspetoria Regional de Fomento Agrícola no Pará* 9: 23–35.

On the use of steam and water to power rice mills

Wallace, A. R. 1853. *A Narrative of Travels on the Amazon and Rio Negro, with an Account of the Native Tribes, and Observations on the Climate, Geology, and Natural History of the Amazon Valley.* London: Reeve and Co. P. 26.

On the antiquity of sugarcane to the Amazon

Betendorf, J. F. 1910. Chronica da missão dos padres da Companhia de Jesus no Estado do Maranhão. *Revista do Instituto Historico e Geografico Brazileiro* 72 (1): 1–682.

Edmundson, G. 1903. The Dutch on the Amazon and Negro in the seventeenth century. Part 1. Dutch trade on the Amazon. *English Historical Review* 18: 642–63.

Lorimer, J. 1989. *English and Irish Settlement on the River Amazon, 1550–1646.* London: Hakluyt Society.

On the technology of sugarcane mills

Galloway, J. H. 1989. *The Sugar Cane Industry: An Historical Geography from Its Origins to 1914.* New York: Cambridge University Press.

On cultivation of sugarcane by Catholic missions

Azevedo, J. L. 1901. Os Jesuitas no Grão-Pará: Suas Missões e a Colonização. Lisbon: Tavares Cardoso & Irmão.

Cruz, E. 1973. *História de Belém*. Belém: Universidade Federal do Pará.

Dias, M. N. 1970. *A Companhia Geral do Grão Pará e Maranhão (1755–1778)*. Coleção Amazônica, Série José Veríssimo. Belém: Universidade Federal do Pará.

Edmundson, G. 1922. *Journal of the Travels and Labours of Father Samuel Fritz in the River of the Amazons between 1686 and 1723*. 2d Series, No. 51. London: Hakluyt Society.

Ferreira, A. R. 1964. Notícia histórica da Ilha de Joanes ou Marajó. *Revista do Livro* 7: 145–64.

Leite, S. 1943. *História da Companhia de Jesus no Brasil*. Rio de Janeiro: Imprensa Nacional.

Lima, R. R. 1994. *Várzeas da Amazônia Brasileira: Principais Características e Possibilidades*. Belém: Faculdade de Ciências Agrárias do Pará.

Teixeira, J. F. 1953. *O Arquipélago de Marajó*. Rio de Janeiro: Instituto Brasileiro de Geografia e Estatística.

ON THE NUMBER, LOCATION, AND PRODUCTION OF SUGARCANE MILLS IN THE ESTUARY

Anderson, S. D. 1992. Engenhos na várzea: Uma análise do declínio de um sistema de produção tradicional na Amazônia. In *Amazônia: A Fronteira Agrícola 20 Anos Depois*, edited by P. Léna and A. E. Oliveira, 101–21. Belém: CEJUP.

Baena, M. 1885. *Informações sobre as Comarcas da Provincia do Pará Organizadas em Virtude do Aviso circular do Ministerio da Justiça de 20 de setembro de 1883, por Manoel Baena Director da 2a Secção da Secretaria da Presidencia da mesma Provincia*. Belém: Typ. de Francisco da Costa Junior.

Brusque, F. C. 1862. *Relatorio Apresentado A Assembéa Legislativa da Provincia do Pará na Primeira Sessão da XIII Lesgislatura pelo Exmo. Senr. Presidente da Provincia Dr Francisco Carlos de Araujo Brusque em 1 de setembro de 1862*. Belém: Typographia de Frederico Carlos Rhossard.

Cruz, E. 1973. *História de Belém*. Belém: Universidade Federal do Pará.

Hiraoka, M. 1993. Mudanças nos padrões econômicos de uma população ribeirinha do estuário do Amazonas. In *Povos das Aguas: Realidade e Perspectivas na Amazônia*, edited by L. G. Furtado and W. Leitão, 133–57. Belém: Museu Paraense Emílio Goeldi.

Le Cointe, P. 1922. *L'Amazonie Brésilienne: Le Pays-ses Habitants, ses Resources, Notes et Statistiques jusqu'en 1920*. Vol. 2:469. Paris: Augustin Challamel.

Lobato, E. 1976. *Camino de Canoa Pequena: História do Município de Igarapé-Miri*. Belém: Gráfica Falangola Editôra.

ON CACHAÇA IMPORTS INTO PARÁ

Brusque, F. C. 1862. *Relatorio Apresentado A Assembéa Legislativa da Provincia do Pará na Primeira Sessão da XIII Lesgislatura pelo Exmo. Senr. Presidente da Provincia Dr Francisco Carlos de Araujo Brusque em 1 de setembro de 1862*. Belém: Typographia de Frederico Carlos Rhossard.

ON IMPORTATION OF ANISE TO FLAVOR CACHAÇA

Spix, J. B., and C. F. P. Martius. 1976. *Viagem pelo Brasil, 1817–1820*. Vol. 3. São Paulo: Edições Melhoramentos.

ON THE NUTRITIONAL VALUE OF CUBIU

Yuyama, K. 1993. Underexploited Amazonian fruits. In *Investigations of Plant Genetic Resources in the Amazon Basin with the Emphasis on the Genus Oryza*, edited by H. Morishima and P. S. Martins,

63–74. São Paulo: Monbusho International Scientific Research Program, Japan/Research Support Foundation of the State of São Paulo.

CHAPTER 7

ON THE NUMBER OF SAWMILLS IN THE AMAZON

Barros, A. C., and C. Uhl. 1999. The economic and social significance of logging operations on the floodplains of the Amazon estuary and prospects for ecological sustainability. In *Várzea: Diversity, Development, and Conservation of Amazonia's Whitewater Floodplains*, edited by C. Padoch, J. M. Ayres, M. Pinedo-Vasquez, and A. Henderson, 153–68. New York: New York Botanical Garden Press.

Pandolfo, C. 1974. *Estudos Básicos para o Estabelecimento de uma Política de Desenvolvimento dos Recursos Florestais e do Uso Racional das Terras da Amazônia*. Belém: SUDAM.

ON LOGGING FOR VIROLA AND DEPLETION OF STOCKS

Anderson, A. B., I. Moussasticoshvily, and D. S. Macedo. 1999. Logging of *Virola surinamensis* in the Amazon floodplain: Impacts and alternatives. In *Várzea: Diversity, Development, and Conservation of Amazonia's Whitewater Floodplains*, edited by C. Padoch, J. M. Ayres, M. Pinedo-Vasquez, and A. Henderson, 119–33. New York: New York Botanical Garden Press.

Macedo, D.S., and A. B. Anderson. 1993. Early ecological changes associated with logging in an Amazon floodplain. *Biotropica* 25 (2): 151–63.

Stone, S. W. 1997. Economic trends in the timber industry of Amazonia: Survey results from Pará state, 1990–1995. *Journal of Developing Areas* 32: 97–122.

Uhl, C., P. Barreto, A. Veríssimo, E. Vidal, P. Amaral, A. C. Barros, C. Souza, Jr., and J. Gerwing. 1997. Natural resource management in the Brazilian Amazon. *Bioscience* 47 (3): 160–68.

ON SEED DISPERSAL OF VIROLA BY BIRDS

Howe, H. F., and E. E. Schupp. 1985. Early consequences of seed dispersal for a neotropical tree (*Virola surinamensis*). *Ecology* 66: 781–91.

Van Roosmalen, M. G. M., M. P. D. Bardales, and O. M. C. Garcia. 1996. Frutos da floresta Amazônica. Parte I: Myristicaceae. *Acta Amazônica* 26 (4): 209–64.

ON THE DUBIOUS ECONOMICS OF SUSTAINABLE MANAGEMENT OF AMAZONIAN FORESTS FOR TIMBER

Laurance, W. F. 1998. A crisis in the making: Responses of Amazonian forests to land use and climate change. *Trends in Ecology and Evolution* 13 (10): 411–15.

McRae, M. 1997. Is 'good wood' bad for forests? *Science* 275: 1868–69.

Rice, R. E., R. E. Gullison, and J. W. Reid. 1997. Can sustainable management save tropical forests? *Scientific American* 276 (4): 44–49.

CHAPTER 8

ON THE USE OF MOBILE FISHING FENCES IN THE NINETEENTH CENTURY

Edwards, W. H. 1847. *A Voyage up the River Amazon, including a Residence at Pará*. New York: Appleton.

ON SHIPWORM DAMAGE AND CONTROL EFFORTS

Cohen, A. N., and J. T. Carlton. 1995. *Nonindigenous Aquatic Species in a United States Estuary: A Case Study of the Biological Invasions of the San Francisco Bay and Delta*. Washington, D.C.: U.S. Fish and Wildlife Service.

Gruson, L. 1993. In a cleaner harbor, creatures eat the waterfront. *New York Times*, 27 June, 1, 32.

Landström, B. 1969. *Sailing Ships in Words and Pictures from Papyrus Boats to Full-riggers*. Doubleday, New York.

Quatrefages de Bréau, A. de. 1854. *Souvenirs d'un Naturaliste*. Vol. 2. Paris: Charpentier.

Turner, R. D. 1966. *A Survey and Illustrated Catalogue of the Teredinidae (Mollusca: Bivalvia)*. Cambridge, Mass.: Museum of Comparative Zoology, Harvard University.

ON SHIPWORM AS HUMAN FOOD

Smith, F. G. W. 1956. Shipworms, saboteurs of the sea. *National Geographic* 110 (4): 559–66.

ON THE ECOLOGY OF MANGROVE CRABS

Diele, K. 1997. Life history and population ecology of the mangrove crab *Ucides cordatus*: Preliminary results. In *Resumos do Terceiro Workshop Internacional Dinâmica e Recomendações para Manejo em Áreas de Manguezais de Bragança, Pará, 11 a 12 de novembro de 1997*, 47–50. Belém: madam.

ON THE SPIRITUAL GUARDIAN OF CRABS

Andrade, J. 1984. *Folclore na Região do Salgado, Pará: Teredos na Alimentação, Profissões Ribeirinhas*. São Paulo: Escola de Folclore.

CHAPTER 9

ON THE DIET OF THE BROCKET DEER

Bodmer, R. E. 1989. Frugivory in Amazonian artiodactyla: Evidence for the evolution of the ruminant stomach. *Journal of the Zoological Society of London* 219: 457–67.

ON THE DIET OF THE PECCARY

Bodmer, R. E. 1991. Strategies of seed dispersal and seed predation in Amazonian ungulates. *Biotropica* 23 (3): 255–61.

Henderson, A., H. T. Beck, and A. Scariot. 1991. Flora de palmeiras da Ilha do Marajó, Pará, Brasil. *Boletim do Museu Paraense Emílio Goeldi, Série Botânica* 7 (2): 199–221.

Kiltie, R. A. 1998l. Stomach contents of rain forest peccaries (*Tayassu tajacu* and *T. pecari*). *Biotropica* 13 (3): 234–36.

ON HUNTING BLACK-BELLIED TREE DUCKS USING CATTLE AS COVER

Lustosa, A. A. 1976. *No Estuário Amazônico "À Margem da Visita Pastoral."* Belém: Conselho Estadual de Cultura do Pará.

ON THE SLAUGHTER OF CAIMANS

Farabee, W. C. 1921. Explorations at the mouth of the Amazon. *Museum Journal* (University of Pennsylvania, Philadelphia) 12 (3): 142–61.

Fittkau, E. J. 1973. Crocodiles and the nutrient metabolism of Amazonian waters. *Amazoniana* 4 (1): 103–33.

Goeldi, E. A. 1902. Maravilhas da natureza na Ilha de Marajó (Rio Amazonas). *Boletim do Museu Paraense* 3: 370–99.

Rebêlo, G. H., and W. E. Magnusson. 1983. An analysis of the effect of hunting on *Caiman crocodilus* and *Melanosuchus niger* based on the sizes of confiscated skins. *Biological Conservation* 26: 95–104.

Wallace, A. R. 1853. *A Narrative of Travels on the Amazon and Rio Negro, with an Account of the Native Tribes, and Observations on the Climate, Geology, and Natural History of the Amazon Valley.* London: Reeve and Co. Pp. 37, 100, 104.

ON THE RATIO OF BLACK CAIMANS TO SPECTACLED CAIMANS

Best, R. C. 1984. The aquatic mammals and reptiles of the Amazon. In *The Amazon: Limnology and Landscape Ecology of a Mighty Tropical River and Its Basin,* edited by H. Sioli, 371–412. Dordrecht: W. Junk.

ON THE DANGER OF CAIMANS TO BATHERS

Edmundson, G. 1922. *Journal of the Travels and Labours of Father Samuel Fritz in the River of the Amazons between 1686 and 1723.* 2d Series, No. 51. London: Hakluyt Society.

Evreux, Y. 1864. *Voyage dans le Nord du Brésil fait durant les Années 1613 et 1614.* Leipzig: Librairie Franck.

CHAPTER 10

ON FOOT-AND-MOUTH DISEASE IN BRAZIL

Integrar a pecuária sul-americana. 2000. *Gazeta Mercantil* (São Paulo), 9 May, A2.

Schelp, D. 2001. Vamos escapar dessa? O Brasil salvou seu rebanho da vaca louca e agora monta um cerco contra a febre aftosa. *Veja,* 9 May, 120–21.

Index

Page numbers in italics refer to photo captions.